If You Remember Metal Skates

A baby boomer's story

NANCY WILLIAMS

ISBN: 1456349856
ISBN-13: 9781456349851
Library of Congress Control Number: 2010916965
CreateSpace Independent Publishing Platform
North Charleston, South Carolina

Introduction

"If there's a book you really want to read, but it hasn't been written yet, then you must write it."

Toni Morrison

I am a bona fide baby boomer, born in 1949, four years after my dad returned from fighting in World War II. For years, I have searched for a book which told the story of us baby boomers. I never discovered such a book about which many of us could say, "This is our story." Although I grew up on the West Side hill of Charleston, West Virginia, I'm sure my recollections about my childhood and youth will resonate with many baby boomers. After reading several chapters from this book, numerous friends and acquaintances, who grew up in other parts of the country, have remarked, "I can't believe we had such identical childhoods."

Our story truly does transcend geographic boundaries. Although all of us boomers have unique personalities, there still remains a close bond between us. There are so many of us close in age, who experienced parallel lives. During our youth, I don't think most of us realized how good we had it. Many young people have told me, "I wish I grew up when you did." They know, that as children, we lived in a less-hectic time, with home-lives very different from what they are experiencing.

While conversing with other baby boomers, there has been one constant, which people ask: "Do you remember skating with those little metal skates, which always came off while we were skating?" Almost all of us boomers remember our heavy metal roller skates, which slid onto the soles of our shoes, and the skate keys we used to tighten them. Many people boast about still having their skates and skate keys. Those seem to be fitting symbols of our youth.

I want this book to put a smile on your face and to tug at your heartstrings, as you read of memories long forgotten. Let me take you down memory lane to a slower-paced era. Together, let's reminisce about a cherished childhood, and recall an awkward adolescence. Go back to the sixties and seventies with me, when most of us were in college, then began our careers. Let's revisit the joys and perils of parenthood, and reflect on aging and coping with elderly parents. Finally, we will ponder our uncertain future.

Acknowledgements

This book has been a real labor of love for me. The past year seemed like one long writing marathon and I have loved practically every minute of it. Many times it felt more like working on a research project, as I was digging up all of the "delicious details" from the past. Numerous acquaintances, friends, and family members have so graciously offered their assistance and support. There are hundreds of individuals who have assisted me in so many ways, and I thank all of you for helping to make *If You Remember Metal Skates* a reality.

I would like to thank the *Washington Times* for asking me to write a story for them in 2009. The complementary comments from their copy editors about my writing certainly helped to give me the confidence I needed to tackle this book project. Working on the article for them helped to rekindle my love and passion for writing.

When the staff at Scribd.com featured two of my chapters, several months ago, I began getting favorable feedback about my work from their readers all over the country. For a debut author, that has been a real boost. So, thanks to all of the Scribd staff for featuring my work and especially for creating such a wonderful Website, where authors can share their documents with one another and with their followers.

I would especially like to thank Peter for his financial support, Becky for the use of her skates and skate key, and my family and two cats, Sophie and Mackenzie, for being "on hold" much of the year. A special thank you goes out to Michael Costello for the great book cover design and awesome front cover photo and to Jerry Waters for providing the creative author photograph as well as several images in the book.

Thanks to Billy Joe Peyton and Henry Battle for their input on the Charleston chapter. Most of my friends on Facebook have served as my consultative team when I needed them...thanks guys. I greatly appreciate the many people who have been instrumental in providing photographs for the book and in allowing me to write about them and their family members. Finally, I would like to thank Gary and Sue for their enthusiasm for reading the chapters as they were written, one by one.

Contents

I would like to dedicate this book to all of our fellow

baby boomers who are no longer with us,

but whose memories remain in our hearts forever.

My First Lessons

On the very first day of school in the second grade, I got into trouble. The possibility of anyone getting into trouble was so foreign to me and my classmates. Our first grade teacher had been strict but was still pretty laid-back. She never raised her voice to any of us. As is the case with all people, our second grade teacher had a completely different personality. Since we were second graders, she expected more from us.

I can still remember the sounds and smells of our classroom at J.E. Robins Elementary on the West Side of Charleston. It was a typical three-story, older red brick school building, which occupied the biggest part of a block on Beech Avenue. Every classroom had hardwood floors and wooden desks, which were attached to the ones in front of them. All of the wood in the room produced a unique, distinctive aroma. The pitter-patter of footsteps on the wooden floor was a memorable sound.

Our teacher began the first day by instructing us to write our names on the top line of our papers. She wanted our entire names. First, middle, and last. Of course, I had written my name before, but not my middle name. Our first grade teacher never made us write our middle names.

I panicked! How do you spell "Sue?" Asking our teacher how my name was spelled was out of the question. I would have been the laughingstock of the entire class. As a veteran student, with one year under my belt, I couldn't possibly reveal that I didn't know how to spell my name. "You don't know how to spell your name?" the teacher would scoff. All of the other students would be rolling in the floor from laughing so hard.

I remembered seeing that my middle name had three letters in it. The first syllable in the name of my friend, who was sitting beside me, was pronounced exactly like my middle name. So I figured that all I had to do was use the first three letters of her name to spell my middle name. Right? Made perfectly good sense to me.

I can so vividly recall how very nervous I was as the teacher walked around the room, checking everyone's papers. We sat towards the front of the room and could hear exactly where she was behind us. No one dared to turn around to see what was happening. Her heels made such a loud, clomping sound on the wooden floors. Clomp, clomp, pause. Clomp, clomp, pause. That was the only sound in the otherwise perfectly silent room, full of petrified second graders, on the first day of school.

She didn't say anything as she checked everyone's papers. An occasional muffled "Uh huh" was offered to indicate that someone's paper was acceptable. My heart began to race as her footsteps got closer. The dreaded moment arrived. She stopped beside my desk, hovering over me. In one quick motion, she reached down and grabbed my paper then started waving it in the air. "You copied from her paper," she screamed, while pointing to my friend's paper. It felt as if I had been caught cheating on a test. "That is not how your middle name is spelled. The name 'Sue' does not have a 'z' in it." I looked over at my friend, Suzette, who looked as puzzled as I. The surprised expression on her face clearly showed that she was equally as perplexed as I that my logic could have been so wrong.

A few years later, I got called into the principal's office. At Robins, no one was ever, ever called into the principal's office.

My mom had arranged for me to go home with my next-door neighbors after school one day. She had a meeting to attend and wouldn't be back before school let out. I walked home with my neighbors, Sharon and Susie. We went in their side door, walked down the steps to their basement, and left our belongings from school on the ping pong table. We grabbed a snack, and then went out behind their garage to work on our makeshift "fort."

After playing for several hours, Mom called me home for dinner. My neighbors and I went back down to the basement so I could get my belongings. To our shock and disbelief, their dog was having a fit, growling so loudly and ferociously. He had what was left of a textbook in his mouth and was shaking it fiercely. As he uncontrollably slung his head back and forth, pieces of paper flew everywhere.

The book had been so badly maimed by its assailant, that we had to use deductive reasoning to determine which book it was. Whose book was not among the stack which remained unscathed on the ping pong table? The book that had been attacked and ruined ended up being mine. I just couldn't believe it… "Their dog…their basement…my book."

The next day, our stern principal called me to her office. Over the loudspeaker, for the entire school to hear, she announced, "Nancy Williams, report to the principal's office." An ominous silence fell over our classroom, as the sounds of a collective gasp faded. Every kid in the room looked up at me with such empathy and visible expressions of concern for my well-being. My chin started to quiver as I slowly walked out of the classroom, all alone, to my unknown fate.

I could not have been more terrified if I had been called before a firing squad. As I shoved the heavy, dark wooden door to the principal's office open, I could see the expression of anger on her face. She held up the shredded, hardly-recognizable book, with a very-recognizable "Shame on you" expression. I quickly glanced at the book, then anxiously kept my eyes on her face to see what might follow. She lectured me about my "negligence" with the book, as if I had deliberately ruined it myself.

My mother had taken the remnants of the book to school that morning. She explained to the principal what had happened and agreed to pay the cost of replacing it. I never dreamed I would be called on the carpet about the incident. That ordeal was my first life lesson in realizing, at a very young age, that sometimes life is simply not always fair.

Backyard Venues

One of my fondest pastimes as a young girl was nightly rituals of performing acrobatics in the backyard. Our outdoor arena was embellished with tall stalks of pink and purple hollyhocks on one side and hearty yellow forsythia bushes on another. Sometimes we would get a whiff of the enticing aroma from neighbors cooking hamburgers, hotdogs, or steaks on their charcoal grills. The familiar clicking sound from men cutting grass with their push lawn mowers could often be heard from nearby yards, as the refreshing smell of newly-cut grass filled the air. With the onset of dusk, lightning bugs mysteriously appeared, glistening in the evening sky.

Back in those days, when I was as skinny as a rail, I mostly wore short, one-piece, gingham seersucker jumpsuits. They had elastic waistbands and white ties at the shoulders. I alternated between my pink, blue, and yellow outfits. My hair was brown and straight, pulled back in a long ponytail, with a wide plastic headband on top. Some of my friends called me "Stick," because I was so skinny.

We kicked off our tennis shoes and began flitting around like little yard spirits, swirling and tumbling with our impromptu yet graceful routines. As prissy and poised as an Olympic gymnast, we held a deliberate stance at the beginning and end of each maneuver. I never, for the life of me, was able to master the cartwheel. I could do about anything else, but there was something about going sideways that threw me off. With our limber and agile bodies, we performed backbends, full and half splits, tumbles, and backward and forward flips. Those who could often circled the yard doing cartwheels.

No sense of competition or threat of being outdone by someone else was present. We were like a sisterhood, lending a helping hand to assist someone who was struggling with learning or perfecting a new or difficult move. There was such a feeling of pride and accomplishment as we learned to master new feats. Boy... those were the days. I can only imagine the disastrous results if I attempted any of those moves today.

Sometimes at dusk, we caught fireflies in clear Mason jars with holes punched in the gold lids. There was something so magical about having a jar full of little flickering lights. In the afternoons, we often stretched out in the grass, looking up to the enormous white clouds overhead. As we gazed up to the clouds billowing across the sky, we looked for any familiar images. Someone would point out an object, then others would chime in with, "Oh yeah, I see it." Many hours were spent in the backyard, making hair garlands, necklaces, bracelets, or long chains out of clover flowers. We made a little slit near the end of one stem, then threaded a stem from another flower through it, and repeated this over and over. The flowers were plentiful, and we often made impressive, long chains.

Sometimes we spent many hours ferreting through several patches of clovers, looking for elusive four-leaf clovers. Believing that these coveted clovers would surely bring us good luck, we thought this was a wise investment of our time. If we were diligent enough with our searching, almost everyone came away with a prized clover. Handling our fragile treasures ever so delicately, we took them home and preserved them by pressing them between the pages of a book. Recently, I was delighted to come across little flattened, brittle clovers in a small, white zippered leather Bible I used as a child. I smiled and remembered our serious and laborious backyard adventures from a slower-paced time. We liked to pluck the petals off of daisies to see if our boyfriends loved us. "Loves me, loves me not, loves me, loves me not," we repeated as we pulled off one thin white petal at a time. Of course, we were always thrilled to have our last petal reveal "He loves me."

Another frequent event which took place in our backyard was "Kick the Can." Our backyard wasn't huge, but it was one of the biggest yards on the street. I'm often surprised to see how small it looks now, compared to how I remembered it. Practically every kid on our end of the street gathered in our yard to play, often with more than twelve kids participating. We usually started playing after supper and continued into the dark evening hours, until parents started calling for their kids to come in. We always determined who was going to be "It" first by our standard, "Eeny, Meeny, Miny, Moe." We didn't know about being "politically correct," and we didn't have one ounce of racism or prejudice in our innocent minds. Without any parental directive, we changed the objectionable phrase to, "Catch a tiger by his toe." This was probably a result of our schools becoming integrated in 1954.

To start "Kick the Can," someone kicks the can as far as possible, down the length of the yard. While "It" runs down to retrieve the can and brings it back up to where it was kicked, everyone else scatters and hides. Being "It" was always such a daunting task. There were so many good hiding places. If "It" found someone, then that person would have to go back to the can with the rest of the caught players. Someone who had not yet been caught could run up and kick the can again. That freed all of the caught players, and "It" had to start all over. Sometimes we would have to employ the standard call: "Ally ally, oxen free. Come out, come out, wherever you are." This usually happened when too many players were being called home, or if the person who was "It" had to leave or simply gave up.

The kids in our neighborhood spent so much time playing together. We also had some fun times playing "Hide and Seek," "Freeze Tag," and "Spotlight." All of us got along pretty well, and enjoyed each other's company. One family's dad frequently came out and played with us. He even participated in races we often held up and down our steep street. Of course, he outran us every time. That didn't bother us. We still thought he was pretty cool.

When Service Meant Service

Jim Harless and General Thaxton at the old Stonewall Station, late 1950s.
Photo courtesy of the Thaxton family.

Several services, which are sadly nonexistent today, were commonplace during the days of our youth. We were so accustomed to having them, that we thought they would be around forever.

Unfortunately, we took most of these services for granted, not realizing how valuable they were.

Early in the morning, several times a week, the milkman delivered quarts of milk in glass bottles to our front porch. He picked up our empty bottles and exchanged them for full ones. My sister, Jean, still has the scar on her forehead from falling on the cement stoop with a bottle in her hand. She had gone out to the porch to pick up the delivered milk one morning. I was recently reminiscing with a childhood friend and neighbor, Margie. She had an old Bonham's milk delivery bill, from 1952. Her mom had purchased six quarts of milk, at a quarter a piece.

Once a month, our Avon lady, Mrs. Daugherty, came calling. She was always dressed so formally and looked and smelled like she was wearing a sampling of all of her products. We girls were so excited when she came. As she opened her suitcase of products to show our mom, we eagerly watched. She always gave us kids little tiny, green plastic tubes of lipsticks, which were samples of her color selection. Mom typically ordered something from her every time she came.

I remember on several occasions, when someone had a serious illness, our family physician, Doc Robertson, came to our house. That's a far cry from enduring an all-night ordeal in an emergency room waiting lounge, or a twenty-four-hour clinic.

The ubiquitous Fuller Brush salesmen scoured every neighborhood. These gentlemen were always very polite and well-groomed, clad in their dress suits. They sold such a variety of products, from cleaning supplies to kitchen utensils. Most of the time, there was just one salesman. Mom usually invited him in, and he opened up his suitcase to display his wares in the middle of the living room floor. My favorite Fuller Brush product was a particular style of their plastic hairbrushes. It had a comfy grip and was what I used for more than twenty years.

Several times during the week, Mr. Douglas, of Bluebaugh bakery, drove his delivery van around the neighborhood. He stopped at a couple of places on each block. When he parked his van in front of our house, he blew several perky, loud toots on his two-toned whistle. Then he walked to the back of his van and opened the two doors. It was quite a sight to behold. At the sound of his whistle, women and children came running out of their houses to his van. He proudly stood beside his mouthwatering display of treats which he was peddling that day. Mr. Douglas was always so enthusiastic and convincing about how delicious his baked goods were. No one could resist his sales pitch. My mom always bought his fresh loaves of bread and scrumptious, cream-filled coffee cakes.

Similarly, the Mister Softee truck driver meandered up and down the streets of our hilly neighborhood. As he filled the air with such loud, calliope-type music, everyone could hear him coming several blocks away. That gave us plenty of time to grab some change from our parents. The driver stopped in front of our playground and wherever people had gathered, waiting for him. We bought his slushy drinks and soft-serve ice cream. My favorite was the swirled chocolate and vanilla ice cream cone.

The big-ticket item which salesmen walked the hillside pushing in those pre-computer, pre-Google days, was encyclopedias. The brand which carried the most prestige was World Book, so, understandably, it carried the most expensive price tag. My parents decided upon a Compton set, which served our needs well. I used the dark red volumes for numerous, intensive researches.

Vacuum cleaner salesmen were abundant, too. My mom bought one of her favorite canister sweepers from a convincing young salesman. Dad was a bit disgruntled when he came home from work, only to discover that she had made such an expensive purchase without first consulting with him.

Mom frequently summoned our very competent neighborhood television and radio repairman, Bill Krebs, who also made house calls. We always enjoyed watching him work on our sets, especially when he opened up the back panel and pulled out all of the "insides" of the television. In those days, the enormous glass tube was the biggest part of the inner workings.

Our mom liked to shop at Evans grocery store, at the foot of our hill. She ground up coffee beans in their stainless steel grinder, then poured them into red and brown bags. Back then, there were no scanners, so cashiers had to type in the price of each item. At Evans and all of the larger grocery stores, we were always helped out to the car by bag boys. Those young men were extremely polite and loaded our paper grocery bags and cartons of glass pop bottles into the trunk. They tipped their hats and thanked us, then wheeled the grocery cart back into the store.

At two of the neighborhood Ma-and-Pa stores, my mom could call the owner and describe what cut of meat she wanted for dinner. Their butcher cut whatever she ordered and wrapped it up in butcher paper. Either my sister or I ran down to the store and picked it up. As was common practice back then, the purchase was added to our tab.

The most noticeable difference in service, or lack thereof, was at the "service" stations. We were loyal customers of the Shell dealer at the bottom of our hill. He eventually switched to become an Esso dealer. The routine at the Stonewall Station never changed. "Ding ding ding ding" went the air hose as Dad pulled up to the pump. The friendly owner, General Thaxton, and his slender sidekick, Jim Harless, cheerfully came running up to the car and greeted us. "Fill 'er up?" General asked. Without Dad requesting anything, the two men checked the air in every tire and looked under the hood, checking fluid levels on everything. They looked and acted like attentive mechanics during a NASCAR pit stop. Finally, they washed the front and rear windshields. Most importantly, they pumped our gas and didn't charge for the air we needed. Air was free in those days. So was service.

Our stops at the Stonewall Station were like going to visit close friends. General and Jim were such a constant, predictable part of our lives. Both men were trustworthy, extremely competent mechanics. They were always busy working on customers' vehicles. In 1965, the two men became business partners and built a new, bigger red brick station across the street, which opened in 1968. At first it was an Esso station, and then eventually became Exxon. Dad knew his car was in good hands when he had them work on it, and he knew they would charge a fair price. Having good mechanics whom you personally knew and trusted was priceless.

Jim Harless and General Thaxton at their new station, 1968.
Photo courtesy of Jim Harless.

Camp Cowen

Shuffleboard courts at Camp Cowen, 1950s.

One of my favorite childhood experiences was attending Camp Cowen. The popular camp, located in beautiful Webster County, West Virginia, near the little town of Cowen, is owned and operated by the American Baptist Convention. I went there every summer for a week for several years, beginning with the summer before my third grade. Usually a few friends from church, Belinda and Linda, came with me. Other years I was the only person from our church. My mother bought iron-on name tags from a mail order catalogue with my name printed on them. We ironed those on every piece of clothing, washcloths, and towels I packed for the week.

On the very first night of my stay, the counselors hosted a watermelon party at the athletic field for us new campers. Numerous campers ate way too many pieces of watermelon. The next morning, mattresses were airing out on the porches of nearly all of the little white wooden cabins. Consuming too many slices of watermelon resulted in numerous campers wetting their beds.

Our little cabins, scattered on the bank and in the woods behind the flagpole, were pretty primitive. They had no phones, televisions, air conditioning, or plumbing. About eight sets of wooden bunk beds were in each cabin, housing an adult counselor and somewhere between twelve and sixteen campers. All of the windows were covered with a big piece of wood, which could be propped open to let in some air. The bare floors were unfinished wood. Heavy gray wool blankets over stiff white sheets were all that kept us warm. A dirt path from each cabin led up to a cinderblock bathhouse. We hiked up the dark path in the middle of the night, to use the restroom and made the walk again in the morning for an invigorating cold shower.

Everyone gathered in a big circle around the flagpole early each morning while the flag was being raised and the bugler played reveille. At the end of the day, we gathered around the flagpole again as the flag was taken down and the bugler played taps. Those flagpole rituals were some of my favorite parts of our daily routine.

Camp Cowen's dining hall had an ambiance all of its own. It was a huge, horizontal, one-story wooden structure, filled with long wooden tables. The food was delicious, especially the cook's homemade bread. All of the groups from each cabin took turns doing chores in the mess hall. One day, when it was our turn to set the tables, I was so crushed when a boy complained that I was touching the utensil end of the silverware instead of the handles. That was especially painful, since he was the most popular boy in camp.

The water in the swimming pool was painfully frigid, but I still signed up for swimming lessons every summer. I remember learning the Dead Man's Float, and how to float on my back. The goal of the classes wasn't to produce skilled swimmers, but to teach us to not be afraid of the water. Not everyone signed up for swimming, but I looked forward to it each year. The summer after my seventh-grade year, I worked on the camp's newspaper, *The News Flash*. I still have a copy of it in my scrapbook.

During the week, we split up into different nature study groups. I was so thrilled to be assigned to Doc Collins' group for several years in a row. He is one of my favorite people of all time. His knowledge about the woods was inspiring. He was an older, extremely fit, avuncular gentleman from Huntington, with white hair, a friendly face, and a tan complexion. Along a babbling stream in the woods, he taught us how to bend a rhododendron leaf into a cup shape. With that knowledge, we would always be able to get a drink of water from the pristine mountain streams. We hiked up into the deep woods every day and worked on our forest home for hours at a time. For carpet, we gathered soft green moss, which was plentiful in those parts. We chose nice large, flat rocks for everyone to sit upon. The frame of our home was made of small branches, which we had cut and fastened together with rope. Those afternoons were such memorable experiences.

Crafts class was another favorite of mine. Fifty years later, I still have the wooden cross I made out of burnt matches. In our free time, we liked to play shuffleboard in the courts between the mess hall and camp store. Once in the morning and in the afternoon, the store was opened, and campers could purchase snacks or camp T-shirts and gear. I bought a maroon and white Camp Cowen pennant one year, which I still have.

Every night we walked through the athletic field to the natural stone sanctuary for vesper services. To me, this place was so tranquil and serene, emitting an awe-inspiring, spiritual presence. Huge stone boulders surrounded the outdoor sanctuary, and thick wooden benches, made from split timbers, were arranged like an outdoor amphitheater. Tall, majestic evergreen trees and rhododendron bushes filled the space around the rocks. The special effects at the beginning of the services were magical to us. Vesper service began when the pastor, behind the stone podium, recited Genesis 1:3: "And God said, 'Let there be light,' and there was light." During that phrase, a baseball-size flame dramatically came shooting out of nowhere from behind the last, highest row of campers. When it stopped, it immediately ignited the campfire, which burst into tall, roaring flames. Doc Collins had rigged a ball of kerosene-soaked fabric, which he shot down a wire that was invisible to us. Presoaked wood in the fire pit guaranteed the fire would ignite with explosive force. Like myself, I bet every camper who witnessed that phenomenon will never forget it.

We often sang "Kumbaya" and "Jacob's Ladder" at the outdoor services, but my favorite hymn we sang around the big campfire was "Spirit of the Living God." I can still picture everyone singing the lyrics as they made the hand movements, which described the words in gestures.

Practically every year, there would be some male counselors who instructed vulnerable, novice campers on how to go snipe hunting. Those of us who were seasoned campers knew better than to go along with that trick, more than once. We had lots of fun relay competitions and volleyball and softball games on the athletic field. The sweat bees were often relentless on the dusty field, and it seemed like we were always getting gnats in our eyes on those hot summer days.

Everyone at camp followed the romance of the most popular couple, who got together every year for the entire week. They made such a cute couple. Susie had big brown eyes and blonde Shirley Temple ringlets. Jim was dark and handsome, with perfect Ken doll features. Most of the rest of us had crushes on the older counselors of the opposite gender. During my first year, I was nicknamed "Moochie" because I was such a cuddly kid. That name stuck with me during my entire camping career.

I always enjoyed the weekend sessions at Camp Cowen, when families from our church and South Charleston Baptist camped together. It was hilarious to see how many of the men played practical jokes on one another. The most popular of these was "short sheeting" the beds. Everyone could tell who the victims of that prank were, as they groaned when they couldn't slide down between their sheets as they climbed into bed.

Gym Class 101

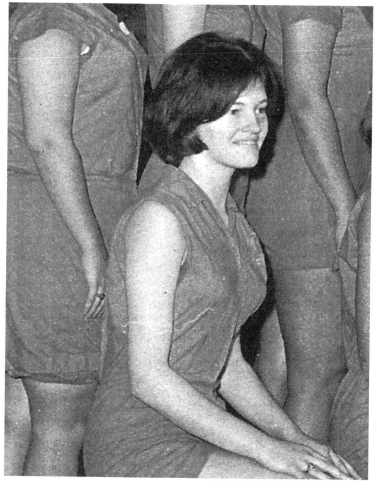

My good friend, Sue Mason Phillips, in her blue gym suit, 1967.

During my first year at Woodrow Wilson Junior High School, I had several phobias, which made my gym class a most unpleasant experience. Unlike today, it was mandatory that we participate and dress for every class. There were no exceptions. Our class was run similar to a boot camp, filled with more than fifty girls. We were required to purchase and wear identical short, blue cotton jumpsuits. On the bodice, right above the pocket, our last name and first initial had to be embroidered with white thread. White socks and tennis shoes completed our uniforms.

After getting dressed in the basement locker room, where there was absolutely no privacy, one by one, we ran up to the gym. We lined up like young Army cadets, forming a large human square around the perimeter of the room. Our very athletic teacher, Miss Whitt, was an attractive, petite lady with short black hair, peppered with gray. While twirling her whistle, she walked around the square, inspecting our uniforms and checking the roll at the same time. It was easy to tell who was absent. We always filed into our assigned placements, so if a girl were absent, there would be an open space.

After attendance was taken, we fell into formation for the predictable calisthenics regimen. We always began with fifty jumping jacks, then went into the "arms up, bend over, and touch your toes with the opposite hand" movements. Our exercise regimen usually followed the same routine, with little variation. Sometimes we played volleyball and basketball after the exercises. Doing sit-ups was the kicker for me. We had a partner, who held our feet down on the red mats and counted aloud how many we had done. At the beginning of the semester, we were required to do fifty, and eventually we worked our way up to the mandatory one hundred sit-ups. Our stomach muscles ached for days after having to do so many.

The activity which I dreaded more than any other was, by far, the ropes. There were two long, thick, twisted jute ropes hanging from our very tall ceiling. I couldn't say exactly how long those ropes were. My guess is they extended up to the equivalent of three stories high. I had a severe case of acrophobia back then, as I still do today. My heart started to pound and my hands began to sweat as my turn to climb approached. When my turn came, with much trepidation, I ever so slowly and reluctantly inched up the prickly rope, one reach-pull-and-push movement at a time. I was careful to never look down at my classmates on the floor, who were cheering me on from below. Once I reached the top of the rope, I was always so relieved.

Unfortunately, I was too eager to get my feet back on terra firma and invariably slid down my coarse lifeline too quickly. Every single time, I ended up with raw rope burns on my thighs from clinging so tightly. They were nearly the size of a tennis ball and usually took several weeks to heal.

The real trauma associated with my gym class experience happened after class, in the dungeon-like locker room. In my mind it somewhat reminded me of what life must have been like in a concentration camp. We lined up on the stairs, which led from the gym down to the basement, then, together, we marched down to the locker room.

Unlike in schools today, back then, taking a shower was a requirement. To show proof that we had taken one, we handed over our wet towels to older student gym helpers. We waited in line stark naked as they checked each person's name off. The lull between handing them our towels and walking over to where our lockers were seemed like an eternity. Every girl's naked body was practically in full view for all to see. This proved to be quite intimidating and embarrassing for most of us. I had just stepped up from wearing a training bra and had very small breasts. On the other hand, there were a number of girls in our class whose breasts were the size of cantaloupes. Theirs certainly dwarfed mine, which somewhat resembled two fried eggs, sunny-side-up. I'm sure the well-endowed were equally as humiliated as those of us who were flat-chested.

Many of my friends loved gym class. For me, the combination of having to undress in front of classmates and climb the ropes was so humiliating. Back in the early sixties, girls were required to wear skirts or dresses to school. We were also having to deal with the nuisance of wearing sanitary belts and taking off and putting back on garter belts and hose. We didn't have the convenience of pantyhose until a few years later. In the locker room, I always got runs in my hose from snagging them on a rough wooden bench or the sharp corner of a locker. I kept a bottle of clear nail polish in my purse to dab on the runs, keeping them from "running" any further.

"Were You a Hippie?"

This is at my 23rd birthday party in my parents' dining room, November, 1972.

"Ms. Williams, were you a hippie?" one of my high school students asked last spring. "Oh, I'll bring in a photograph and you can decide for yourself," I replied. Another student, Chris, who knows me very well and is the most conservative person I've ever known, answered: "Ms. Williams, you are still a hippie, and that's perfectly all right." Chris has always been wise beyond his years.

The Google dictionary definition of a hippie/s is: "Hippies were young people in the 1960s and 1970s who rejected conventional ways of living, dressing, and behaving, and tried to live a life based on peace and love. Hippies often had long hair and many took drugs." I don't know why, but every single time I read that definition, the last part comes off as "and took *many* drugs."

The next day, when I showed several students the photograph of myself, from 1972, one girl said, "That doesn't look anything like you." I responded: "Give yourself forty years, and see if you look the same." The younger version of me looked like many of us did back then: a pretty, slender, wide-eyed young lady, with hair down to my waist, parted in the middle. My 120-pound figure resembled that of the *Venus de Milo*. In those days, my favorite outfit, which I wore when I wanted to get dressed up, was a black cotton turtleneck sweater and a long, flowing, knee-length vest with large green and black herringbone patterns. Matching wide bell-bottom pants and tan lace-up leather boots were the finishing details.

Several years ago, when my two sons were in their early teens, we were purchasing a new van. The salesman was a former student of mine from my first year of teaching, 1971. When he was in his office alone with the boys, he told them: "Your mother used to be a real 'fox' back in the day." They snickered about that all the way home and still get a good laugh reliving the moment. No one is supposed to say that about your mom.

Often I was referred to as "the hippie on the staff" when I started teaching. I remember Margaret, one of the more revered older teachers, approaching me in the hall after school one day. As if she were the designated spokesperson for a group, she said: "Several of us have been discussing this, and we think you need to gain some weight." And so I did.

Like many of us, I am right on track in upholding the frequently-used statistic that adults usually gain two pounds a year. Instead of looking like the *Venus de Milo*, I now look in the mirror, and see more of a resemblance to the *Venus of Willendorf*. I take great comfort in knowing that she was a symbol of beauty twenty-six thousand years ago.

I no longer have the hair down to my waist. This is still shocking to most people, since that was my signature look for more than thirty years. The first summer when I was taking graduate classes, I had an epiphany about my hair. My schedule was so grueling, every waking moment was precious. It became more and more absurd to blow-dry my long, thick hair for twenty minutes every morning, simply to pull it back in a ponytail. The only thing that made sense was to get it whacked off.

These days, I wear a very short buzz cut that feels too long when it grows out much more than half an inch. It seems like the older you get, the more you realize that the length of a person's hair, just like his or her clothes and outward appearance, doesn't have much to do with what that person is really all about.

Frequently, acquaintances I run into have no idea who I am until they hear my voice. Often these are people who knew me very well but just don't recognize me without the long hair. They are shocked and often embarrassed that they didn't recognize me. I don't mind it, really. I've actually enjoyed having a little anonymity.

Over the years I have developed a horrible aversion to clothes. I especially dread shopping for clothes. It's as if the department stores have "three floors of ugly" on display. These days, it's nearly impossible to find anything which isn't decorated with sequins, beads, or gold, glittery paint. I am none of those things and feel very uncomfortable wearing them.

When I was coaching a middle school forensics team several years ago, one of my students was competing in the "Impromptu" category. In this event, students are given well-known phrases, on which they have to give an impromptu speech. My student drew the phrase, "Beauty is only skin deep." I was flabbergasted when he started giving his speech. He had no clue what that phrase meant and spoke about it as if it had a literal meaning.

His generation may not know what "Beauty's only skin deep" means. Ours certainly does. And I'm glad the Temptations did too.

Birds, Bats, and Baby Rats

For my entire lifetime, I have been the perpetual nurturer. Even as a child, I was always taking in birds who were injured or squirrels and turtles who had been hit by a car. As an adult, I am completely cognizant of the fact that these rescue missions usually don't have happy endings. Even knowing that, I still will try to help any animal who needs to be nursed back to health.

Back in the early 1980s, when I had my glass studio, a desperate pigeon showed up one day on my front stoop. He had somehow been injured and was unable to fly. Although he couldn't speak, he stared into my eyes and clearly sent me the message, "Please help me." I kept that pigeon at my shop for several years. On the days when the shop was closed, I drove into town from our farm to feed him and change his water.

When my sons were young and we lived out on the farm, there were numerous incidents of animals needing help. A groundhog who had been wounded by dogs was my patient for about a week. I took him to work, where I was teaching at a center for gifted students. He stayed in a box, in the workroom between our two classrooms. I didn't mention to the students that I had him, not wanting them to disturb him. One little girl nearly fainted when she walked into the workroom and saw him. She was certainly not expecting to encounter a big, furry creature.

One summer night, inside our fairly primitive little farmhouse, a bat found its way inside. I ducked from him as he flew over my head in the hallway. Before we knew what had happened, he had become plastered to the sticky strip of fly tape hanging in the bathroom. His thin, delicate wings were spread out, firmly attached to the gummy surface of the tape.

What a nightmare! I have always had a bit of a phobia about bats. At camp, when we were out in our johnboat at dusk, we were afraid they were going to dive-bomb our heads. I could never have imagined that I would ever have such an up-close-and-personal, one-on-one encounter with a bat.

I took the little, brown, entangled victim outside and gently placed him on a towel on our round, white metal patio table. Under the light from a hanging mechanic's lamp, I worked on the scared little critter until daylight came the next morning. Fortunately, alcohol dissolved and removed the glue from the fly tape. Very carefully, and extremely cautiously, I pulled the tape off of the delicate wing tissue, a tiny bit at a time. Then I took cotton balls saturated with alcohol and wiped off the wings. Many hours later, the stickiness was completely removed. The frightened little bat was as uncomfortable as I was with this bizarre situation. He never attempted to bite me, but he frequently turned his head towards me and hissed. It was as if he were voicing his disapproval of what I had done to him.

Since it was already daylight by the time I had finished getting all of the tape and glue off of his wings, I placed him in our root cellar. When the door was closed, it was pitch black inside. Once evening came, I opened the door to the cellar. My family and I watched, with great hope and anticipation, then jubilation, as the little bat flew effortlessly up to the dark night sky, where he belonged. That was indeed a rare, happy ending.

Out of all of the farm critters I encountered, the one I became most attached to was a baby rat. One of the cats had caught it, brought it inside, and then placed it at my feet, as though she were presenting me with a gift. I had seen plenty of baby mice before at camp, but this little one-inch baby was a rat. No question about it. He had a much longer snout than a baby mouse.

I named him Oscar, because the name seemed to fit. He became my constant companion for a little more than a week. Oscar cuddled up in the palm of my hand and accompanied me everywhere I went. With a medicine dropper, I gave him warm milk. He was so small, that no one could tell he was even there. On Saturday, I was shopping with my sister and took Oscar with us. She had run into a drug store while he and I waited out in the car. All of a sudden, his breathing became noticeably shallow. I was so saddened when he inhaled such a huge, deep, final breath, and then exhaled a loud, long breath that seemed impossible for such a tiny creature.

I think some of my fellow teachers were beginning to question my sanity over this Oscar episode. Several voiced their confusion and disapproval about my wanting to save a baby rat. Too bad Oscar didn't have a fluffy tail, like a squirrel. Then they would have thought he was cute and worthy of living.

Sweet Hour of Prayer

My parents with my sister, Jean, and me at our church, 1960.

I grew up in Emmanuel Baptist Church on the West Side of Charleston. The large, red brick building, on the corner of

Washington and Florida Streets, has been a prominent landmark of the community for many years. We have photographs of my grandparents at the groundbreaking ceremony, in the early 1940s, when construction was beginning on the massive sanctuary. They were referred to as being one of the "pillar" families of Emmanuel. Our family was one of those families who fit the description, "If the church doors were open, they were there." We attended Sunday school, Sunday morning and evening services, and Wednesday night prayer meetings, as well as the annual Vacation Bible School, School of Missions, and revival services. My parents served on various boards, which met regularly. I had youth choir practice once a week.

I think all of us try to delve into our memories to see what our very earliest memory is. Surely mine must be playing "London Bridge" in our church's nursery. I remember singing the tune and walking around the "bridge," only to be caught in the middle of it from time to time. I also remember our teacher showing us how to do the hand movements that went along with this saying: "Here is the church" (clutch hands with fingers tucked inside), "here is the steeple" (bring up the two index fingers and make them touch), "look inside and see all the people" (turn over your hands palms up, to reveal the "people" while wiggling your fingers). That seems like it was only yesterday.

Another vivid memory I have is of the night when the Haynes girls and my sister, Jean, and I got into trouble during a Sunday night service. We were very young and had such a difficult time sitting perfectly still and quiet for an hour. Those hard, wooden pews were pretty uncomfortable for sixty minutes. Somehow we began laughing uncontrollably. Once we started getting so slap-happy, all it took was just a funny look or expression from someone else to make us laugh even harder. Knowing that we weren't allowed to make any noise at all made it twice as difficult.

Thinking of all the times we spent at church brings back such fond memories. Many of the real heroes of my lifetime were men and women from Emmanuel. They had a tremendous part in shaping who I am today. Della Smith always told all of us kids: "Stand up straight. You'll end up with a hunched back if you don't." Some of my dearest friends are from our extended church family. We have been so close for such a long time that they really do feel more like relatives to me. I miss our young and old friends from church who have passed on. Some have been gone for many years now, but their memories live on forever.

In the days of our youth, everyone was so much more formal in their attire. This is especially true with what people wore to church. Men wore dark suits, with starched white shirts, ties, Oxford wing-tip shoes, and fedora hats with wide brims. Some men wore taps on the bottom of their shoes. Women wore colorful dresses or suits with large brooches, pointed-toe high heels, hose with seams, veiled hats, and white or black gloves. Especially on holidays, we girls wore gloves and hats too. Many women had mink stoles or capes. I always tried to avoid sitting behind a lady wearing a mink stole. Having to stare at those poor little minks' faces and paws for an hour was too disturbing. After every service, many people congregated on the sidewalk at the Florida Street entrance to shoot the breeze and have a smoke. A few ladies smoked out there too, but it was mostly men, smoking cigarettes and sweet-smelling pipes and aromatic cigars.

Of course, these days, everyone is so informal with what they wear. A woman wearing a hat is the exception. It's common for men to wear tennis shoes and sweaters, not suits, to church. Pantsuits are perfectly acceptable attire for women. When I was in from college one weekend, I attended a Sunday morning service at Emmanuel, wearing a pantsuit. A girl my age, who didn't realize I was within hearing distance, called out to her friend: "Nancy Williams is here, and she's wearing slacks." That's how much of an anomaly it was back then. No one would even think of making such a remark today.

As a child, our sanctuary at Emmanuel seemed so enormous. The extremely high ceiling and tall windows emitted such a feeling of spaciousness. During our youth, practically every family in Charleston attended church somewhere. Like most churches, the pews at Emmanuel were usually packed every Sunday. The seating arrangement of the congregational faithful never changed. Everyone knew that Mr. and Mrs. Allen, with their daughters, Ruth Ann, Dorothy, and Beverly, would be sitting in close proximity to our family. They were either in the pew in front of or directly behind us, on the right side of the sanctuary. Bonnie Lanham and her daughters, Betty and Sue, and their families always sat in the front on the right side. The Haynes and Young families could always be found on the left side. My Aunt Floda and Uncle George Craft, who never, ever missed, were always seated in the middle section, a few pews back from the front. These seating patterns were as predictable as night and day.

The handsome black walnut Communion table, which sat below the podium in the sanctuary, was handcrafted by my grandfather, Doc, and my Uncle Ralph. The table is still used for displaying gold Communion trays filled with tiny cups of grape juice and broken pieces of crackers. Christ's commandment, "This do in remembrance of me," is spelled out along the front, in large, three-dimensional wooden letters. Knowing that this table was a gift from my family always meant so much to me. It was presented to the church, in 1950, in honor of Doc's mother, Varina. The tiny glass cups, which we used years ago, have been replaced with disposable plastic ones. Torn pieces of bread have been replaced with small squares of crackers.

Many emotional moments at the end of our services often took place. The pastor always extended an invitation for people to "come forward," and accept Christ, or to rededicate their lives. As individuals started parading down the aisles to the front of the church, most of us got a lump in our throats, and tears in our eyes. Time after time, the preacher kept extending the invitation with,

"One more verse" of a hymn, such as "Just As I Am," or "I Surrender All."

In the fourth grade, I made my own trip down the aisle and was baptized by submersion on a chilly November night in 1958. My friend Bert Bostic and I were baptized during the same ceremony. He was my age, and the two of us had grown up together. It was helpful to have a friend share the experience. We donned our long white robes and bravely walked down the steps into the waist-high water. Except during baptismal services, the red velvet curtains behind the choir loft were never opened. To us children, the closed curtains made the baptismal pool seem very secretive. It felt so strange to finally be standing in the mysterious pool, looking out onto the congregation, from an entirely new and rare perspective. Reverend Gordon Withers, our pastor at the time, stood in the water with us. He gave a brief explanation to the congregation about the symbolism of baptism. Bert and I stood by, visibly shivering from being nervous and from the cool temperature of the water.

Reverend Withers walked over to me first and positioned me in the middle of the opening. He asked me: "Do you accept Jesus Christ as your Lord and Savior?" to which I replied, "I do." Right before he dipped me backwards into the water, he quoted from Matthew 28:19: "I baptize you in the name of the Father, and of the Son, and of the Holy Spirit." In one fell swoop, he dipped me back then raised me out of the water. Then, I waited along the side of the pool as he repeated the same motions and words with Bert.

Actually, the whole experience of getting baptized was not as frightening as it could have been. I had plenty of practice for the occasion. For years, all of us kids had played like we were "baptizing" one another in the bathtub, swimming pools, or river. We had most of the words down perfectly, although not quite the pronunciation: "I batize you in the name of the Father, Son, and Holy Ghost."

My two favorite occasions at church were Candlelight Service on Christmas Eve and Easter Sunrise Service. For me, both of these events reached beyond the realm of mundane human experiences. On Christmas Eve, everyone walked to the front of the sanctuary and lit their candles while singing "Silent Night." An atmosphere of love and hope filled the air. Sunrise Service was held right at daybreak at a local cemetery overlooking Charleston. Every year I tried not to miss it. In high school, my friend Tom and I attended a very rare community Sunrise Service at the Municipal Auditorium. The enormous choir, overflowing with talent, consisted of people from every denomination across the city. One of the most moving services I ever attended was at Key West. What a glorious service we experienced that morning as the sun crept up from the horizon and shone across the ocean.

During my grade school years, I spent many afternoons hanging out in the church kitchen beside the long fellowship hall. My grandmother and mother were deaconesses, which was the group who, among other things, prepared all of the meals for any occasion. Back then, there were such large crowds, especially at the Mother-Daughter Banquet. The classrooms adjacent to the fellowship hall had to be opened up for overflow areas. Everyone always had fun watching the men of the church waiting on tables for a change, wearing red and white gingham aprons.

All of the ladies who worked in the kitchen wore full aprons. Many were elderly women who were expert cooks and were revered by everyone. Although cooking for such large crowds was a serious job, there was always a lot of laughter and lively conversation going on. Frequently, one of the women would start singing a familiar song or hymn, and the rest would chime in with such beautiful harmonizing. The song I remember hearing most frequently was Eddie Cochran's tune, "Tell Me Why."

Several women were experts when it came to making bread. My favorite kitchen activity was watching Aunt Ruby and Macie Price make their signature dinner rolls, the kind with three balls on top. The two ladies worked at one of the long kitchen tables for hours, often passing down their expertise to other women. Pinching out the precise amount of dough, they rolled it in between their palms until it was perfectly round. Then they gently tucked three balls of dough into each greased cup of the large metal muffin pans. There were definite perks from hanging out in the kitchen with the cooks instead of playing shuffleboard with the other kids. One of those perks was getting to lick chocolate icing off of the gigantic beaters from the huge stainless steel mixer. The ultimate perk, however, was getting to devour one of those delicious, steaming hot rolls, right out of the oven, with a little bit of butter melting on top.

Our BYF group, Baptist Youth Fellowship, was very active. We met on Wednesday nights during the adult prayer meeting, and sometimes during the Sunday evening worship services. We went Christmas caroling and skating together, had Halloween parties in the fellowship hall, put on plays and services for the entire congregation, and attended annual statewide conferences. On Halloween nights, we went door-to-door, collecting money for the Trick-or-Treat for UNICEF program. Afterwards, during our party, bobbing for apples was always pretty embarrassing. I could never seem to open my mouth wide enough to sink my teeth into any of those floating targets.

We had several adult BYF leaders throughout the years. One leader, Dayton Ford, always called me "Miss Peach," after a character I had portrayed in a play. Even as an adult, he calls me that whenever we see each other. He and his wife, Carolyn, were our youth sponsors for many years. The older I get, the more appreciative I am of all of the adults who so willingly gave their unwavering dedication, time, and energy to our group.

The BYF programs we used each week were in booklets from the national Baptist headquarters. Many of us didn't take these structured, more formal parts of our meetings too seriously. We took turns having the program, and, as with anything else, it was easy to tell who came prepared or not. A friend of mine and I still laugh at the faux pas we pulled one night. We were reading from the booklets, and part of our lesson had the lighting of candles as an important symbolism. We lit the candles, then picked up our booklets and proceeded to read, "As we light the candles..." She and I couldn't help but laugh at ourselves. It was so obvious that we hadn't read over the material. From then on, we made sure that never happened again.

One of the most memorable things we frequently did was to stand in a circle and sing Kurt Kaiser's touching hymn, "Pass It On." At the beginning of the song, each person held an unlit candle. As we started the lyrics: "It only takes a spark to get a fire going," one candle was lit, then from that candle, the next one was lit, and so on, continuing from person to person. Finally, we were standing in a beautifully-illuminated circle. That little ceremony was always very moving to me.

One year, our BYF group attended a statewide convention in a town about an hour from Charleston. The host church had a lovely Saturday night banquet for everyone, catered at the local armory. During the Sunday morning service at their church the following day, practically everyone who had eaten at the banquet began to show symptoms of food poisoning. Anyone who has ever experienced the exhausting ordeal of getting food poisoning can surely appreciate the nightmare which ensued. The two common symptoms are simultaneous projectile vomiting and severe diarrhea. As in most churches, there were only a few small restrooms in the building, not nearly enough to accommodate hundreds of people needing them at the same time. The crowd quickly dispersed. Everyone needed to fend for themselves and seek out a restroom wherever they could find one.

We also had many dedicated men and women who were our Sunday school teachers. One of my favorite teachers was Ray Ranson, who taught our sixth-grade class. He was such a gentleman, with his serious, soft-spoken demeanor, never getting upset. As he presented the lessons, he raised his eyebrows while he spoke. We could tell he enjoyed being our teacher as much as we enjoyed being his students. Traveling to foreign countries to help build schools or churches was one of his passions. He often helped the elderly of the church, through Project Love, with any building or maintenance needs they had. Those were two missions which gave him great joy.

Ray passed away last year. At his funeral, during the touching eulogy, Reverend Stoner told of how Ray took a Polaroid camera to Haiti, on one such trip, to take pictures of the village children. He said the kids' eyes grew so big as the images developed on the film. Many of the boys and girls had never seen a picture of themselves. They ran home to show their parents the miraculous photographs. In no time, all of the parents showed up, dressed in their fanciest clothes, to have their pictures taken too.

In junior high school, many of us girls were on our church's basketball team. Emmanuel didn't have a gym back then, so we weren't very good, especially compared to the teams who had their own gyms. I don't remember winning a single game, but we still had fun with it. Our coach, Homer Armstrong, was extremely patient with us, always keeping a smile on his face. He was athletic, tall, and lanky, with a flat-top haircut. His coaching instructions to us along the sideline never varied: "Get the ball to Sara Beth." She was an outstanding basketball player but, unfortunately, was practically the only one on our team who had much of a handle on how to play the game. It's pretty impossible to have a successful one-woman basketball team. I'll never forget the Saturday morning game at First Presby's gym, where I made a complete fool out of myself. Someone threw the ball to me. I tucked it under my arm, like a football, and ran down the court with it, without dribbling at all. I was completely oblivious to the official's whistle. Being a member of Homer's team was such an honor.

Almost everyone who was in our BYF sang in the youth choir. One year, a guest choir director from a church in South Charleston came to work with us. She was an attractive, vivacious, red-haired woman, the age of our parents. As only great teachers, coaches, and directors have, she had the ability to bring out the best in us.

We performed, under her direction, on a completely different level, sounding better than we ever had before. One of the girls in our choir, Joyce Lanham, had such a strong soprano voice. She was always being picked for solos. Interestingly enough, she and her husband, Jim Downey, are both soloists in the adult choir today and sing so beautifully together as a duet. I'm sure many of us remember their exciting, romantic reunion, when he showed up at church one night on leave from the military.

In the choir and congregation, I liked to harmonize by singing the alto parts. It was always fascinating and surprising to me when the men sang the "response" parts, such as in the hymn "Love Lifted Me." Sometimes those parts were written in the hymnals, but many times, they were just passed down from one generation to another. There are numerous hymns which hold a special place in my heart, but my favorite of all time is, "Come Thou Fount of Every Blessing." One of my favorite evening services used to be when the entire hour was devoted to singing hymns that the congregation requested. I am such a hymn junkie.

In 1970, when I was in college, our pastor at that time, Reverend Archie Snedegar, and his late wife, Sally, organized a trip for about eight of us girls in our youth group. Their young son Steve accompanied us. It's overwhelming to think of how much planning was involved on such a long trip. Looking back on it, I am so appreciative of their efforts. We traveled in two station wagons across the country to work with Hopi Indians at Third Mesa, Arizona, near Flagstaff. One of the cars had a huge hand-painted sign across the front which read: "Arizona or Bust." Baptist churches along the route agreed to let us sleep in their gymnasiums or basements. One night we slept under the stars, at the bottom of a rocky cliff, at a campground in one of the western states. Some kind of wild creature, possibly a bobcat, let out blood-curdling shrieks from atop the cliff all night long.

Two congressional members, Momma and Poppa Shank also drove and chaperoned on the trip. I was usually the designated map reader in their car. Since we were on a shoestring budget, we usually ate pimento cheese spread or peanut butter and jelly sandwiches at rest stops. We kids got so tired of eating the same thing, that we begged the adults to stop at a McDonald's one day. The final destination on our trip was the Shank's nephew's church in California. All of the men with long hair at his church looked so odd to us. We had never seen the lyrics to hymns projected on the wall. Nowadays, of course, that is common practice. While we were in California, we spent a day at Disneyland. My great aunt, who lived in Anaheim, met me there for lunch.

During our weeklong stay in Arizona, we slept in the basement of a church on a Navajo reservation at Keams Canyon. We became pretty attached to three little Navajo sisters, Caroline, Ruthie, and Rebecca, who lived by the church. Most of the girls in our group taught Bible lessons, but I taught the Hopi ladies crafts. They seemed very appreciative to have the attention from us. During crafts, they especially liked making burlap wall hangings, with big, colorful, cut-out flowers. A pleasant lady with the common Indian name of Mamie Begay served as our interpreter. The Hopi ladies showed us paint rocks, which they used to decorate pottery. These were small, rough, gray, round rocks, not quite as big as a golf ball. When they were split open, a little round, reddish deposit, which looked like iron ore, was found in the center of each rock.

I became quite fond of one elderly lady, Lucy, who was completely blind. She came every day, decked out with a red velvet blouse, a long, fuchsia cotton skirt, and a white turban over her hair. A large silver and turquoise necklace hung down from her neck. She sat patiently, waiting for me to show her, with my hands, what she needed to do. At the end of every day, we rode in the back of a big white Dodge pick-up truck, as the driver delivered the ladies back to their homes. On the last day, when we stopped at Lucy's wooden hut, we said an emotional goodbye to one another, then, to my surprise, she invited me inside.

The interior of her home was one open room, with sparse furnishings. The floor was dry red clay, the same as the ground outside. A few thicknesses of blankets on the floor served as her bed. Clothes were hanging on several hooks along the walls. A wooden stool and an enormous loom sat in the middle of the room. The loom must have been five feet tall and six feet wide. Although it was very primitive and made of rough wood, the blankets which she had woven on it looked professional. With great pride, she showed me the impressive stack she had made. When I tried to take a picture of her beside the loom, I got the message on my camera: "Replace Batteries." Although that was disappointing, I will always cherish the priceless images in my mind.

Lucy, on the right, outside of her home, at Third Mesa, Arizona, 1970.

As Mamie and I walked back to the truck, she explained that no one had ever been invited inside Lucy's home before. Upon hearing that, my eyes began to water and my chin started to quiver. I felt so humbled. Lucy was the only person on their reservation to hold out and refuse to leave her shanty. All of the other families had moved into cinderblock dwellings which the federal government had built for them. During the next year at college, I painted a palette knife portrait of Lucy and proudly displayed it in my senior art show. It has hung in my parents' living room for nearly forty years and has sparked many conversations.

Emmanuel is celebrating its one hundredth birthday this year. I think it is altogether fitting and appropriate that the sitting pastor, Ron Stoner, and his wife, Jan, are the current "first family" of the church during this celebration. They have been such a vital part of Emmanuel for twenty-six years. He continues to preach meaningful, perceptive sermons. Ron holds the record as the pastor having the longest tenure. His years of service at Emmanuel cover more than a fourth of the century being celebrated. Jan, who was diagnosed with multiple sclerosis fourteen years ago, has been such an inspiration to all of us. She is always so cheerful, determined to not let her debilitating disease get her down.

Carefree Livin'

Robins playground, 1952.

Summer days back in the fifties and sixties were such carefree times. In our neighborhood, the only concern we had was that it might rain too much, forcing our city-run playground to close. It was exactly like the lyrics in the famous Gershwin and Heyward tune: "Summertime and the livin' is easy." Most of the time, we ran around our hilly neighborhood barefooted. Occasionally, we stepped on a bee or shard of glass. The sweltering heat shimmied up from the streets and smelled like a boiling, bubbling tar pit. Sometimes the steaming pavement burned the bottoms of our feet so badly, we could hardly stand it. Wasting no time, we raced across the scorching streets to seek some relief in a grassy spot.

Occasionally we got banged up skating, riding our bikes, or tripping on the uneven sidewalks. Then, we worried about how the mercurochrome or Merthiolate our moms always used would burn like liquid fire. Even our mothers' quick blowing on the treated wounds wouldn't do much to help ease the sting. "Blow faster, blow faster," we pleaded. We were ignorant of the fact that we shouldn't be chasing the peculiar-looking gray pesticide trucks as they circled the neighborhood, filling the air with a big white cloud of DDT. In retrospect, the overwhelming majority of us did lead pretty carefree lives.

Many a night, I looked up to the first star of the evening and recited to myself: "Star light, star bright, first star I see tonight. I wish I may, I wish I might, have this wish come true tonight." I believed that there was some truth about the success that might follow upon reciting this regularly, just like making a wish before blowing out the candles on a birthday cake. During the summer of 1956, after my first grade, Doris Day's hit "Que Sera, Sera" first came out. This song was popular for years. It was a great descriptor of our carefree mind-set back then: "Whatever will be, will be."

We played in halters, shorts, and other lightweight clothing, during extremely hot days. On weekdays, practically every waking moment was spent at the playground. It was just at the foot of our street. Occasionally we ran up to my house, since it was so close, and cooled off with half of a Popsicle or a glass of Kool-Aid. Mom was always so nice to all of the kids in the neighborhood, welcoming them into our home. We were drawn by the inviting fragrance from the honeysuckle bushes along the fences in our yard and behind the school. We plucked the light orange blossoms and gently pulled out the stamen to expose one tiny, sweet drop of nectar. On the chain-link fence along the lower side of our front yard, the most delicate, beautiful blue flowers adorned a twisted morning glory vine, woven in and out of the fence openings.

One of our favorite pastimes at the playground was to scavenge for coins in the sand underneath the jungle gym. The money had fallen out of the pockets of kids hanging upside down. We were always successful in our search for the buried treasures. With our newfound wealth in hand, we rewarded ourselves with a shopping excursion to Maple Grocery. It sat diagonally across the street from the playground. Back then, we could buy everyone a Black Cow or Sugar Daddy for just a few pennies. We frequently bought candy cigarettes and puffed on them, pretending that we were really smoking. Most of our dads and some of our moms smoked, so we wanted to look cool like they did. Often we bought everybody several pieces of penny Dubble-Bubble gum, and then had bubble-blowing contests on the front stoop of the store. The winner was not only whoever could blow the biggest bubble, but who could hold it the longest. Many times, the kids who blew gigantic bubbles ended up with pink masks covering their faces.

I can still hear the store's owner, Buzz, answering the phone, with his drawn-out, "May-a-ple Grocery." Tuck, the store's butcher, was always busy behind the glass panels of the meat counter, towards the back of the store. In those days, little family-run grocery stores like Buzz's were scattered all over the West Side. There were four of them just within four blocks of our house. Part of their success when they were flourishing was that they allowed customers to charge their purchases, plus, they had delivery service. Today, not one of those stores remains.

The activity we spent most of our time on at the playground was Block Ball, or Four Square, as it is called today. Practically the entire day was spent standing in long lines, waiting for our turn to play. All of us become pretty skilled at that game. Whoever could advance to block four and stay there always gained a lot of clout. It was so much fun to watch older, very athletic kids take a beating from much younger, unpretentious players. Two little guys, Leon and "Peanut," were small in stature but could beat the socks off anyone when it came to Block Ball.

We also played our fair share of Hopscotch. Drawing the court accurately, throwing our markers on the right spot, and hopping and jumping through the court successfully took some practice. Leaning over on one foot, while picking up our markers, then pivoting around on that same foot proved to be the most challenging moves for me. Sometimes we brought pieces of waxed paper from home, to make for a faster trip down the slicky slide. Robins had a pretty large slide, so it was thrilling to go down it so fast. The metal surface of the slide became so hot some days that we had to hold our bare legs up, to keep them from touching the scorching surface.

Jumping Rope was another activity we spent a lot of time doing at the playground. Timing was everything on the Double-Dutch jumping. I never really got the hang of figuring out precisely when to run into the two moving ropes at the opportune time. It always felt pretty clumsy to get tangled up in the limp rope when it fell down on my head. Our favorite chant while jumping rope was: "Linda and Jerry sitting in a tree, k-i-s-s-i-n-g. First comes love, then comes marriage, then comes Linda with a baby carriage."

We played Badminton on the grassy front lawn of the playground, and pitched horseshoes in the sandy pits towards the back of the school. Since we played these games so often, most of us became fairly adept at both of them. When "Peanut," Bobby Wesley, and "Appleseed," Charles Price, played Horseshoes, they always drew a crowd. They were so incredibly skilled at the game, it was a special treat just to watch them. Once a week, a visiting crafts teacher came to our playground and had something fun and interesting for us to do. Over several years, our moms collected plenty of colorful potholders that we wove with stretchy loops on small metal looms.

Frequently, kids brought their yo-yos to play with and show off their skills. The extent of my yo-yo repertoire was simply making it go up and down, so I marveled at those who could do tricks. "Walk the Dog" always looked so difficult to me, and there were several kids who had that down pat. Others did such complicated moves, swinging the yo-yos around their heads and behind their backs. Those feats looked impossible to me. Sometimes we took our metal Slinkys to the playground. Over and over, we watched the Slinkys "walk" down the concrete steps, seeing whose could go the farthest. Not many of us learned how to play the game of Marbles. We did, however, gather around to watch as a few boys shot marbles on the shady front yard of the playground. They played for hours at a time and became so involved in the game. Even though I didn't play Marbles, I loved my marble collection. My favorites were the colorful cat's eyes. Many times during the day, at the playground, we could hear the loud train whistles, from several blocks away.

Every summer, the playground directors held special events. We participated in bike parades, pet shows, talent shows, and doll shows. For the bike parades, we decorated our bikes with balloons and crepe paper streamers, which were woven in and out of our spokes and hanging from our handlebars. My tiny little turtle placed third in the "Smallest Pet" category one year, beaten only by guppies and goldfish. Another year, I won second place in the "Most Unusual Doll" category, with my little doll made of corn husks. The judges of these contests were always so kind. Everyone who participated walked away with some kind of ribbon. All of us had a pretty impressive collection of colorful satin ribbons from those competitions. Of course, most of us had more of the pink "Honorable Mention" ribbons than any other kind.

We idolized our playground directors, who were usually college students. One of our directors, Jake, was a big, athletic football player and was very popular with us kids. He was our director for several summers. Whenever it rained, we crammed into his car, like clowns in a circus act, and waited out many downpours in the steamy interior.

Many times we got cleaned up and changed clothes after dinner. An entirely different group of people showed up at the playground after suppertime. In the evenings, we had many spirited Volleyball games. A group of older boys from the flat part of the West Side frequently came up to our playground for a serious game against the kids in our neighborhood. That was always a special occasion, and exciting to watch. The rivalry was extremely intense, the skill level of the players was off the charts, and, most importantly, those visiting, older boys were so good looking. C. G. and Bobby were two of my favorites.

One event which drew a huge crowd every summer was the playground's street dance. This night was the big deal of the summer for everyone. The music was loud, and the packed street was fairly dark, with the only light shining down from a few streetlights. Most of us stood along the sideline as we watched the older, popular kids dance. One year, Piccolo, an extremely popular older girl from school, showed up, and was quite the center of attention. She was such a talented dancer.

Every night after the playground officially closed its gates at eight o'clock, many of us walked across the street to sit on the Duff family's big stone wall. We hung out and visited there until our parents started calling us in for the evening. A lot of good times and conversations took place on that wall.

On extremely hot days, our mom took us to visit friends who lived across the street from the playground at Tiskelwah Elementary, not far from our church. In front of their playground, firemen regularly opened up the fire hydrant like a huge fountain. We squealed and laughed as we frolicked and jumped in the cold spray. It was a much-welcomed relief from the hot summer sun. On rare occasions, firemen opened the fire hydrant near our playground, too.

In the sixties, our family joined Edgewood Pool, a brand new swimming pool in our neighborhood. We spent most of our summer days there. My very favorite thing to do was to swim in the water after dusk. That's when the water was illuminated from the lights down in the pool. There was something so heavenly about that. I remember opening my eyes under the water and seeing the refracted light patterns. We swam up to the lights and touched their glass surface, enjoying the warmth they emitted down in the cold water. My friends and I mastered some impressive feats on the high dive at the pool. There was a friendly competition among us. Graceful dives and forward and backward flips from high in the air were what we enjoyed doing. This is so intriguing to me, because I don't have the slightest desire to even get on a high dive these days, much less flip or dive off of one.

Another fun treat that we got to do several times a summer was load up the car with friends and go to the popular drive-in theater. Those were such great times. We hung the speaker box on the outside of our car window and turned it up loudly enough to hear it. Watching the movie from our blankets, spread out beside the car, was more fun than staying cooped up inside the vehicle. It was cooler, too, as the pleasant evening breeze whipped all around us. We always got a kick out of seeing the older teenage couples making out in their front seats. Snickering and giggling, we walked by them as we headed over to get popcorn and snacks from the concession stand. Sadly, all of our drive-in theaters have bitten the dust.

There was such a strong sense of community during those years. Our mothers visited with one another and often borrowed baking ingredients from each other. Our dads frequently chatted with one another while they washed their cars out on the streets. In the evenings, after the sun went down, families usually sat out on their porches to cool down and visit with their neighbors.

Neighborhood friends Toey Goff and Georgette Otten with Jean and me, 1952.

We kids were always running in and out of each other's homes. Our kitchens were so similar to one another. Practically everyone had white metal cabinets and porcelain over cast iron sinks, a can opener on the wall, silver canisters with copper lids, a chrome kitchen table with a Formica marble-pattern top, and chrome chairs with padded vinyl seats. So many kids who were extremely close in age to one another lived in our neighborhood. We were very fortunate to have plenty of friends and playmates at the pool, playground, or on our street.

Occasionally, the ominous sound of the distress whistle could be heard from a nearby chemical plant. The kids and wives of the men who worked there always stopped in their tracks whenever they heard the whistle. The pattern of the toots from the whistle communicated which part of the plant was having an emergency. The plant workers' families carefully listened to the whistle patterns to hear if their loved ones were in danger. Whenever we heard the whistle, all of us stopped whatever we were doing and looked at each other, wondering what might be happening.

Ida Dell

My maternal grandparents, Doc and Ida Pierson, 1916.

My grandmother and I had a real mutual admiration society. We were so close. On October 12, 1890, she was born Ida Dell Craft, in her parents' home in rural Braxton County, West Virginia. Her husband, William "Doc" McCauley Pierson, grew up over the hill on a nearby farm. He was named after Doctor McCauley who delivered him. Since he died a week after my second birthday, I don't remember him. Doc was a traveling dry-goods salesman for Guthrie-Morris Campbell. He drove to general stores all over the central part of the state, selling fabrics and other merchandise. Back in those days, traveling salesmen were called "drummers." My grandmother was a registered nurse at Memorial Hospital in Charleston. She worked many years after Doc's death. She never drove, so we either picked her up at the hospital when she finished her shift or she rode the bus home.

As a young couple, they first lived in Rosedale, then Sutton, West Virginia, before settling on the West Side of Charleston in 1921. They raised a son, James Ralph, and daughter, Betty Jean, my mom, in a crowded little court called Woodward Court. It ran off of and perpendicular to Garden Street, which was brick-covered, as were many of the streets in the neighborhood. Houses lined both sides of the narrow walkway, which extended down the court from beginning to end. They were crammed together so closely, that the overhangs from their roofs nearly touched. In between the houses were small, three-foot spaces.

My grandparents' brown, one-story, wooden frame house was typical of the vernacular architecture of their neighborhood. Doc was a master furniture maker and built a woodworking shop behind their home, overtop the garage. The house and shop were connected by a stairway, which led up to the shop and down to the backyard. After he died, the gray wooden door to his shop remained closed and locked, as if there were memories behind that door too precious to be disturbed.

Being a devout Baptist and the matriarch of the family, Ida, or "Granny," as we called her, set the standards for much of what we children were allowed, or not allowed, to do. Decks of regular playing cards, which were used to play poker, were never allowed in our home. We couldn't discuss our going to dances with her, since she didn't approve of such behavior. To me, the most fanatic rule she had was her ban on root beer, because of the obvious reason…it was some kind of "beer."

My immediate family, Mom's brother, Ralph, his wife, Virginia, and their daughter, Joyce, visited with Granny often, especially since we all went to the same church. We spent a lot of time together at camp and in each other's homes. Our houses were only a few blocks up the hill from hers. Whenever we went for visits, we rang her front doorbell and waited for her to open the door. She pulled up the blind on the door window and was always so thrilled to see us. Every time she rolled up the blind to reveal who was there, she threw her hands up, raised her eyebrows, and dropped her jaw from excitement.

More often than not, when we went to her house, she was making medical bandages to send overseas. This seemed to be her self-imposed, personal mission. For many years, she tore up white sheets into long, thin three-inch-wide strips, and then rolled them tightly into bandages. These were mailed overseas to missionaries, who were in dire need of medical supplies.

She was also active in the local chapter of the WCTU, the Women's Christian Temperance Union. It was the nondenominational, worldwide women's group which spearheaded the Prohibition Movement. Her chapter sponsored coloring contests every year at local grade schools. Among other things, it held annual White Ribbon Ceremonies at local churches. These were for parents of young children to pledge that they would never expose their children to any form of alcohol.

Sometimes when we visited her, she stood at her ironing board for hours upon hours, starching and ironing her crisp, white nurse's uniforms. After she retired, she ironed for other families.

I'm sure she was only paid a pittance for ironing their baskets of clothes, but she was happy to earn the spare change. Frequently, she washed curtains for other families, having to measure them carefully, then stretch them back to their original size. She used wooden stretcher frames to keep the sheers from shrinking as they dried. Granny liked to quilt, and often had an enormous wooden quilting frame set up in her living room. She painstakingly made beautiful hand-stitched quilts to give as gifts. All three of us grand-daughters received a custom quilt, made especially for us. The quilt she made for me, with large, pink dogwood blossoms, is one of my most cherished possessions.

When I spent the night with her, it always looked so strange to watch her sit at the vanity and brush out her long, gray hair. This was such a rare sight, since she always wore her hair pulled up in a tidy little bun or French twist. At her home, I used the Colgate tooth powder to brush my teeth. After sprinkling some out in my palm, I added a few drops of water, and made a paste with it. She loved for me to spend the night with her. Every time I came home from college, she called and invited me to come visit and spend the night. I usually took her up on the offer. That's why we were so close. I was still single, unlike my cousin and sister, so I could willingly give her quite a bit of my time.

She and I often sat in front of the dark, wooden mantle in her bedroom, and snuggled up next to the gas space heater. Sometimes, we watched her favorite television show, *The Price is Right*. When I was in the fifth grade, while we were visiting in her bedroom, she commented that I had dirt on my knee. When she realized it was the dark hair on my legs, from then on she became my advocate in convincing Mom to let me remove the hair with Nair cream.

Even though we had given her an electric blanket one year for Christmas, she preferred not to use it. She slept in a handsome walnut bed Doc had made. He had hand-turned the tall wooden posts on his lathe. The mattress sat a little higher than on most beds. When we went to bed for the night, I climbed up to her icy cold sheets. The weight from all of the blankets was so heavy, it was nearly impossible to turn over.

While we visited with her in the kitchen, she loved baking sugar cookies for us. She often offered her visitors treasures which she had hoarded from the hospital cafeteria…assorted flavors of jellies. She kept the little rectangular packages on a serving platter and only got them out on special occasions. Queen Elizabeth couldn't have been more proud to have offered her guests exquisite caviar than Granny was in presenting us with the packaged jellies. She acted as if those were rare delicacies.

We always celebrated Thanksgiving and Christmas meals at her home, as we gathered around the large, round, wooden dining room table. It had a leaf for the middle to accommodate our big family. Each meal was a feast of epic proportion. My favorite mouthwatering dish was turkey dressing with chestnuts. The dish of sweet potatoes with marshmallows melted on top was always a big hit. I liked to help grind up the ingredients for the cranberry salad, shoving the orange peelings down into the sturdy, metal, hand-cranked grinder. It was a real honor to get to break the wishbone with someone else. Whoever ended up with the bigger half was supposed to get his or her wish.

At Christmastime, Granny had a small artificial tree, which she sat out on a dark round coffee table. I don't consider myself to be a materialistic person, but some of my favorite memorabilia is from her house. They are striped, fragile, glass Christmas ornaments, which I remember seeing on her tree when I was a child. I take great pride in hanging them on my tree every year.

One of my fondest things in her house was the pair of beautiful tapestry rugs she had in her living room and dining room. The rugs in both rooms were identical and were so large they nearly covered the entire floor. The tightly woven rugs had a handsome pink and black floral design. That has always been my favorite color combination. I still love to see the one in my mother's upstairs guest room, which we fondly call "The Shrine." Granny had us help her take the rugs outside and clean them by hitting them with large wire rug beaters.

Wash day at my grandmother's family's home, circa 1913.

As a young lady, Granny was accustomed to washing clothes by hand, out in her family's yard, using large wash tubs. So, to her, a wringer washing machine was a real luxury. For years, we watched her force her wet clothes through the wringers of her electric washing machine. One day, she caught her little finger in the wringer, crushing it. The machine had a large, round, white tub and stood on four legs. It sat out on her back porch, which was enclosed with small windowpanes and also served as a greenhouse. She had a beautiful display of large-leafed, magenta and purple coleus plants and a magnificent crown of thorns cactus plant. It was at least five feet wide, occupying a large part of the porch.

For the longest time, Granny didn't own a clothes dryer. She hung her wash out to dry either on the line in the backyard or on her back porch during bad weather. While we were young, she had a delivery man from the North Pole Ice Company bring a gigantic cube of ice a couple of times a week to refrigerate her ice chest. At that time, she had no electric refrigerator.

One of Granny's neighbors had an incredible green thumb. Her backyard was very visible from Granny's porch and yard. It was a beautiful palette of rich colors from plants and flowers blooming all year long. Granny never saw the neighbors on the other side of her house. They were blocked off by the big two-story shop and garage. We certainly could hear them from time to time. The couple frequently got into screaming matches. Their domestic disputes always escalated into throwing clay flower pots or anything else within reach at each other. When my sister and I heard the screaming begin, we hurried out the back porch door and excitedly tiptoed up the gray wooden steps which led to the old workshop. We hunkered down on the dusty landing at the top of the stairs and, with outstretched necks, peeked down onto her neighbors' backyard. Staying absolutely quiet and perfectly still, we watched as the drama unfolded.

The neighbors were an elderly couple. He was short and stocky with gray hair, and she was thin and spunky with dyed red hair. Stage one of the mayhem was loud screaming and swearing at one another. Then the real ruckus began. One at a time, they would pick up an object on their patio and heave it at their partner as they let out a loud, primal scream. The wife often ran into the kitchen to fetch dishes and pans for more ammunition. The flying objects were hurled across the yard or porch with such force and intensity, that they surely had the potential of hurting someone. We never knew if both the husband and wife couldn't hit their spousal targets because they were such bad shots, or if this was a case of deliberate misses. Thankfully, their ability to duck from flying obstacles far outweighed their ability to aim at and hit their targets with any accuracy.

These episodes went on for quite a long time. It was like watching a Neanderthal version of dodge ball. Instead of throwing a red rubber ball, the objects they used were loud as they crashed onto the patio, sometimes shattering upon impact. The couple was so completely engrossed in their fight. They were totally oblivious to the fact that they had an audience on the landing above them, taking in their every move.

The Pierson family, left to right: Guy, father James Floyd, William "Doc," John, mother Varina Frame, and Clara, circa 1899.

Even though I don't remember my grandfather, I have very fond memories of visiting with his siblings. His brother John and his wife, Erma, raised four kids on a beautiful farm near Frame-town. It was just over the hill from where he grew up in Braxton County. When we visited with them, John took my sister and me to the chicken coop to help him gather eggs and showed us how to milk a cow up in their red barn. He got a kick out of squirting us with milk. We had many cousin reunions at their farm, always with such delicious food. John led the singing at the Middle Run Baptist Church, where we went on Sundays when we were staying at camp. Another brother, Guy, was also a fine woodworker like Doc. When I was in the second grade, he made me a custom wooden doll bed, which I treasure. My mom always thought I looked like their sister, Clara. When we were young, she managed the Blossom Dairy restaurant on Quarrier Street. She often waited on our table in her gray and maroon uniform.

Ida's family on her wedding day, June 16, 1915, at her family's home. Back row, left to right: brothers Ernest, John, George II and David. Middle row: sisters Mabel, Fanny Mae, brother Wilbur, Ida and bridesmaid, Carol Cunningham. Her parents, George and Mary Elizabeth Craft, are seated.

We often visited with Ida's brother George and his wife, Floda, up on their Vandalia hilltop farm, overlooking Charleston. He was a fine gardener, and she served mouthwatering, light and fluffy chicken and dumplings. Their son, Paul, with his powerful bass voice, sang "How Great Thou Art" at Granny's funeral. We traveled to Marietta, then Athens, Ohio, to visit her brother Wilbur and his wife, Thelma, and their two daughters. He had the most lavish flower and vegetable gardens. Before they moved to Ohio, Wilbur managed the company store at Widen, a coal camp in Clay County, West Virginia. His customers paid him in tokens called "scrip," which was what the coal companies used to pay their miners. Sometimes we drove to Widen to visit Ida's coal miner brother, Ernest, and his wife, Ethel, and their children. We traveled to Union, a small town in rural Monroe County, West Virginia, to visit her brother David and his wife, Hazel, and their family. He was a Baptist minister at a local church. One Sunday afternoon, we were visiting Granny's nephew Doc Craft, another minister, at his farm near Sutton, also in West Virginia. He was out slopping hogs when we arrived. While we were visiting with him and his family on their porch, a love-struck young couple showed up and asked Doc if he would marry them. He went inside and washed his hands, then came back out and proceeded with the impromptu ceremony.

I never met Granny's brother John, but I often go by and pay my respects to him, at the War Memorial in Charleston. His name is engraved among the other casualties of World War I. Not long ago I found a postcard from the war, which he had written to his mother, telling her he would be coming home in a week. He died in combat, on October 3, 1918, and never made it home. John is buried in the Meuse-Argonne American Cemetery in Romagne, France, with thousands of other brave men who lost their lives far too young. We have a certificate which reads: "The state of West Virginia in profound appreciation of the Supreme Sacrifice for Country and Mankind made by John E. Kraft in the War for Civilization, offers to his Family and Friends this token of Gratitude and Sympathy." It's unclear as to why his name was written as "Kraft" instead of "Craft." Two of my grandmother's sisters, Daisy and Mabel, also died at a young age.

Granny was a stickler for what was proper, and was not one to embrace change. She told one pastor at our church that she thought it was only appropriate for preachers to wear white shirts at the pulpit. He had shown up one Sunday wearing a pastel pink shirt. On the day I was to get married, she called our pastor who was going to conduct the ceremony, Reverend Archie Snedegar, to ask him if he thought the wedding "could be pulled off" with all of those men in the wedding party wearing long hair.

One of the few times I remember Granny not being able to cope with a situation very well was when Ralph and his family decided to attend a different church. I never understood why this stirred up such a brouhaha. As adults, they surely should have had the freedom to decide where to worship. They seemed so enthralled with their new church. Still upset about their departure, she refused to attend my cousin Joyce's wedding because it was being held at their new church. Thankfully, at the last minute, love conquered her stubbornness.

When my first husband, Doug, and I moved to Columbia, South Carolina, Granny was one of the reasons I was so homesick and wanted to come back home. A few days after we had moved back to Charleston, in April of 1974, my mother called her on the phone one morning and didn't get a response. Doug and I were staying with my parents for a few days until we could move into our own home. I volunteered to go down to the court and check on her.

I rang her doorbell, but she didn't answer, so I walked around to her bedroom window. Looking through the window, I could see that she was still in the bed. I crawled through her window and tried to wake her, but she was completely nonresponsive. Perfectly positioned in her bed, under the covers, she was still breathing, albeit it ever so shallow.

She had suffered a stroke and was taken to Charleston General Hospital, where she never would regain consciousness. For three days, we kept a constant vigil over her. We were clinging to hope, which started to fade with each day of seeing no improvement in her condition. On the third day, April 19, she peacefully stopped breathing and was officially declared dead.

I always thought that the way she died was the perfect way to go. There were no signs that she had struggled, and she never experienced any pain. A few days before the stroke, at 83 years old, she was up on a ladder, removing the leaves from her gutters. After witnessing many friends and relatives endure such excruciating suffering over prolonged periods of time, I believe Granny was truly one of the lucky ones.

She was buried beside Doc in a little cemetery at Middle Run Baptist Church, near her birthplace. There are at least three generations of her family, the Crafts, and of Doc's, the Piersons, buried on those hallowed grounds. One of my favorite annual excursions is to go to the little white pristine church's Memorial Day picnic and decorate graves. That is a family tradition we have observed ever since I can remember. During our youth, hundreds of people attended the picnics, which were held on long, weathered wooden tables under ancient shade trees on the church grounds. Now the picnics are held in a picnic shelter. Every year, the crowd gets smaller, as the old timers pass on, one by one.

The once bountiful, delicious spread of chicken and dumplings, baked hams, fried chicken, deviled eggs, fresh green beans, and homemade breads and pies has changed, too. There's still plenty to eat, but not many ladies are left from the older generation, who took so much pride in preparing their signature homemade dishes for the picnic. They have been replaced by a younger generation, with different preferences and offerings: store-bought fried chicken and desserts, hummus and pita bread, and tossed salad. Even though the menu has changed, it is still one event which I look forward to every year.

Camp Pierson

Our typical crowd at camp: clockwise, Dad on left, Jean, Aunt Virginia, me, Hazel Withers, Granny, Uncle Ralph, Becky Shelton, Joyce, and Mom, 1963.

Like many families in West Virginia, we owned a fishing camp, and spent quite a lot of time there during my youth. It was nothing fancy, just a two-room wooden structure. The tan siding resembled thick tar paper, with a coarse, textured, fake brick pattern. Our screened-in porch served as the rustic kitchen. It hung over the bank, which led down to the flat grassy bottom beside the river.

The main room served as a dining room, living room, and bedroom. It had a double bed and three roll-away beds. An eclectic collection of old wooden chairs was scattered across the room. Beside the front door was the long wooden dining table with a narrow bench lining each side. A small bedroom on the back side of the camp had two double beds. Each half of the room was partitioned off by a privacy curtain.

Our camp was located in the remote part of Clay County, near the little community of Ivydale. It sat snuggled up against the steep hillside, which led down towards the Elk River from Route 4. A set of steps, which seemed so arduous and precarious, headed down the sharp slope from the highway to the large concrete patio. A grassy path out the back door, where snakes liked to sun, led to the primitive outhouse. On the highway side of the building was an oxen yoke and a two-foot, professionally painted sign which simply read "Camp Pierson."

We didn't have running water, so we transported water from home in large, steel milking cans. When we ran out of water, the men took the empty cans down to the river to fill them up. That water was used for bathing and doing dishes. To replenish our supply of drinking water, we often journeyed several miles up the road, to Hizer's small grocery store. They were generous and neighborly, letting us get water from their well. Riding up to Hizer's was an exciting day trip to us kids. Our parents bought us several pieces of penny candy, or a nickel ice cream treat.

At the onset of every trip to camp, we stopped on the outskirts of Charleston at a big white cinderblock building called the Ice House. Dad purchased a big square-foot block of ice, which was our only source of refrigeration at camp. It kept food cool in the ice chest, which resembled a small refrigerator, with no electricity. In the main room, the big, black, coal-fired, potbelly stove provided our heat. For most of our stays, we didn't need to crank up the stove. When it did get chilly, especially at nighttime, it felt so good to gather around our welcoming source of heat. We usually backed up to it, or stretched out our hands in front of it. Sometimes we dried our wet clothes and towels near the stove.

My grandfather, dad, and uncle built our camp. We took a great amount of pride and pleasure in having it. In good weather, in the days of my youth, my immediate family, my mom's brother, his wife and daughter, and our grandmother traveled to camp practically every weekend. In the summertime, we often stayed for weeks at a time. There was no interstate in those days, so the trip up Route 4 took several hours. As I got older, my family's ability to go to camp gave way to junior high and high school band and majorette practices.

Keeping up with the maintenance at camp, especially weed control, was a never-ending ordeal. The men used long scythes to cut the big bottom. My grandmother, who was in her seventies at that time, never wore slacks except at camp. When she pulled weeds and cleared brush, she changed into tan work pants and a plain white T-shirt. Weeds often took over the steep bed of irises beside the patio, so she chopped away at those for hours at a time. Since she was so susceptible to getting poison ivy, she invariably ended up with it all over her face and body. Her standard treatment for the rash was Gentian Violet, a bright purple liquid which was commonly used back then. It stained everything it touched. Granny worked as a registered nurse in Charleston. Frequently, we would travel to camp ahead of her, while she was still working. When she finished her shift, she rode the Greyhound bus, which made daily runs up Elk River Road. We waited up for her and could hear the bus stop on the highway at the top of our steps. It was well after midnight when she finally arrived.

I enjoyed working in our vegetable garden. It usually fell victim to the circumstances of our not being able to be there during the week. Whatever the critters didn't eat was always overtaken by weeds. I often questioned the laws of nature: "How could weeds grow so much faster than vegetables or flowers?" Occasionally we enjoyed fresh corn, green beans, and tomatoes from the garden.

Granny and cousin Joyce out in the johnboat with Jean and me at camp, 1956.

The river was our main provider of recreation. We fished, swam, bathed, and took boat rides in it. There were several shoals, where the men had to get out of the boat, and pull it through the rapid, shallow water. Special afternoon boat rides always took place when visitors came. They were usually carried out in shifts, to accommodate so many people. Those rides were a real treat for all of us. Sometimes the men dropped off us kids to explore a nearby island while they took out another load. We searched through the hot sand, finding treasures which had been washed up from the high waters. When our guests wanted to try his or her hand at fishing, Dad or Uncle Ralph paddled us into one of the damp, shady coves, where fishing was the best.

There was something so serene and tranquil about being on the river. The still, calm waterway was a quiet channel surrounded by a host of chirping birds in the lush green vegetation of swaying trees and tall ferns along the damp, sandy banks. Watching the thin water strider's effortless gliding across the water's surface always fascinated me. Occasionally a snake doctor or a dragonfly, with its beautiful iridescent wings, briefly stopped by, as if to be checking us out. Several times we spotted graceful water moccasins as they swam by the boat. If we kept real quiet, we could come upon a beautiful, rare blue heron standing in its favorite spot in the middle of the shoals just up from camp.

Our little dog, Skipper, tried to follow us whenever we went out in the boat. He followed our boat along the river bank, and then climbed out on one of the numerous horizontal tree trunks which lined the water's edge. To everyone's chagrin, he usually fell into the water and swam out to us. We lifted him up into the boat, and then braced ourselves for his inevitable shaking. After he shook several times, everyone in the boat was soaked...and smelled like the unmistakable wet-dog stench.

Some pretty serious fishing took place at camp. All of us enjoyed the benefits from that, with many scrumptious fried fish dinners. Fried catfish was my favorite, with the delicious, mild white meat. A lot of great fellowship took place as we gathered with family and friends around the long, wooden dining table. We were often awakened by the captivating aroma of bacon, hash browns with onions, and eggs being fried in the kitchen. Sometimes we had pancakes and sausage for breakfast. Camping, great food, and good company...it doesn't get much better than that.

Except when we had company, I didn't get to go out in the boat fishing with my dad and uncle, since I was the youngest of the three cousins. My father always said: "The oldest kids get to go," meaning my cousin and sister. I sure thought that wasn't fair. I couldn't help being the youngest child. "Why am I being punished for my age?" I pondered. Obviously, those circumstances would never change, and the fate of being the youngest cousin, deprived of any fishing privileges, became the perpetual law. Sometimes Dad let me go with him when he drove down the road a few miles to seine for minnows in a nearby creek.

Sister Jean with me on the front patio at camp, 1952.

Since I was the lone kid out, many days, I entertained myself by playing in the sand. We had a sandy beach area by the boat landing, shaded by the branches of a large oak tree. I built very complicated, sophisticated networks of bridges, tunnels, and highways. These structures were unlike the sand sculptures at the ocean, which are vulnerable to being erased by the tides. My sculptures lasted for days, until they were flattened by a downpour or until I decided to change them. My grandmother used to yell, from the screened kitchen: "Ralph Pierson, come home. Dinner's ready." When I heard that, I knew it wouldn't be long until the gang out in the boat would be coming in. I got a lot of chigger bites at camp, especially playing in the sand. My mom would put a dab of nail polish on them, to ease the sting and itch.

My dad and uncle liked to set trot lines. These are fishing lines which run from one side of the river to the other. Multiple hooks are strategically placed along the lines. The men went out very late at night and checked their lines to see if they had caught anything. One night, a real surprise awaited them. They had managed to catch the strangest-looking creature any of us had ever seen. Dad brought it up to the front patio and called for us to come see what he had. It must have been from the "ugly branch" on its family tree. This oddity looked like it would have been right at home in the Mesozoic era. It resembled an enormous lizard, with short legs and a slimy body. The scared critter was the size of a small dachshund and walked around the patio, making barking sounds. Appropriately, these animals are called "mud dogs." After a brief viewing, our dad took it down the bank, and released it back to where it belonged, in the deep waters of the river.

We shared the camp with several critters, who were more permanent residents than we were. At the beginning of each stay, when we unfolded the roll-away beds, we always found nests of little baby mice. They had stayed warm and cozy, tucked in the folds of the mattresses. Almost during every visit, Aunt Virginia or our mom let out an ear-splitting, terrifying scream. We knew they had found another black snake peering down upon them from a kitchen shelf. The kitchen was made of rough lumber and was not very tightly enclosed. Upon several occasions, one of the men found a rattlesnake skin under the camp, in the dirt area where we kept our garden tools.

My cousin's boyfriend, Larry, who would become her future husband, joined us one weekend at camp. An avid fisherman, he went out in our johnboat to fish with my uncle and dad. To their astonishment, Larry pulled in an enormous muskie, the likes of which no one had seen come out of the river near camp. This was a little difficult to swallow for the two master fishermen. They had fished those waters for decades. The only bragging rights they had were stories about trophy catfish and wide-mouth bass. Compared to the size of Larry's muskie, Dad's mounted bass hanging in our den look like a sunfish.

For many years, we were fortunate to have our camp not bothered or ruined by vandals and thieves. There used to be several year-round residents, like Tom Hyer and his wife, who lived nearby and always helped to keep an eye on it. Eventually, those folks moved or passed away, and there were no close neighbors left. Sadly, several years ago, our camp finally fell prey to hoodlums who torched the place.

My cousin Joyce, her parents, and her son, Jon, went up to assess the damage. They sifted through the ashes of our beloved camp, which was so unjustly and swiftly reduced to rubble. She was thrilled to find even the smallest remnants of memorabilia among the ruins. A china tea cup had been perfectly preserved and unscathed by the fire. It was down in a metal tin with a tight-fitting lid. Joyce guessed that the tin had probably been used as a flour or sugar canister, with the cup serving as a scoop.

Vandals may have been able to ruin a physical structure, but they could never erase all of the treasured memories we will have forever. Understandably, the shared experiences at camp, helped to make our family closer. Many friends and relatives often recall special memories they have kept over the years from their visits and stays at camp. We were so lucky to have owned Camp Pierson. It provided such a perfect setting for many cherished memories.

Company's Coming

The Haynes family with Dad and my sister and me at Blackwater Falls State Park, 1953. Back row, left to right: Austin, Ruby, Dad. Middle row: Mary, Sharon, Jean. Bobby and I are in the front.

When we were kids, we always had a lot of company and frequently visited in other people's homes. Our birthday parties were big deals, often with more than twenty kids. On many occasions, Mom filled up our inflatable swimming pool on the back porch, and we invited several kids to come for a swim. It wasn't a very large pool, but it was often crammed full of playful children. My sister, Jean, and I always had to wear bathing caps, even in such shallow water. Our halter-clad mothers looked on from white wooden lawn chairs, sipping on iced tea as they visited in the yard. We played in the pool, on our swing set, or in the yard, hitting the badminton shuttlecock to one other.

There were four or five families which we visited with all of the time. We went on vacations together and frequently visited in each other's homes. At mealtime, in every single household, we heard the same thing: "Eat everything on your plate. There are children starving in China." Such a closeness and familiarity existed among our families, we felt more like relatives. Even today, the grown children of these families refer to my mom and deceased father as "Aunt Betty and Uncle Russ." I still call Ruby Haynes and her deceased husband "Aunt Ruby and Uncle Austin." Most of these families had children my sister's age, three years older than I. A few families had kids who were a little younger than the two of us. We were their role models and idols.

In the fifties, the Haynes family traveled with us to the Cincinnati Zoo. They didn't own a vehicle back then, so we all went in our black Buick. Ruby and Austin had three children: Bobby, who was a few years older than my sister, and Sharon and Mary, who were close to my sister's age. As we were en route to the zoo, the luggage, which was strapped to the top of the car, flew off and scattered all over the highway. We must have looked like circus clowns each time all nine of us emptied out of the car. For meals, we stopped along the highway at roadside parks and ate sandwiches our moms had packed. My mother's reliable Mason jar of soapy water was always kept in the trunk for washing our hands before each meal.

Another incident, which I have heard of numerous times, happened before I was in grade school. Mom and Aunt Ruby had driven us five kids out to a friend's house. Since it was crowded in the car, I was sitting on a cake pan on the floor of the back seat. Everyone got out of the car, but I was left sitting on the pan. The car rolled over a steep embankment, with me in it.

Since their family didn't have a television back then, the Haynes girls frequently came to our house to watch *The Big Top* on Saturday mornings. We ate together during many Sunday lunches, which were usually big spreads of fried chicken or pork chops. Sundays were lazy afternoons, since we weren't allowed to go swimming or bike riding on the Sabbath. On Sunday nights, no one was ever very hungry, so our mothers made gravy and served us gravy on toast for supper. The Hayneses' home was within a block from our church, so all of us walked over from their house to Sunday night worship service.

Each week, before every evening service, all of us children memorized a Bible verse, which we recited for the entire congregation. This had quite a competitive feel to it, since one of our friends, Charlie, always outdid everyone else. He impressed the congregation by reciting such lengthy verses. It was unthinkable to not recite a verse. We never considered shirking our responsibility of this obligatory task. John 11:35 was often recited by the slackers of the group. It is the shortest verse in the Bible: "Jesus wept." Such a display of minimal effort never got anyone's respect.

Jean and I often spent the night with Sharon and Mary. They lived on the flat part of the West Side of Charleston. There was a tremendous amount of street noise and action, which took place during the wee hours of the night. That was pretty exciting to my sister and me, since our hillside neighborhood was so quiet once everyone went in for the evening. At nighttime, the four of us girls climbed out one of their second-floor bedroom windows onto the roof over their front porch. It was a good, safe vantage point for watching the goings-on in the middle of the night. The piercing noise from screeching sirens was an omnipresent background, and swirling, flashing, red lights from police cars, ambulances, and fire trucks lit up the night sky. They lived within a few blocks of Cunningham's ambulance service, and the busy Firehouse # 3 on Florida Street.

As most children do, we sometimes got into mischief when we needed to entertain ourselves. All of us gathered around the phone one evening as Mary, who was probably put up to this prank, called a local Pick 'n Pay grocery store. We excitedly hushed each other, as she bravely asked the store employee on the other end of the phone: "Do you have Prince Albert in a can?" Of course, he answered, "Yes," since it was a popular pipe tobacco. We could hardly hold back our giggling as Mary replied: "Well, you better let him out before he suffocates."

Playing a joke like that on some stranger seems like a pretty silly thing to do, in retrospect. But at the moment, it sure was hilarious to us. Another similar call kids made was: "Is your refrigerator running?" To the answer in the affirmative, the reply was: "Then you better go catch it." Those kinds of calls were easier to carry out back then, before the days of Caller ID.

One night, the Hayneses were visiting with us in our home, and all of us were watching some kind of play or movie on television. It had the character of a little bratty girl called "Baby Elizabeth." That became my nickname. It has exhibited a tremendous amount of staying power, since five decades later the Haynes clan still fondly calls me "Baby Elizabeth." I was always the baby, out of the five kids in our two families. As an incentive for me to stop sucking my thumb, my mom promised to buy me a Mister Potato Head kit. Back then, there were no plastic bodies, so we used a real potato. I was so excited to get it, and all of the older kids liked to play that with me.

One afternoon, Uncle Austin helped me lose a tooth, which had been dangling for days. He tied one end of a string around my little loose tooth, and then tied the other end of it around the doorknob of their opened front door. In one quick motion, and before I could become too scared about the situation, he slammed the door shut. In a split second, my tooth was freed at last. It was such a relief to finally get rid of that nuisance tooth. I felt nothing but gratitude towards him. Besides, the Tooth Fairy would surely leave me a few silver coins under my pillow that night, to boot.

Most households back then used Melmac plates and dishes, like we did. They were made of a lightweight, hard, durable plastic. Aunt Ruby served meals on the famous Homer Laughlin Company's Fiestaware. As a child, I always thought that was so special. These brightly colored ceramic dishes are manufactured in West Virginia and are available in a multitude of rich colors. Uncle Austin bought the Fiestaware over a long period of time at McClung and Morgan, a South Charleston department store where he worked for nineteen years.

My Fiestaware is one of my most treasured, nostalgic possessions. I have a multicolored collection, taking advantage of the vast array of colors. Looking at vintage Fiestaware in antique shops is one of my favorite things to do. Ironically, the building where Uncle Austin had worked and bought the dishes is now an antique mall. The vintage dishes on display these days are exactly like the ones originally sold there decades ago.

One of my fondest memories from my youth is about Uncle Austin. He could whip up the most delicious batch of made-from-scratch chocolate fudge. On winter evenings, when there was snow on the ground, we frequently had the ultimate treat of all time, "Snow Pepsis and Fudge." We tucked glass bottles of Pepsi down into the snow and left them there, just long enough to become slushy. Snow Pepsis and Uncle Austin's fudge was a divine combination. My mouth keeps watering just thinking about it.

The Haynes kids taught Jean and me how to ride bikes. Thinking back on it, we must have looked like a scene right out of a Laurel and Hardy routine. Their backyard had an ever-so-slight incline to the entire length of it. Someone, usually Sharon's and Mary's brother, Bobby, held one of us up on the bike at the top of the slope, then gave us a gentle push off. Every single time, we rode uncontrollably down the yard, swaying from side to side, for about twenty yards or so until we inevitably fell over.

I couldn't guess how many times this happened, but there were numerous rides, repeated over and over again. Eventually, Jean and I got the knack of balancing ourselves and graduated from being confined only to backyard rides. Unlike our hilly street, their neighborhood was so conducive for bike riding, since it was perfectly flat.

Bobby was five years older than I and had three close friends who lived nearby, two named Bill and Leslie. The four of them were always hanging out together. Needless to say, there was quite a bit of hero worshiping that took place. The four of us younger girls looked up to the older, attractive boys.

The Hayneses' family pet was a handsome dog named Romeo. He was a big, white, loveable mutt, with beautiful black markings and a laid-back personality. Our dog, Skipper, and Romeo were such pals. One Easter Sunday, we looked out our front door, and to everyone's disbelief, Romeo had walked up to our house. He played with Skipper as our visiting relatives joined us in the backyard for our traditional Easter egg hunt. We could hardly believe he found our home, since our two houses were at least twelve blocks apart. His shocked owners eventually drove up to retrieve their adventuresome friend.

Mary Haynes was a talented beautician. After attending beauty college, she opened her own salon in Charleston. While I was still in college, she asked me to paint the sign for her shop on the storefront window. In large letters, I painted, "Peachie's Beauty Parlor," since that was her nickname. As fate would have it, shortly after her shop was established, Mary cut her hand on a glass jar. She was getting some frozen food out of the jar, when it shattered on her hand. The tendons and nerves were so badly severed, it was impossible for her to continue a career as a beautician.

Sharon Haynes had the remarkable gift of playing piano by ear. I'm not talking about simply pecking out an easy tune on the keyboards, like "Heart and Soul." That popular song, and a fraction of my first and only recital piece, was the extent of my piano repertoire. When Sharon played, she moved up and down the keyboard, playing complicated chords and incredible, complex arrangements. She reminded me of a New Orleans jazz pianist. I never understood how anyone could play the piano by ear. She made it appear to be so effortless. Watching her play was like witnessing a miracle.

My parents insisted that Jean and I performed whenever company came. That was so humiliating to me. It was difficult for anyone to fake that they were enjoying listening to my squawking clarinet, which I was just learning to play. My choppy, torturous clarinet solo of "Mary Had a Little Lamb" was a pitiful excuse for any performance. It was a far cry from the usual concept of entertainment and was definitely not music to anyone's ears, other than, I guess, my parents'. Before my clarinet days, during grade school, I was required to show our guests the twirls I had learned at Joan Basham's backyard baton lessons. This was equally as painful, sensing that my captive audience wasn't really enjoying the show.

On the other hand, Jean had several years of playing the piano under her belt and was pretty proficient at it. Listening to her performance was both entertaining and pleasant. She had stuck with taking lessons from Francis Holbrook, our neighborhood's stellar piano teacher. I, on the other hand, was a piano lesson dropout. The ticking sound of my teacher's metronome, which sat on top of her piano, is what I remember so vividly about those lessons.

Rick, Mary, and Larry Wolfe, 1957.

Our forced performances were especially embarrassing when the Wolfe family came to visit. Their older sons, Larry and Rick, were such talented musicians. I could only imagine how they had to hold back laughing out loud, when I stood at the front of our living room and started squeaking at them on my horn. Like us, they too, begrudgingly, had to play their trumpet and trombone for our family when we visited them. The difference was overwhelming, to hear them perform with such skill and perfection. It was always fun visiting with Mary and Russ, the boys, and their big, friendly collie, Jake. They often came up to our camp, and sometimes we joined them at their favorite campground in the Blue Bend Recreation Area of the Monongahela National Forest. Mary and Russ Wolfe were my mom's best friends in high school.

The most trouble I remember getting into was when we were visiting in my friend Belinda's home. Our family had stopped by her home after church one evening. Her mother, Evelyn, always kept such an immaculate house. Jean and I went to Belinda's room with her, and the three of us started jumping on her bed, as if it were a trampoline. At that very moment, our parents opened the bedroom door and were in complete disbelief of what they saw. They were outraged that we were behaving so badly in someone else's home. We never lived down that episode.

1983 Myrtle Beach trip with the Youngs. Clockwise, starting with me in the sunglasses: my mom, Kay's husband Jeff Biddle, Steve's wife Donna, Kay, Lynn, Mabel, Charlie, my son Michael, and my dad. Photo taken by Steve Young.

The Youngs also attended our church, and our two families became very close. We often took summer vacations together, frequently renting beach houses at Myrtle Beach or rustic cabins at Watoga State Park. They had three children, Lynn, Kay-Kay, and Stevie, who were a few years younger than my sister and I. Their parents, Charlie and Mabel, were about ten years younger than ours, and in my mind, they always seemed pretty young. It was a little surprising when we celebrated Charlie's eightieth birthday last year. At his party, Kay explained to one of her sons that when we were growing up, I was just old enough for her brother and her to want to follow me around, and pester me, everywhere I went.

On our beach trips, we girls frequently went shopping for clothes while the men played golf. Charlie was always so strict about his girls not wearing revealing clothes. This was especially true of bathing suits. With everything they tried on, we would have to discuss and debate whether or not it would get "Chuck's approval." As most people did back then, we stupidly sunbathed most of the time at the beach, slathering on baby oil, trying to get as dark as we could. I remember having to ride the Tilt-a-Whirl carnival ride by myself. The Young children weren't tall enough to ride it, and I couldn't talk anyone else into going on it with me.

The other place where we vacationed with the Youngs was Watoga State Park. It is one of West Virginia's oldest and most beautiful parks, located in Pocahontas County. We liked to stay in the older "standard" cabins, which are rugged log structures with huge, stone fireplaces. Many of our older state parks had the same sturdy, rustic cabins, which were built between 1833 and 1942 by Roosevelt's CCC, the Civilian Conservation Corps.

The park's pool had some of the coldest water you could ever imagine. We spent many fun-filled afternoons there, swimming and shivering. Driving around the park at dusk every night, hoping to see deer, was one of our favorite pastimes. In an ironic twist, these days, deer have taken over our old neighborhoods. What used to be such a special, rare sight is now commonplace in our parents' backyards. Before we had a driver's license, Dad let Jean and me drive in a huge grassy field near the park's entrance. That was so thrilling to us.

We also enjoyed hiking on Watoga's numerous trails, many lined with rhododendron bushes. Visitors who came during the weeks when the rhododendrons were in full bloom were in for a real treat. The park had huge, stately trees with lush, dense forest beds, which let visitors sense that these woods had been around for centuries. Only old forests are capable of emitting such an aura.

One afternoon, some of us kids were walking beside the road which ran between the lake and our cabin. Simply by happenstance, we discovered one of the greatest finds of a lifetime. Someone in our group reached down to pick up a rock beside the road. To our surprise, the bottom side of it had a perfectly-intact fossil on its surface. We couldn't have been more elated if we were pirates discovering lost treasures. The rocky bank had dark gray, flat layers of what looked like shale. The more rocks we flipped over, the more fossils we found of what resembled small, lacy ferns.

Our family also visited with the Carpers. Charlie was one of Dad's fellow workers at DuPont. He and his wife, Mary, had a daughter, Charlene, who was around eight years younger than I. Since she was so much younger, Jean and I did our fair share of spoiling her. She had deep dimples and beautiful red hair, which I always insisted on calling "strawberry blonde." When she was little, Charlene's favorite food was cottage cheese and pineapple, mixed together. It was Mary and Charlene who taught me to enjoy this tasty combination, which remains a favorite of mine. As a visitor in their home, I was always intrigued with their unusual, circular bathtub.

We tricked Charlie one night with our fake ice cube, which had a bee inside it. Another time, we got him with our realistic-looking rubber "chocolate" candy. It was great fun to trick the trickster. Charlie was a real character, always showing a great sense of humor, especially with the stories he told. We thought it was a big deal when he brought his own boat with an outboard motor to camp. Our little johnboat only had oars and paddles. He passed away last year. As his son-in-law pointed out so appropriately in his eulogy, it was altogether fitting that Charlie appeared to have a smile on his face, lying in the open casket.

Charlie and Mary Carper with baby Charlene at our camp, 1957.

At the funeral, Charlene introduced me to one of her sons and husband by saying I was her childhood idol. For many years, I knew that was how she thought of me. She had followed in my footsteps by being a majorette in junior high and in high school. I was always a little uncomfortable with being placed on such a high pedestal and trying to live up to her expectations.

Another family we visited with frequently was the Griffiths. Bonnie was a tall, attractive lady with the face of a model. Her husband, Everett, was shorter than she, with a friendly grin which never stopped. They had two sons, Butch and Greg, who were close to Jean's age. One night when we became a little too rowdy, Greg got a pretty bad burn from falling on our big floor furnace in the hall. We were taken aback one evening when they came to our house to visit and the boys enjoyed playing with our dolls. Back then, a boy playing with dolls was such a taboo. Looking back on it, I think those guys were just ahead of their time. These days, there are so many single dads and househusbands, who are often the primary caregivers to their children. I always thought men who took an active role in changing diapers and raising their kids had a special attractiveness.

Cousin Joyce with Jean and me, in our front yard, on Easter day, 1953.

My cousin Joyce and her parents, Ralph and Virginia, spent a lot of time visiting with us, too. We always got together on Easter Sundays, and the three of us girls shared the goodies from our Easter baskets. My favorite things in our baskets were the fancy, hollow white eggs made of compressed sugar. They were decorated with colorful, hard, yet edible icing. Each egg had a peephole on one end. A small, very intricate scene was inside each egg. When we visited at their home, we always marveled at their cat, Black Boy. He taught himself how to urinate in their toilet bowl. That sounds like it couldn't have been feasible, but he actually could aim very accurately. When he was finished, he rattled the commode handle until someone flushed it. That was an unbelievable sight.

Many times, we had multiple families visiting at the same time. Most of these people knew each other. Often, my parents set up cardboard card tables in the living room for us kids to eat on. The adults got to dine at the dining room table. All of the families mentioned in this chapter had to endure hours upon hours of watching home movies of our family. These movies became a little more interesting when they finally had sound. At least there were scattered bits and pieces of each family injected into these movie marathons. That always resulted in a lot of loud bursts of laughter.

We served soft drinks and popcorn, to help create a going-to-the-movies atmosphere. Dad proudly projected the 16mm movies on a huge white screen, which he had set up in the living room. I can still hear the clicking sound from the reels and the Bell and Howell projector. Their sometimes fuzzy, unclear, jumpy images were a far cry from Blu-ray or the high definition we enjoy today. With all of their imperfections, those old images are precious and dear, cherished treasures from our youth.

The Williams Clan

Grandparents Alfred and Flora Williams on their wedding day, November 5, 1894.

My paternal grandmother, Flora Belle, was born on February 11, 1876, in Walzenhausen, Switzerland. She was one of nine children born to Jakob and Albertina Barlocher Kellenberger. When she was ten, her family immigrated to the United States. They entered the country at Castle Garden, New York, America's first immigrant receiving center, where Battery Park is today. Her family brought with them two of their prized Swiss dairy cows. They settled in Helvetia, in Randolph County, West Virginia. The small Swiss community was, and still is, commonly referred to as "Little Switzerland."

Flora's brother Jakob had seen a booklet about West Virginia and was instrumental in convincing his family to move here. Only one sibling, Eugene, stayed behind. In 1864, the West Virginia Legislature had passed an act "for the encouragement of immigration to this state." The legislators appointed Joseph H. Diss Debar, of Doddridge County, to be the State Commissioner of Immigration. He designed *The West Virginia Hand Book and Immigrant's Guide*, which was first printed in 1870. The guide was subtitled *A Sketch of the State of West Virginia*. It had chapters on each county, and on subjects such as education, worship, land and farms, fruit and wine-growing, coal, timber, and other job opportunities. More than eighteen thousand of the pamphlets, printed in English and German, were distributed in other states and across Europe. Diss Debar had previously designed the West Virginia official state seal in 1863.

In her late teens, Flora moved to Upshur County, where she lived in Rock Cave and worked as a cook at a logging camp in Alexander. There, she met Alfred Lee Williams, a tall, dark-haired logger from Lubeck, West Virginia. He was thirteen years older than Flora. Alfred was born in 1863 to James Edward and Matilda Johnson Williams. His ancestors, John Williams, his wife, and son had come over from Stafford, England in 1651, on the *Assurance*. They first settled in Stafford, Virginia, and then moved to Lubeck in Wood County, West Virginia.

Flora and Alfred were married in Buckhannon, Upshur County, at the Methodist minister's home on November, 5, 1894. They lived in Alexander, where their first child, Lettie Maude, was born in 1896. Alexander was a small community near Helvetia. Alfred and Flora then moved close to his family, in Wood County, where they farmed and she gave birth to their second and third child, Glenna Belle, in 1898, and Jacob Alfred, in 1901. Then they moved to Centralia, Braxton County, and eventually settled in the new, developing town of Gassaway, also in Braxton County. There, they built a combination residence and grocery store. Flora ran the store, while Alfred returned to the woods to log, coming home only on weekends. Flora often voiced her disapproval, feeling overwhelmed with six children to care for and a store to run on her own. In 1914, they became the third proprietors of the grandiose Valley Hotel, formerly the Gassaway Hotel, which they owned and operated until 1931. The hotel had been constructed by a development company when the town was being built. It was located across the street from the train depot and was used often by traveling salesmen and other rail travelers.

Over twenty-three years, Flora and Alfred continued expanding their family, until my father, Russell Lee, their eleventh child, was born in 1919. When Flora gave birth to him, at the age of 43, there were plenty of older siblings to help take care of him. Sadly, like so many babies back then, two of their children, Wanda and Donald, died during infancy. From oldest to youngest, their children's names were: Lettie Maude, Glenna Belle, Jacob Alfred, Carl James, Nellie Blanche, Clara Marie, Everett Clark, Robert Woodrow, Wanda Louise, Donald Harold, and Russell Lee. Most of the Williams children inherited their mother's outstanding gardening skills, and many followed their parents' footsteps in becoming successful entrepreneurs.

The oldest three daughters, Maude, Glenna, and Nellie cooked for the guests of the hotel. Maude and Clara played the piano at the Lyric Theater on Elk Street in downtown Gassaway. They provided the music during silent movies, before the "talkies" were invented. Maude and Glenna rode the train down to Frametown once a week to give private piano lessons.

The Williams children in 1910. Clockwise, beginning with the baby: Everett, Nellie, Jacob, Maude, Glenna, Carl, and Clara.

The family also owned and operated Williams Quality Store on Elk Street. It first opened up as a pharmacy, then became a general store, with a soda fountain, pharmacy, and dry goods department. Later, they opened Williams Brothers' Garage beside the store. Carl, Everett, and Bob worked as mechanics in the garage. As kids, we were never encouraged to go into the garage, since there were calendars with revealing images of pin-up girls hanging in the office and at every work station. The place always seemed bustling with plenty of customers.

Maude attended West Virginia Wesleyan College, where she studied music. While she was working in the kitchen of the hotel, she met and fell in love with a young meat salesman, Sam Vande-vender. His wife, Grace, had died from pneumonia, leaving him with a young son, Sam Junior. Sam made frequent stops to pick up the hotel's orders, while getting to visit with Maude. The two of them married on Christmas Day of 1920 in Philippi. They and Junior settled in Elkins, West Virginia. Sam worked for the Wilson meat packing company, and Maude played the piano for the First Baptist Church. She gave birth to a daughter, Dorothy Mae, who was called "Dot." Dorothea, as she was later named, worked in Randolph County as a home economics teacher. In 1952, at her step-brother's home in Charleston, she married Hugh Nestor, the woodworking teacher at her school. They had two daughters, Dama Maude and Julia.

Glenna graduated from Glenville State Normal School and became an elementary teacher at Davis Elementary in Gassaway. She gave private piano and accordion lessons in her home and was the pianist in the Gassaway United Methodist Church. Although she never married, she and a friend, Lee, shared a camp on the Elk River, south of town. She and Bob, the only brother who never married, lived with their mother. He was fifteen years younger than Glenna, being born in 1913. After Flora's death, they continued to live in the big brick house and make their home together. The family owned two of these identical houses on River Street behind the hotel. The houses served as overflow areas for the hotel guests. When we spent the night with Glenna and Bob, it looked so odd to see brass numbers nailed to each of the bedroom doors.

Bob Williams with the family's workhorses, circa 1921.

In the afternoons, Glenna often worked in her vegetable garden after school, still wearing her high heels and dress clothes. She and Bob were both what some might call eccentric characters. Sometimes when we visited them, they had their coins drying out on towels from where they had washed them. They were simply ahead of their time. These days, all of us are so conscientious about sanitizing everything, even our grocery cart handles. When we visited them, Glenna always gave us performances with her pearl-toned accordion. Bob was a quiet, serious man, whose expertise at the family's garage was glass cutting. He was somewhat of a homebody and enjoyed collecting pocket knives. Glenna was involved in numerous community and church organizations. She had the art of tatting down to perfection. It was so intriguing to watch her use her fingers and little shuttle, to create beautiful tatted designs.

Glenna often called our dad, asking him if she and Bob could go to the beach when we went. They joined us on several beach trips. Sometimes when we went out to eat at the beach, after looking over the prices on the menu, they refused to order anything. That was pretty amusing to us, knowing that they certainly could afford it. While we were down along the ocean, they sat out on blankets with us. Glenna wore a scarf on her head, and Bob did some serious girl-watching. On the Fourth of July in 1981, Glenna died of a heart attack as she and Bob were walking downtown to the annual Gassaway Days. Unfortunately, Glenna never knew that at the celebration, she was to receive an award for teaching fifty years in the elementary school. Bob continued installing automotive glass until he retired. Ironically, he died on the exact same day, and in the same hospital, where my first son was born, in September of 1983.

Jacob, or "Jake" as he was called, was the eldest son. One of his first jobs was to meet the trains from Charleston and Elkins to solicit customers for the Valley Hotel. He worked for the Gassaway Coal and Coke Railway for a brief period before operating his own businesses. Jake had several stores in Gassaway and near Frametown, then later opened the Williams Wholesale Candy Company in Gassaway. My cousin Everett, or "Skeeter," loved riding in the delivery truck with Jake when they distributed candy all over central West Virginia. Next, Jake and his first wife, Lakie, opened the

Kane Motel in Lookout, West Virginia. After they divorced, he returned to Braxton County and, in 1950, took over what became the Williams Restaurant and Truck Stop on Route 4 at Granny's Creek, north of Sutton. There, he fell in love with and married one of his young waitresses, Alice Hamner, from Newville.

They had two daughters, Barbara and Sandra. Barbara came along nine years after all of the other Williams grandchildren. She graduated from Wesleyan College, and became a teacher in Braxton County. Sandra also graduated from Wesleyan with a business degree and works as a certified public accountant. Jake passed away at the age of eighty-five.

Carl was two years younger than Jake, born in 1903. He settled in Parkersburg, where he worked as an engineer for the B&O railroad. He met Mary Elsie Snyder, from Jackson County, and the two were married in 1929. They had one child, "Jim," Carl James II. He attended Notre Dame, and worked as an engineer for Kodak, in their Rochester, New York, headquarters. There, he met his wife Carol. The couple's wedding in Lexington, Kentucky, was the fanciest occasion my sister and I had ever attended. It was a beautiful outdoor wedding with enormous white tents, and an impressive spread of food and plenty of bubbly champagne.

Carl was a master gardener and died a premature death, under his grapevine in their backyard. He was only fifty-four. For many years, we visited his widow, Elsie, in their large, white, wooden house on Williams Street in Parkersburg. She always had the best fresh-baked pies and cobblers on the table in her welcoming, sun-filled kitchen. Elsie's sister, Jess, usually visited with us, too. They were such fun-loving, jovial ladies.

Nellie was born in 1905 and was one of the sisters who cooked in the hotel kitchen. She stayed with Maude in Elkins while she attended Davis & Elkins College. After graduating, she returned to Gassaway and took an elementary teaching job at Exchange, down the road a bit from Gassaway. Every Sunday afternoon, she walked down the railroad tracks for several miles to Exchange, where she stayed with a family during the week. On Fridays, after school, she walked the tracks back to Gassaway. She dreaded walking through the long, dark railroad tunnel, worrying that a train might come barreling through at any time.

Nellie met her husband, Steve Dyer, an auto mechanic, while he was working for her family in their garage. He was from Philippi, West Virginia, and had attended the Detroit Automotive School. They raised their family on a beautiful farm in rural Berry Siding, between Heaters and Flatwoods, also in Braxton County. They had three daughters, Mary Ellen, Flora Ann, and Jane. When we visited with them, Janie and I liked to swing on the hammock in their front yard. She was our only cousin close to my age. Mary Ellen and Flora Ann were in their high school band, and my sister and I were so impressed whenever they put on their band uniforms. The mythical Braxton County Monster was sighted near their farm. Of course, like all of the local residents, they were curious about it. On September 12, 1952, the same night it had been sighted, Flora Ann had witnessed a strange light going across the sky.

All three of Nellie's and Steve's daughters attended Glenville State College. Mary Ellen moved to the big city of Charleston, to work for the state, then eventually, Union Carbide. She married her childhood boyfriend, Don Stout, from 4-H camp. Flora Ann and her husband, Rod Oldham, both became teachers in Parkersburg, where she taught home economics. Jane lives in Gassaway and taught in Braxton County Middle School. She served as the mayor of Gassaway in the late 1980s. Steve passed away in 1973, and Nellie died five years later, in 1978.

Flora and Alfred's fourth daughter, Clara, was born in 1908. She married a minister's son from Gassaway, Arthur Thorne. The two of them took her parents' car and moved to Illinois, where several of her mother's siblings lived. They were married in 1933 in Columbia City, Illinois. Clara and Art were employed at a clothing manufacturing plant in Elgin. During World War II, they moved back to West Virginia, to Charleston, where he worked at South

Charleston Naval Ordnance Plant. It was a defense metal stamping plant, which made armor plating, big ship parts, and was touted for producing the most gun barrels in the country during the war. Thousands of women were employed at the plant, since so many men were overseas, fighting in the war.

Clara worked at The Baby Shop, on Quarrier Street, while they lived in Charleston. She also took organ lessons at Woodrum's furniture store, and became an accomplished organist. The couple's only child, William, "Bill," was born on the West Side of Charleston at the end of Woodward Court. When the war was over, on August 15, 1945, the entire town celebrated, with church bells ringing, sirens sounding, and people clapping and cheering from their porches. Little Bill joined in the hoopla by riding up and down the court on his tricycle, with a cooking pan dangling and clanging on the sidewalk. It was a joyous day of celebration across the country.

Cousin Bill with Jean and me, at Gassaway, 1952.

After the war was over, the family returned to Gassaway, where they took over and ran the Williams Quality Store. As a young child, Bill played with the children who lived in the apartments above the store. The older girls liked dressing him up in girls' clothes. One day, when he was dressed up like a girl, the town's loud warning siren went off, and before he realized it, he had run out into the middle of the street, to watch the fire trucks, still wearing girls' clothes. While my sister and I were young, Clara and Bill spent a lot of time with us at our home and on trips. It was impossible for their family to go on vacations together, since Art had to stay home and tend to the store. Bill was nine years older than I, so he seemed like the older brother my sister and I never had. He was tall and good looking, and we admired and idolized him. We went to Daytona and Myrtle Beaches, the Smokies, and hit many tourist stops around the state. While they were visiting us in Charleston one week, Clara bought Bill a pet turtle. I was teething at the time, and before anyone could stop me, I had the turtle in my mouth, chewing on it.

Clara Thorne behind the marble counter of the soda fountain in the Williams Quality Store, 1940s.

We often visited with their family at the store. Clara would play her organ for us, which was always such a treat. She was an extremely talented organist, often playing by ear. While we were at the store, we got milkshakes from the fancy soda fountain with chrome and brass fixtures, wrought iron stools, and a marble counter. In the kitchen area in the back of the store, she fixed us mouthwatering meals. Clara was usually busy with knitting or crocheting projects whenever we visited her. After Art died, in 1986, Clara continued to run the store for eight more years. Bill and his wife, Kay, had one son, Billy. To Clara, her grandson was the delight of her life. At her funeral, on February 11, 1998, at the Gassaway Baptist Church, her pastor delivered a touching eulogy. He had such an admiration for Clara, since she had been the church's organist for fifty years. At the funeral, he mentioned that Billy was "the apple of her eye." To that Billy replied: "I know I was."

Everett was born in 1910 and was nicknamed "Feets" because he had such large feet. He also worked in Williams Brothers' Garage. Feets and his first wife, Mabel, had two children, Alfred Lee, or "Skeeter," as he was called, and Joan. Sadly, Mabel died when the kids were just four and five years old, leaving Feets with two young children. He hired a live-in nanny, Thelma Bright, from Newville, to help raise the children. They fell in love, and he proposed to her by asking: "Would you take a chance on life with me?" Thelma and Feets eloped to Greenup, Kentucky, and were married on June 6, 1940. She was nineteen and he was twenty-nine. Together, they had a daughter, Sherry. When he was hired to work with the B&O railroad, the family moved to Buckhannon. They operated a sandwich shop, which was a popular eatery for high school students.

Alfred Lee operated the print shop, as a civilian, at Patrick Air Force Base. Joan attended West Virginia Wesleyan College, where she met her husband Ted Cooperman. She had a long career as an elementary school teacher, where they live in Tappan, New York. Sherry met her husband, Charlie Fansler, at her house, when he was visiting with relatives. They got married and lived in Parkersburg for ten years before moving to Orlando, Florida. There, they both worked at a community college, where Sherry worked as a student advisor. After being together for many years, she and Charlie discovered that, as a young child, he lived in the exact same house in Gassaway where she was born, several years later. Everett and Thelma moved from Buckhannon back to Gassaway, where he died in 1981. Thelma spent the last seven years of her life in Orlando, before she died in 2006.

Russell playing beside the train depot, across from the Valley Hotel, 1922.

My father, Russell, was the youngest of the Williams clan. His life is very well-documented in photographs. We have many wonderful old pictures of him as a young child, playing in the train yards near their home in Gassaway and playing with his pet rabbits and raccoons. He often said that his oldest sister, Maude, felt more like a mother to him, since she was twenty-three years older. Russell was only twelve when his father died from heart disease in 1931. Dad told us that he was never interested in drinking, because as a kid, he would sometimes have to escort an older brother home, who had one too many drinks at a local bar.

After high school, Dad moved to Charleston to attend a business college, Charleston School of Commerce. During that time, he lived with his sister Clara, who introduced him to my mother, Betty Pierson. They married in 1941, then shortly after that, he was drafted to fight in World War II. When the war was over they started their family. Dad's mother, Flora, died in 1952, when I was only three years old. We have a photograph showing many of us cousins in her living room, gathered around the Christmas tree with her. I was too young to remember that, since I was only two.

Not long ago, when my sister and I were sorting through some old boxes under Mom's eaves, we discovered three large, black, cloth-bound books. They were registries from the Valley Hotel, dating as far back as 1914. We also found a crystal ink bottle and an old quill pen. It was fascinating to look through the names of the guests in the registries, some written with such commanding or impressive handwriting. To my surprise, at the top of each page was the message: "Guests without luggage must pay in advance." I had conjured up such glorious images of the grandiose hotel, with guests dressed to the hilt, elegant wooden furnishings, elaborate architectural details, and fine dining and sleeping accommodations. I never dreamed that "Guests without luggage" would have been a topic which needed to be addressed.

During our youth, the Williams family gathered for huge picnics in Parkersburg to decorate Flora's and Alfred's and their parents' gravesites. They are buried at Bethel Baptist Church cemetery. A terrific sadness came over me at my father's funeral in September of 1998, knowing that he was the last living sibling of their remarkable family. My mom and I still make the rounds on Memorial Day to decorate many of Dad's family's gravesites. Most of them are scattered across Braxton County, at several cemeteries.

On the outskirts of Gassaway, four siblings are buried at Little Otter Cemetery on a shady knoll, surrounded by ancient cedar trees. The red clay road is impassable to these hallowed grounds, where the lonely call of a phoebe is the only sound that breaks the peaceful silence. As I slowly climb up the steep hillside to where my ancestors were laid to rest, the familiar smell of the red clay and damp banks fills the air. Many of the tombstones are moss-covered and weathered from age. On the older ones, the names have been completely erased over time.

I have such fond memories of our relatives, touring their elaborate gardens and visiting with them in their homes over lively conversations and savory home-cooked meals. I am so proud of the rich heritage passed down to me and feel fortunate to be a part of "The Williams Clan."

School Daze I

Betsey and Johnny Hill with me on the first day of school in front of our homes, 1958.

Our grade school, J. E. Robins, was only two houses down from our home. It was one of several similar, massive, old red brick structures, which were built during the same era. These gigantic buildings were scattered all over Kanawha County. Like the majority of these older schools, Robins was a tall building with three floors. "J. E. ROBINS 1929" was carved in the slab of granite above the front doors. As students, we never knew who J. E. Robins was. One would think that if J. E. had the school named in his honor, then the students there should surely learn about him. He was never mentioned by any of my teachers.

The first year public schools in West Virginia were desegregated was 1954. That was the year before I started school and my sister's third year. The change wasn't a big deal to the children of our neighborhood. The city-operated summer playground we attended at Robins had been integrated for years.

When my sister, Jean, was in the first grade, she had a horrible phobia about going to school. Every morning, when it was time for school to start, she threw one heck of a conniption fit. We never really understood why. As the younger sibling, I always suspected that she was just jealous because I got to stay home and she didn't. For the first week, every morning, our mom had to walk Jean down to school, since she was unwilling to go on her own accord. Our next-door neighbor, Patricia, brought her daughter, Betsey, and son, Johnny, who was my age, to our house so Mom could drag Jean down to the prison guards, or so it seemed. Betsey was only a year younger than Jean, so she started school the next year.

An old photograph of Johnny and me shows us standing on our sidewalk one morning in our pajamas and robes. We are holding hands and waving good-bye to Jean and Betsey as they headed off to school. Mom told me we did that every day. While our older sisters were at school, Johnny and I spent a lot of time together while our mothers visited. One day, I tried to tell Patricia and Mom that I didn't think Johnny could talk very clearly. It took me several times of repeating myself before they could figure out what

I was trying to tell them. Their dog, Mitzi, was a cute little black and white Boston terrier with a hyper but pleasant personality. She always sucked or chewed on a wet, knotted-up sock which she carried around their house, everywhere she went.

Three years passed by quickly, and it was time for Johnny and me to start school. Our first-grade teacher was the quintessential schoolmarm. As was desirable for a first grade teacher, she was gentle, with a pleasant smile and personality, but still very strict. She had a rather unexpected difficulty in dealing with me. I could look out through the windows which lined the outside wall of our classroom and see my house. This allowed me to watch my mother's comings and goings. It was quite the distraction to me, and a problem for my entire class. Whenever I saw her leave, I panicked and started bawling. My fear of her not being there when I got out of school was overwhelming, albeit not very substantiated. Mom had only missed being there a time or two. On each occasion, she returned within a matter of minutes. As calming and comforting as my teacher tried to be, I still became very upset every single time I saw my mother drive off.

Our class was a pretty typical group of students. We grew up with one another, usually traveling as a group, from first to sixth grade. Most grade levels had two teachers, so sometimes the groups got shuffled around. There were a few misfits, who were always jeered at and made fun of at recess by the bullies of the class. I was always impressed with my friend Terry, who, by himself, stood up for these underdogs. There were differences in race and our families' socioeconomic status. But to us kids, there was never a feeling that other children were more important or discriminated against because of their race, or how wealthy or poor their families were. The children at our school ran the gamut of the middle-class range, from lower middle class to upper middle class. My family was smack dab in the middle.

The PTA, Parent Teachers Association, drew large crowds for its evening meetings, which were held several times a year. As with most families, my sister and I attended the meetings with our parents. I always thought it was interesting to see everyone's parents. Unlike these days, back then, the overwhelming majority of parents were actively involved in their children's education. They supported and respected their children's teachers. The PTA sponsored a school carnival once a year. It always proved to be one full day of fun. The school was packed with adults and excited kids. My very favorite thing to do at the carnival was the cake walk. We played many rounds of musical chairs in the cake walk, trying to win a prize. There were so many delicious-looking cupcakes, cookies, brownies, pies, and cakes for prizes. I also loved to visit the fortune teller and go "fishing" in the fish pond. Everyone was guaranteed a prize in the fish pond, just for throwing a line behind the curtained booth. The general store offered various items for sale, often handcrafted and baked goods.

All of the classrooms in Robins were identical to one another. They had hardwood floors, and wooden desks mounted to the floor. Each desk had a flip-up seat, a groove for a pen or pencil, and an ink well. Hissing radiators lined the walls, and blackboards, which were actually black, spanned the entire width of the front wall. A wooden teacher's desk sat in the front of the room. Every classroom had one outside wall, which was covered with tall windows made of small panes. Each window had a dark tan roll-up blind. Large ivory lights, which somewhat resembled upside-down mushroom caps, hung from the ceiling. The loudspeaker box, covered with shiny burlap-looking fabric, was mounted on the wall over the blackboard. A large, round, black wall clock hung in each room. In the front of the room, a full-size American flag hung down from a dark wooden floor stand.

With no exceptions, every classroom had hanging on the wall *The Athenaeum Portrait*. This was Gilbert Stuart's 1796 portrait of President George Washington, "The Father of Our Country." I am sure millions of young schoolchildren across the United States, stared up at that portrait and were mystified, as I was. It always kept me wondering what the artist had in mind, with the white, cloudy effect at the bottom of the painting. This looked to me like some kind of ethereal enhancement, similar to what professional studios often use in their portraits. I never realized back then that Gilbert had simply left the painting unfinished.

In addition to *The Athenaeum Portrait*, almost every classroom had one of Franz Marc's famous horse paintings. He was a German painter and printmaker whose works often show a heavy influence from the Futurism movement. The ones I remember the most are *Blue Horse I* and my very favorite, *Grazing Horses IV*, sometimes called "The Red Horses." They were in several of my classrooms. I liked Marc's rich color blending of the blue horse and on the reddish-brown horses in the background. None of the teachers ever referred to these paintings, but it would be interesting to know exactly how Marc's paintings became the artworks of choice for our classrooms.

The regimented routine in every classroom was pretty similar, too. Every morning, we carried out our morning exercises. We stood and recited the Pledge of Allegiance and followed that by singing a patriotic song, such as "The Star-Spangled Banner" or "My Country, 'Tis of Thee." Then we bowed our heads and recited the Lord's Prayer. Around ten o'clock every morning, for a snack break, small bottles (then eventually cartons) of milk were delivered in crates to the door of each classroom. The milk cost three cents a day. At the beginning of each week, our teacher collected fifteen cents of "milk money" from those of us who opted to purchase it. I never bought the milk because I didn't like white milk, which was the only choice back then.

All classes had recess either in the morning or afternoon. During that time, we usually played teacher-led games, such as Dodge Ball, "Red Rover, Red Rover," or "Duck, Duck Goose." The part I dreaded the most about Dodge Ball was waiting so long for one of the captains to pick me for his team. The same girls and I were part of the group that everyone referred to as "Slim Pickin's." I was pretty terrified, too, about getting slammed so hard by some of the bigger, stronger boys. It always seemed to me that Dodge Ball was pretty cruel and didn't have many exercising benefits, either. When the weather didn't permit us to go outside, we stayed in our classroom and played games like "Gossip," "The Farmer in the Dell," and "Button, Button, Who Has the Button?"

Each classroom took periodic bathroom breaks. Our class formed two single lines at the door, a girls' line and a boys' line. We followed our teacher down the dimly-lit hallway to the restrooms, like ducklings in a row. We lined up again in the hall when we were finished, waiting to be walked back to class. Students never wandered the halls on their own. Unless someone was sick, it wasn't even a possibility to ask to go to the restroom outside of these group breaks. A friend of mine recently reminded me of how she wet herself one day in class when we were in the first grade. She was too afraid to ask permission to go to the restroom. Our teacher took her to the furnace room to wash and dry her clothes.

At lunchtime, most of the school emptied out, since practically everyone walked home for lunch. No one had to ride a school bus, since all of us lived within walking distance. Around a hundred students ate in the cafeteria on the bottom floor, but the majority of us went home. Most mothers were full-time housewives and fixed lunch for their children. Occasionally I ate lunch with my friend Barbara. Her grandmother fixed us potted meat sandwiches, and the greatest chicken and dumplings. It was just chicken noodle soup with uncooked, rolled biscuits heated in it for the dumplings. I thought that was such a delicious treat.

Once a month, we had an itinerant art instructor visit each class. The one bit of advice which I gleaned from her instruction was: "The trunks of trees are gray, not brown, like everyone wants to color or paint them." That was more than fifty years ago, but it seems like yesterday when she gave us that wise advice. One of my favorite activities we participated in was interacting with a radio show, *Musical Pictures*. Every month, our teacher tuned into the program, and we listened to the host read a captivating story. Each adventurous tale had a number of musical tunes incorporated into the script. At the end of the program, we drew a scene from the story. This was right up my alley, since I loved a challenge to be creative. It was always so intriguing to see the display of artworks by several classes, hung in the halls, from this assignment. The same story had been visualized and interpreted so differently by each student.

I loved hearing our classes sing in rounds. To hear "Row Your Boat" or "Make New Friends" in perfect three or four-part harmony was priceless. It was so enjoyable to listen to the harmonizing, even though people were singing different lyrics at the same time. After the two first groups stopped singing, the final group remained alone to sing the last lines: "Life is but a dream" or "One is silver and the other one gold." On rare occasions we would have "Show and Tell." I usually brought my black metal Viewmaster with the discs of pictures showing the Grand Canyon, Yosemite, and other national parks.

During our grade-school years, on Halloween nights, we went trick-or-treating in small groups. We plodded up and down the steep streets of our hill, knocking on every door. For three years in a row, I tripped on my costume as I climbed up the same steep, concrete steps to a house on Westwood Drive. Every year, I skinned my shins. We took old pillowcases for our trick-or-treat bags. The neighborhood was so safe, our parents never accompanied us. When we came back home, we dumped our candy onto the living room floor to evaluate our loot. My favorite candies were Mary Janes, Hershey Kisses, Tootsie Roll Pops, and butterscotch Lifesavers.

For our school Valentine's Day parties, we decorated shoe boxes with construction paper and lacy, white paper doilies. The familiar smells from the thick, white LePage's paste and yellowish mucilage glue still linger in my memory. One of our classmates had an uncontrollable fetish for the paste and liked to eat it. Everyone brought little valentines for the entire class. We dropped them into the slits on top of each person's box. At every party, "Pin the Tail on the Donkey" was our favorite game. In the first grade, my class walked up to my home for an Easter egg hunt in our backyard. Every year, there were several dedicated homeroom mothers who made all of the arrangements and provided the goodies for our parties.

In an attempt to teach us the importance of saving money, once or twice a month, a local bank representative set up a makeshift "bank" out in our hallway. Most of us put in a quarter or fifty cents, but one girl made substantial deposits every time. We were so impressed with how much money she had accumulated in her account at the end of each year. Her parents ran their own business and seemed to take this banking opportunity more seriously than the rest of our parents. I purchased a brand new blue and white Schwinn bicycle with money I saved over several years. Picking it out at Currey's Bike Shop at the foot of our hill was an exciting experience. While we were in the first grade, we received the Salk polio vaccine shots. Everyone was so frightened and apprehensive as we waited in line to go up on the auditorium stage, where a nurse was administering the shots.

In the second grade, our teacher drilled us and drilled us on writing properly with cursive letters. She held our noses to the grindstone every day. Frequently she tapped us on the knuckles with her wooden ruler as a reminder to hold our Zaner-Bloser pencils precisely the right way. I always thought the capital "Q" and "Z" looked like they should have been written differently.

Our third-grade teacher used to shake us if she caught us talking. One day, a girl sitting behind me asked me a question, and I turned around to answer her. Before I knew what was happening, the teacher had pulled me up out of my seat and was shaking me as hard as she could. Back then, that was a perfectly acceptable means of disciplining. A friend of mine was reminding me of all the poems our teacher had us memorize and recite. To my surprise, more than fifty years later, she could still remember "Birdie," by Robert Lewis Stevenson: "A birdie with a yellow bill, hopped upon my windowsill, cocked his shiny eye and said, 'Ain't you 'shamed, you sleepyhead?' "

Cute little blond-haired Chuckie was my first boyfriend. On Valentine's Day in the fourth grade, he bought me a heart-shaped box of chocolates. We didn't have the same teacher, so we never saw each other at school. When he delivered the candy to me in my front yard after school, we gave each other a peck on the lips. It didn't matter to us that I was at least a head taller than he was. We used to have some pretty lengthy phone conversations every night. One evening, his mom told him to get off the phone, and, more like an adult's response, Chuckie said: "Like they say, all good things must come to an end." During class in the fourth grade, a friend of mine and I were so fascinated by all of the naked natives in the *National Geographic* magazines which we were supposed to be reading. That was such a strange-looking and unfamiliar sight to us, we could hardly contain ourselves.

Our fifth grade teacher had us purchase Esterbrook fountain pens for penmanship lessons. I purchased a red one from Lowman's drugstore. We placed our bottles of blue Carter's or Scrip ink in the inkwells on our desks. I loved to fill up my pen then watch the ink dry as I wrote with it. We purchased special Palmer paper from our teacher, two sheets for a penny, to use with the pens. If we made a mistake, we were allowed to use ink eradicator, the precursor to Wite-Out. Our little ink blotters were kept nearby in case we needed them.

While my fifth grade class was lined up at our door one day to go out for recess, I had an unforgettable experience. My hair was dark brown, and the short hair on my legs was very visible, since it was the same color. Some of the guys in the boys' line looked over at me and started whispering to each other, giggling about the dark hair on my legs. These were my classmates, and I thought my friends, so the experience was extremely hurtful. Not many years ago, I was listening to one of the evening news magazine shows, such as *Sixty Minutes*. They had surveyed adults to see whether positive or negative childhood memories were most prevalent. Overwhelmingly, the negative memories were what everyone remembered and what stayed with them the longest. Those results didn't surprise me one bit. I can flash back to that incident in a heartbeat, reliving the pain and embarrassment.

In the sixth grade, I was honored to be invited to participate in the school's Safety Patrol program. I so proudly donned my silver badge and white canvas belt, which fit over my shoulder and around my waist. Every day I headed out to the crosswalk in front of our school. My guard duty consisted of assisting the younger kids who were crossing busy Beech Avenue. I felt like a junior version of Mrs. Vance, our patrol lady who directed traffic at the intersection of Beech and West Avenues. Before our sixth grade class was to perform in a Christmas program, I got stage fright and had to throw up. That was a pretty embarrassing episode, but it was comforting that my mom was there.

On the last day of every school year, right before the final bell rang at the end of the day, we belted out Jim Reeves' tune, "May the Good Lord Bless and Keep You." This was always so heart-warming and touching to me. We sang the words with quivering chins and tears in our eyes. I always fell for the part: "May there be a silver lining, back of every cloud you see." Listening to Reeves' version of the song on the Internet brought back such fond memo-ries of us standing in the classroom, swaying back and forth as we somewhat sadly sang the lyrics to each other.

Phone Queen

Betty at her parents' house, 1941.

My mom, Betty Jean, was born in 1923 in a little white house in the town of Sutton, West Virginia. The house sits right beside the road, just down from the Sutton Dam. She was the second child of Ida and William "Doc" Pierson. When she was three, her family settled on the West Side of Charleston, in a little brown frame house in Woodward Court, off of Garden Street. Her parents were devout Baptists with strong religious habits and convictions. They raised Betty and her brother, James Ralph, four years her senior, in Emmanuel Baptist Church. The family faithfully attended morning and evening services on Sunday, and Wednesday night prayer meetings. Doc and Ida took an active part in the church, serving on the deacon and deaconess boards.

Mom was a member of the first class to attend J. E. Robins Elementary in 1929. For part of her first grade year, she attended school in a classroom at Wilson Junior High until construction was completed on Robins. She and her two good friends, Marida and Betty Sue, went to school with one another and played in the court together. One of their favorite pastimes was playing Marbles in the front yard. Sometimes they used the old smokehouse in the backyard for a playhouse. Occasionally, they hid and rolled up grape leaves from the arbor and tried to smoke them, like cigarettes. They walked down a ways on Garden Street to roller skate beyond where the brick part of the street was. Trying to skate on bricks, with those heavy metal skates, was pretty difficult.

After school on Thursday afternoons, Betty walked to church, where her mother was working in the kitchen. As a fundraiser, the ladies of the church cooked supper once a week for the faculty of Tiskelwah. It was an elementary school diagonally across the street from Emmanuel. At that time, the church didn't have folding tables, so they made tables by placing wide, long planks of rough wood over workhorses. While the women were cooking, the kids used the planks for slides and seesaws.

There were alleys which ran behind the houses on both sides of Woodward Court. When Betty was in junior high school, her mother had her deliver a death notice to a family from Gassaway who lived down the alley. Betty introduced herself and told the lady that her sister-in-law had died. Clara replied: "Well, I didn't know Ida Pierson had a daughter. You'll have to come down and play darts with us sometime, when my younger brother, Russell, is here."

Russell had come down from Gassaway to attend business school and was staying with Clara and her husband, Art. Betty did go back to their home that evening to play darts and meet Russell, who was four years older than she. From that time on, he was her steady suitor, although he kept it a secret from Clara and Art. One day Clara told my mother: "We don't know where Russell goes every night. He gets real dressed up and goes somewhere."

Betty and Russell Williams were married on December 20, 1941, halfway through her senior year of high school. Relatives from both families came down from Gassaway and Braxton County to attend the wedding. After the ceremony at Emmanuel, the wedding guests were invited to an open house reception, which Ida hosted in their home. Following the reception, the out-of-town visitors walked down the court to see the house which was to be the excited newlyweds' first home.

Like so many other couples at the beginning of World War II, shortly after they were married, Russell was drafted to serve in the Army. After boot camp, he was stationed at a base in Alabama. Of course, the newlyweds were pining for each other. Betty took the money she received as graduation gifts, recruited Russell's sister Glenna to accompany her, and the two of them rode a Greyhound bus down to visit Russell. She moved back in with her parents, while he served his country in Hawaii and Japan. During their time of separation, they kept in touch by writing numerous love letters to each other. In their letters, Dad lovingly called her "Sadie," and she affectionately referred to him as "Butch." I can only imagine the celebrating that took place the day she received a telegram from him in 1945, advising her to stop sending letters, because he was coming home. The war was over at last, and Russ returned home to be reunited with his young wife. Wasting no time to start a family, my sister, Jean, was born the next year. I came along three years later.

Before I was born, my parents bought a brand new house, in 1947, on Alexander Street. It was in a developing, middle-class neighborhood on Charleston's West Side hill, not far from where Betty grew up. The street was still being finished, house by house, by the Fredericks, father and son contractors. For many years, a large greenhouse, which was opened to the public, had occupied the property where the new street was being built. It had been torn down to make way for new occupants.

Our neighborhood was full of families just like ours. Most of the fathers had been off to war, and the families were started when the war was over. There were many children my sister's age, some my age, some in between, and a few younger than I. Practically all households had two parents pretty close to our parents' age. Everyone took great pride in caring for their cars, new homes and in keeping their yards nicely-landscaped and tidy. It was a bona fide baby boomer neighborhood, where everyone was living out the middle-class American dream.

I always thought that our mother was so beautiful she could have been a model. While Dad was in the Army, she frequently had a professional photographer take pictures of herself so she could send them to him. I always thought she looked so pretty in her swimsuit with a big plaid skirt. During our youth, even when she was home, she usually wore a dress, or skirt and blouse. She almost always wore hose and extremely pointed-toed shoes.

People often tell of when they ran away from home during their youth. My sister and I still remember the day our mother "ran away." We must have been giving her fits and getting on her nerves that afternoon. I was five years old and Jean was eight. Mom said: "I am just going to run away," then ran out the front door. Jean and I were beside ourselves. Finally, after what seemed like an eternity, we found her hiding behind one of the bushy evergreen trees in the front yard.

Mom was a good seamstress and made many tiny doll clothes for our Jill and baby Ginnette dolls. They were two popular Vogue dolls in the 1950s. Sometimes Mrs. Otten, Georgette's mother, came to our house and the two women spent the day together sewing doll clothes. One year for Christmas, Mom made me two of my favorite dolls, Raggedy Ann and Andy. Another year she made matching long red flannel gowns for my sister and me and our dolls. She sewed my majorette costumes and Jean's fancy piano recital dress made of pink dotted swiss. When we were young, she made us dresses with smocked bodices.

We gave Mom several nicknames when we were younger. The first one, and the one she had the longest, was "Phone Queen." To us, it seemed like she was always talking on the phone. The phone jack has been in the same place for sixty years, behind an end table at the end of the couch. Our piano used to sit within reaching distance from the phone, so she could chat nonstop with her friends while dusting off or buffing the piano or end table. I seriously think that this quick, back-and-forth hand gesturing has become so ingrained in her mind, that she can't stop doing it. Nowadays, when we wait for her to get out of or into the car or wheelchair, every single time, she wipes off the dashboard or car door, or brushes off her clothes, using this same gesturing.

There were certain friends she called every day, and others a few times a week. The conversations we heard were always so mundane, often repeating conversations with other people or describing a situation to the most minute detail. I was always a little guarded with what I confided in her, knowing it would be repeated to everyone else. There were several little old ladies whom she talked to for endless amounts of time. She knew no one else was giving them any attention. That epitomizes what our mother was all about. She always took care of those in need. Driving these lonely elderly women to church functions, the grocery store, to a doctor's appointment, wherever they needed to go, also kept her busy. She took care of our elderly next-door neighbor, often helping her apply medications.

Whenever I run into friends who grew up in our neighborhood, they consistently want to know how my mom is doing. Everyone tells me how much they love my mom. Jackie, a friend who grew up on the hill with us, commented recently on how she was "the neighborhood mom." One of our buddies, Bob, who was close to my age, came over to our house nearly every day. He hung out with Mom, even if my sister or I weren't home. During the summer, he often showed up early in the morning and stayed until late at night.

Mom served as the nursery director at church for many years, taking care of the babies while their parents attended services. My sister and the girls in her troop were fortunate to have our mom as a Scout leader. She had two great co-leaders over the years, Charlotte and June. Their troop was very active and went on many camping trips, with my dad and me tagging along.

Middleburg Auditorium Ice Skating Rink sat in the middle of Charleston in the space now occupied by the parking lot of the main post office. Mom took her Scout troop there once a week for ice skating lessons. I got to skate with them and loved every minute of it. There was such a wonderful feeling about gliding over the ice on skates.

Since our family very rarely went out to eat, our mother prepared dinner for us every night. On weekdays, we always ate at five o'clock sharp, as soon as Dad got in from work. It seems like we ate pork and beans several times a week. The staple meals we had usually once a week were: fried chicken, homemade spaghetti, breaded pork chops, Buzz buttered steaks, chili, fish sticks, baked steak, and, when we were in high school, lots of casseroles. Usually each person was served a salad plate with slices of fruit on iceberg lettuce, topped with a dollop of mayonnaise, sprinkled with shredded cheese. She made her delicious chicken pot pie on Dad's birthday, since that was his favorite. On Easter Sundays and Mother's Day, we sometimes went out to eat at Rose City Cafeteria or Humphrey's Pine Room.

We were always entertaining guests at our house. Mom was the consummate hostess, thriving on serving and pleasing her visitors. She often fixed some pretty fancy meals. One of my favorites was the delicacy "popovers," which she baked for special luncheons. The scrumptious rolls, which were hollow inside, were usually stuffed with tuna salad or homemade jam. She liked to make cut "roses" out of radishes to serve on her relish trays. It was a special treat when she made colorful, multilayered Jell-O in glass parfait dishes. She had hospitality down to perfection.

Fondue dinners were trendy, fun, and different. Sometimes Mom had our guests or our family fondue pieces of steak or chicken in sizzling oil on color-coded skewers. Other times, she had delicious chocolate fondue, in which we dipped fruit or squares of angel food cake. Cooking marinated chicken breasts on the grill, with Aunt Thelma's famous barbeque sauce, was everyone's favorite. The mouthwatering chicken was usually served with fresh half-runners and Mom's signature potato salad. The combination of those three tastes made such a splendid meal.

She often baked real shortcake for a delightful dessert of strawberry shortcake. I can still taste how yummy the strawberry shortcake was, with fresh strawberries, the thick, sweet cake, real whipped cream, and a little bit of milk poured over it. Another favorite of mine, which she frequently made, was cornbread, baked in her black cast iron pan, which made muffins shaped like ears of corn. We often had those with a bowl of soupy pinto beans, sliced onions, and spinach or kale. Back then, women kept bacon fat in jars or canisters. They used that bacon grease as the seasoning for anything that needed additional flavoring. When I was in junior high school, my mother thought it was a good idea to have my sister and me cook one meal a week, to give us some experience. That experiment proved to be disastrous. My gravy was so thick one day, it looked more like biscuits.

The two most humiliating things my mother put me through were spit baths when I was younger, then later, picking at the blackheads on my face. I cringed every time she spit on her handkerchief and wiped off my dirty face. Towards the end of grade school, and while I was in junior high, she sat on the couch and had me lay my head on her lap, to pick at my face. This ordeal reminded me of female monkeys, picking through their babies' fur, looking for mites. Zits were a huge problem for most of us during adolescence. We went through many jars of Clearasil.

Mom spent a lot of her time doing laundry for the four of us. In those days, everything needed to be ironed. Unlike today, there was no putting a cotton blouse in the dryer to "fluff out" the wrinkles. Using her water sprinkler, she ironed Dad's shirts, our John Meyer and Villager dresses, Garland skirts, and Pandora outfits. Many of our angora sweaters had to be hand washed, and our mohair sweaters, with the big cable designs, had to be washed very carefully in Woolite to avoid shrinkage.

As a family, we went clothes shopping in downtown Charleston. Occasionally, we drove to Columbus, Ohio, to shop in their bigger department stores. Germantown was my favorite part of Columbus to visit and to eat lunch, in one of their pubs. I always thought it was pretty cool that our dad tagged along with us whenever we shopped. He spent many hours sitting in that lonely chair beside the women's dressing rooms. That's how much he enjoyed being with his wife and girls.

Being the good seamstress that she was, Mom sewed several outfits for me to take to college. In many of my college photographs, I am wearing the dresses she made. They were some of my favorite outfits. I was especially fond of a long-sleeved blue cotton dress with an empire waistline, which had tiny white buttons and lace sewn on the bodice. It was so thrilling to recently find that blue dress, buried in a cardboard box at Mom's.

Mom babysat several different kids over the years. While I was away at college, she cared for a cute little blonde-headed baby, Sandy. Whenever I came home to visit, I was so surprised how much her vocabulary had grown since the last time I saw her. During that time, Mom got into making crocheted bead rings and barefoot sandals. They were so popular that people from all over town ordered them. She made a little bit of money on those and had saved some to help pay for a beach trip. On the way to the beach, all of her earnings were wiped out from a traffic violation ticket she got in Virginia. She was so crushed.

While I was in college, secondhand clothing stores first opened in Charleston. I started buying used clothes in those stores. Mom thought that was just about the most unsophisticated thing anyone could do. She was so amused by this that she bought a hideous-looking used purple dress and wrapped it up for a Christmas present for me as a practical joke. I was thin in those days and could find many nice clothes at local thrift shops. A soft, mauve corduroy jacket was one of my best finds. I'm still a fan of secondhand shops.

Another nickname many people called our mother was "Wheels," because she was always on the go. Right up to a few years ago, when my sister and I insisted that she stop driving, she drove herself everywhere. She often drove to conventions, which were hours away. Even now, she still loves to get out of the house and go places with my sister and me, despite the fact that she spends much of the time waiting in the car.

For years, Mom and several of her friends got together once a week in one of their homes and played the card game Hand and Foot. That has slacked off now, since most of the women don't get around so easily. Mom and Dad often invited other couples to our house to play Rook or Canasta. There were four couples from our church, the Ransons, Reeds, Youngs, and my parents, who constantly ran around together. They referred to themselves as "The Crazy Eights." After church every Sunday morning, my parents were part of a group called "The Lunch Bunch." That group was a mix of couples and widows who went out to eat at local restaurants. For many years, Mom continued to be a part of the group after Dad died.

The last nickname Mom was given, when she got a little older, was "The Energizer Bunny," because she never slowed down. Until a few years ago, she was active in the statewide WCTU association, in her church circle, and in the American Baptist Women's group. She frequently visited shut-ins and took food to families for various occasions. Then her feet and knees started refusing to move when she needed them to, confining her to a wheelchair. One evening, as she was riding with me on the road where I live, she was philosophizing about the situation with her knees. She said: "I've decided that life is like a deer. You never know what's going to hit you." Within seconds of her saying that, as if on cue, a deer ran out of the woods and hit the front side of my car. It fell down upon impact, then immediately got up and ran off. What an unbelievable fluke. All we could do was sit there for a moment, and take in what had just happened. I think we were as stunned as the deer.

Mom enjoyed being a mother to us, but she really loves being a grandmother to my two sons. Before they were in school, she kept them while I worked and Peter went back to college. Mom and Dad took the boys camping to various state parks in their new camper. They often loaded them up and went on many day trips. I think those are some of her most cherished memories. Every year during spring break, my parents went with the boys and me on vacation. We usually went to the Outer Banks, or someplace near Myrtle Beach. The spring after Dad died, we went to Disney World and Key West.

These days, we continue to take Mom for her long-standing hair appointments every week. She still wears her silver hairdo of many years, which is short and very teased, and flattering to her face. An attractive lady at eighty-seven, she enjoys primping in front of her bathroom mirror as much as teenage girls do. She prides herself in getting all dressed up and loves to buy new clothes. Probably the one thing she misses as much as anything, with her immobility, is not being able to be the hostess which she was for so long. Without being able to maneuver on her own, cooking is nearly impossible, not to mention dangerous. As a consequence from wearing pointed-toed shoes all of her life, she now has a severe case of hammertoes on both feet. Her toes have crossed over one another, like people do when they cross their fingers to make a wish. It is very difficult for her to find any shoes that she can get her feet into.

After my grandmother died, Mom took over the presidency of the local chapter of the WCTU, the group which opposes drinking any alcoholic beverages. I was amused with her being upset because we didn't invite her to go with us to the local Wine and Jazz Festival last year. She would have been miserable, seeing all of those people drinking wine in broad daylight. We would have been even more miserable, listening to her complaining about it nonstop.

These days, my sister and I usually alternate taking her to church on Sunday mornings. It seems a little nonsensical to go to all of the effort to load her in the wheelchair, push her into the church, only to have her sleep through most of the sermon. I think her main motivation for attending every Sunday is to see the preacher and her friends and have everyone make a fuss over her. So many people lean over to her and comment on how pretty she looks. She loves the attention and wants to stay until we are the last ones to leave. It really is the highlight of her week.

I have to scream when talking with her on the phone to get her to hear me. Most of the time, she still doesn't understand what I've said. In warmer weather, when the windows are open, I'm sure my neighbors think I am really being mean, yelling at her so loudly. At her home, I have seen her talking to someone on the phone, and the mouthpiece is resting on her lap. No wonder we can't hear her.

Recently I took Mom to visit an assisted living manor. We were hoping she might like it enough to want to live there. As much as she falls, we know she needs around-the-clock assistance, with plenty of help to lift her. During our visit, several nice-looking older men in wheelchairs were very welcoming and friendly towards her. In the car, on our way home, she said: "I didn't realize there would be so many men there." I think that helped to spark an interest.

It saddens me to see our parents' generation disappear, leaving us as they pass on, one at a time. They were so influential in our lives. Their generation seemed to make having a good time and visiting with one another a real priority. Above all, most of them had strong religious convictions. They always gave us such a comforting feeling...a sense that everything was going to be all right. As a child, when I was as sick as could be, lying on the couch with the mumps, measles, chicken pox, or whatever, my mother was always able to comfort me. Sometimes she rubbed my chest with Vicks VapoRub or put a cold, wet washcloth across my hot forehead. Her cure-all combination of chicken noodle soup, ginger ale, and saltine crackers seemed to make any ailment a little better.

You're Bored?

Photograph by Jon Browning.

As a teacher, one phenomenon that tried my patience over the last few years was students announcing, "I'm bored." This was in our new art room, where each student had every opportunity in the world to pursue unlimited, creative endeavors. Self-motivated students were throwing pots on the potter's wheels, painting on canvases, and making stained glass panels and boxes. Others were pursuing their own creativity, with all kinds of incredible projects. Still, there was a handful of students who consistently thought it was in vogue to be bored. They missed out on so much.

It seems like many young people today think they have some kind of entitlement which guarantees them to be entertained by us. Thankfully, I don't recall ever saying to any of my teachers or my parents, "I'm bored." We were good at keeping ourselves busy and didn't expect someone else to entertain us. Being bored was never a consideration. Before we were in grade school, my friends and I played "school." I, of course, was always the teacher, as I liked to boss the younger kids around, even back then. We lined up chairs in a row on my back porch for our classroom. My "students" sat properly with paper, pencils, and a book. I led them through rigorous assignments and activities. Sometimes this entertained us for the entire afternoon.

My friends and I spent many afternoons after school playing *Sergeant Preston of the Yukon.* As we ran around our hilly neighborhood, we pretended to be leading our team of sled dogs. We yelled: "On King, on you huskies. Mush, mush, you huskies," mimicking our hero. To us, these were pretty important, serious adventures. They became more exciting and more real whenever we were fortunate enough to play in the snow. Sometimes we hiked up very steep streets, for about a mile's distance, to play on a golf course which was mostly idle in the wintertime. Once we were there, we magically became a herd of wild horses. Each of us had our own special horse name. We galloped up and down the rolling hills of the golf course, kicking up our "hooves" and neighing.

Sometimes we pretended to be riding horses all over our hill. We had a special place along our neighbors' fence which was our hitching post. Each of us had a designated place to tie up our horse. Frequently, we played cowboys and Indians, mimicking what we saw on television. We often shot our metal cap guns, with the red paper rolls and little round caps. When we pulled the trigger, they made a loud, popping noise and smoked after being shot.

Roller skating was another popular sport in our neighborhood. We frequently got out the shoebox on the floor of our coat closet, which held our collection of metal skates. They were heavy, with crusty brown leather straps, which were usually the first things to wear out. Since the skates were adjustable, we could change the length, to fit our friends and visitors. I can still hear the clang, clang, clomp, clomp sound of the metal wheels hitting the pavement. If we didn't tighten them real well with our skate keys, they invariably came off.

As if we didn't know better, every kid on the West Side hill had a bicycle. We rode them on the streets which ran across the hill, and sometimes had to walk them up and down the steeper streets going up the hill. A scar on my arm reminds me of my worst bike wreck. I was foolishly trying to ride down the extremely steep street next to ours when I lost control and slammed into a tree. Once a bike gets going too fast on any steep downslope it's very easy to lose control.

One of our favorite activities to counter boredom was to work on our "forts." We had a small one behind our neighbors' garage, but the real significant one was at the top of our street. It was on a hilly, vacant lot, covered with brush and briars. For hours at a time, practically every weekday, we worked on clearing out and making improvements to our fort. Sometimes we had lunch or snacks in the fort to take a break from our hard labor. Every time I drive by the house which sits upon that tall hillside where our fort once was, I remember those adventurous times.

When weather didn't permit us to play outside, we usually went upstairs to my bedroom and played with my collection of hard plastic or ceramic horses. The craftsmanship and detail on these statues were amazing. Some had removable saddles and cowboy or Indian figures. My favorite horses were the white family group by the Breyer Company. Over several occasions, I received the colt, mare, and stallion. I still have a few of these statues from my childhood collection, which is more than five decades old now. When I see familiar models in antique shops, it feels like running into old friends.

Sometimes we put on our little plastic high heels, with the elastic straps, and played "Dress-Up." We often draped our mothers' mink stoles around our shoulders and wore their old, fancy, wide brim hats. We made up our faces with lipstick and rouge. My mom donated several old purses to the cause. As we strutted around the house, and looked into the mirror, we thought we were the cat's meow.

I don't remember playing a lot with dolls, but I do recall spending quite a bit of time playing with our paper dolls. Their clothes had little tabs, which folded over to the back side of the doll to keep them in place. We had to cut the clothes out with scissors, since they came on flat sheets of paper. My favorite thing to do was to design new outfits for our dolls. Blank templates were sometimes provided with the dolls. We came up with several attractive, original outfits.

Makeshift tents were always fun, especially at friends' houses, where two twin beds were parallel to each other. We draped a sheet or blanket from one bed to another, for our ceiling. Then we used another sheet, going the opposite direction, to make doors for the tent. Anything was always more fun, when we did it in a tent. At our house, we got out our dad's white silk parachute that he brought home from the war. When we draped it all over the furniture, it made an enormous tent.

For many hours we hovered over the Ouija board, asking poignant questions such as, "Does Steve love Nancy?" I always questioned the validity of the answers, knowing that someone was more than likely trying to skew them. It was fairly easy to manipulate the pointer to produce the outcome we wanted. This was especially true on the "No" and "Yes" answers. We also used our black Eight Balls to get "genuine" answers for important questions. One fun thing we did to occupy our time was to construct colorful chains from folded "links" of chewing gum wrappers. Some days we set up lemonade stands in our front yards. On my own, I sold greeting cards door-to-door in our neighborhood, for extra spending money.

While we were eating at the Cracker Barrel restaurant recently, part of its décor jogged my memory. Along with other memorabilia, hanging on the wall above our table was an old Parcheesi board. It was identical to the one we used to spend hours around. We also played a lot of Candy Land and the game Cootie, then when we were older, Monopoly and Scrabble. The neighborhood kids often came to our house and played many strategic games of Pick Up Sticks with us on our living room floor. Other times, we played some pretty competitive games of Jacks. The kids who were really outstanding at Jacks gained everyone's respect. That game was a lot more difficult than it looked. All of us tried our skill at tabletop Skittle. It seemed like the secret to having a good run had everything to do with how tightly wound the string was around the bobbin.

In 1958, the kids in our neighborhood, as well as millions of children all over the country, became fanatics about hula hooping. The hoops we used were bigger, heavier, and harder than the ones sold today. There weren't any fancy designs on our hoops. Mine was a muted blue color. I was never really a standout at anything except for hula hooping. We often held contests on our street and I could outlast anyone. In the fourth grade, I participated in the hula hoop contest in Kanawha City at Shoney's drive-in restaurant. Hundreds of contestants started out early in the morning and by the time dusk rolled around, there were less than twenty of us left. When the sun went down, the air got pretty chilly. Being so cocky, I tried to put on a sweater, without taking an official timeout. Sure enough, as I slipped my arm into the last sleeve, my elbow nicked the hoop, bringing it down and erasing my chances of winning.

The summer before my fifth grade, I got a hankering to start reading. We had a collection with numerous volumes of colorful, beautifully-bound *Reader's Digest* condensed books on our shelves in the living room. One day I started leafing through the books and began to read them. That was the first time I remember reading for enjoyment. I read several selections over the summer, but by far, *The Yearling*, by Marjorie Rawlings, was my favorite.

Trends of the Fifties, Sixties, and Seventies

Sister Jean wearing a sack dress, and I have on my typical jumper, 1958.

There were a number of trends which achieved great heights of popularity when we were young. Some were very short-lived, and others withstood the test of time. Surprisingly, there are so many of these trends which are still around today, some fifty years later. Much of the candy we enjoyed as youngsters is still available. As a child, I used to save the cards in Mallow Cups to redeem them for "valuable" prizes. My favorite candy to buy at the movies was Good & Plenty, with the bright pink and white pieces. Black Cows, chocolate-coated caramel suckers, and little small wax "Coke" bottles, filled with colored sugar water, are two candies I miss seeing. As kids, those were two of our favorites.

One trend which was popular in our elementary school was the Zaner-Bloser pencils and pens. Our teachers handed out these peculiar-looking plastic pencils and pens, which were specifically designed to have a good grip. Those were our tools when we practiced handwriting skills. Several years ago, before he retired, a friend of mine asked me if I wanted to go through an old box of teaching supplies. It looked like they had come over on the Mayflower. The erasers were hardened from age, the ballpoint pens and markers were all dried up, the scissors had rusted, and most of what was in the box was useless. But, to my delight, a small box of red and blue Zaner-Bloser pencils, just like the ones we used in the second grade, was in the bottom of the box.

Cardboard composition books have definitely withstood the test of time. I was shopping a few days ago and was surprised to see these familiar books with the peculiar mottled black and white design and bound edge. The notebooks looked like they would have been at home in any antique shop. They were identical to the ones we used in grade school and looked a little out of place. Next to them were spiral notebooks and binders in neon colors, many adorned with teen idols. I still like to use the composition books, because the thick covers provide a stiff writing surface.

Metal lunchboxes with very intricate, embossed, painted designs were real status symbols for school kids in the fifties and sixties. These brightly-colored boxes featured popular television shows or actors, like *Lost in Space* or Roy Rogers, and favorite cartoon characters, such as Superman. Some had favorite dolls or toys, like Barbie, or idolized musicians, such as the Beatles. A friend of mine told me that the one thing she coveted when she was in grade school, and never had, was a Hopalong Cassidy lunchbox.

All of us listened to our favorite tunes on palm-size transistor radios, which came in a variety of colors. In our bedrooms, we had pastel-colored clock radios, which were also alarm clocks. These were horizontal, about twelve to fifteen inches wide, and five to seven inches high. They had antennas, a circular dial, and a clock face on one side of the front. One year, when I was in junior high school, I got a beige one as a Christmas gift. It served me well for many, many years.

Small stuffed animals called "Autograph Hounds" were popular when I was in grade school and in junior high school. I kept mine until just recently. Everyone in my fifth grade class had signed the white cloth dog, which had a black bowtie and graduation cap. Several of my friends and I had ant farms. Mine was in my bedroom, for a couple of years. I was so fascinated with watching the ants, especially their digging and nonstop activity.

At my house, we had three magazines delivered during my entire youth: *National Geographic, Life* and *Look.* This was true for many of the families I visited. Yesterday I came across two of these relics while helping to sort through piles of accumulated mementos my mom has kept. One was the *Life* issue from November 25, 1966. It had cost thirty-five cents. The other was a *Look* issue from March 7, 1967. The price on it was fifty cents. Both covers had topics about JFK's assassination.

Telephones very noticeably evolved from the classic, rotary dial, black desktop ones, which most household had. This model, the Kellogg 500 "Banjo Phone," was eventually offered in colors. I thought we were real trendsetters when my family got a beige one. Then the thinner, Princess style was introduced, still with the rotary dial. Next came the wall phone. The real innovation came with the touchtone dials. That's how we could tell if a family was "with it"…whether or not they owned a trendy touchtone telephone. For years we were on a party line without any real privacy. All of the phone numbers in our neighborhood started with the prefix "Dickens."

Most houses in our neighborhood had built-in corner china cupboards in the dining rooms. They were well-constructed and usually had a fancy top, similar to a Queen Anne highboy dresser. Fine china and cut crystal stemware were displayed in these cabinets, where they were kept safe from us rowdy kids. Practically all of the households I visited had fancy china and sterling silverware, the kind which frequently had to be polished. Those were brought out only on special occasions.

In our homes, almost everyone had chenille bedspreads with soft, textured, pastel floral designs. Most newer carpet like Bigelow was very thick, with deep-cut patterns. It never wore out, so sometimes people just replaced it, getting sick of looking at it. "Shag" carpet was the big, new fad when I was in college. Tupperware parties were really popular during our youth, and practically everyone had a set of the company's tall, plastic, pastel tumblers. They came in different colors, making it easier to tell where each person's drink was.

Boxes of detergent often had dish towels or glasses in them. Usually little plastic toys were prizes in our cereal boxes. Plastic-coated cardboard records, which could actually be played on a phonograph, were sometimes printed on the backs of cereal boxes. They had to be cut out with scissors along the dotted circle. For the longest time we shaved with thin metal, double-edged razor blades. Twisting the handle of the razor open it so you could replace the blade. Band-Aids came in metal tins with hinged lids. Dry hair shampoo, Minipoo, was sold in round, pink and black cardboard canisters, with a shake top. The description on the canister read: "New 10-minute way to clean hair. No wetting. No resetting."

Certain baby boomer girls' names, in particular, followed definite trends. In our school and town, one of the most popular girls' names was mine, Nancy. There were always several girls named Nancy in each of my classes throughout my school career. All of the faculties in the various schools where I taught had several women named Nancy. Yet, during my entire thirty-four years of teaching, I never once had a student with that popular baby boomer name.

Other popular boomer girls' names were Carol, Judy, Barbara, Linda, Mary, Donna, Susan, Sharon, Karen, and Brenda. Interestingly, most of these girls' names are very seldom chosen by the parents of today. On the other hand, the time-honored boys' names, which were given to many baby boomers, are still popular today. James, John, Michael, Robert, Richard, David, Charles, and Gary are such examples.

In the fifties, the first popular exercise equipment that was heavily advertised was the vibrating belt machine. It had a very wide belt and vibrated so much, it looked like it would shake the living daylights out of anyone. The belt was placed around the waist, or whatever part of the body needed to be "exercised."

More affluent and progressive-thinking families in our neighborhood took the Eisenhower administration's advice. They had fallout shelters built in their basements. These were lined with cinderblocks and had ample supplies of food, water, towels, and blankets...anything a family might need as they waited out the imminent Soviet nuclear assault.

One popular trend which spanned several decades was getting S&H Green Stamps and TV, Top Value, Yellow Stamps. We got these in the checkout lines at the grocery stores and at some service stations. How much money we spent determined how many stamps we received. At home, we licked and glued the stamps inside little booklets. After accumulating a substantial amount of filled booklets, we traded them for something at the redemption center. There was a good variety of items from which to choose:

toasters, electric blankets, fans, china, lamps, towels, tools, and camping lanterns…all kinds of things. It took such a large number of books to get something of any value, but it always felt so satisfying, thinking we were getting something "for free."

In the fifties, bathroom fixtures and kitchen appliances started coming out in colors. Ironically, those were the hot trend back then. Nowadays, they can outdate a house as quickly as anything. In the sixties and early seventies, almost everything was decorated with rather nondescript geometric designs, especially dishes, furniture, and curtains.

Poodle skirts and Ben Casey doctor shirts were popular when I was in grade school. My older cousin and sister wore their poodle skirts and Ben Casey shirts to school. They also wore round, stiff taffeta skirts which had wide elastic waistbands and were cut out like a large circle. All of us wore hoop skirts. We wore itchy crinolines under them, often with stiff hoops on the bottom. Sitting down while wearing these skirts could be somewhat problematic, when the hoops flew up in our faces. Sometimes we wore multiple layers of petticoats to achieve the full skirt look.

During the latter years of grade school, and when my sister was in junior high, we all wore sack dresses, which resembled their name. They certainly weren't very flattering. Without any real definition to their shape, they hung straight down, just like a sack. Thankfully, these didn't have a very long lifespan. From grade school through high school we wore a lot of jumpers.

In junior high school, wool, plaid, pleated skirts were popular. We usually wore those with starched, white cotton blouses. I remember the blue and gray skirt I wore, which was the product of an assignment in Miss Hall's sewing class. Black and white saddle oxfords or cordovan Weejun penny loafers were our standard school shoes. I think we used to stuff just about any coins, other than pennies, in the little slots on the tops of those penny loafers.

On rainy and snowy days, we pulled on clear, rubber galoshes over our shoes.

During our youth, for such a long time, so much of what everyone wore was white. Men's dress shirts and T-shirts were plain white, never with any designs on them. Older teenage boys often rolled up their T-shirt sleeves and tucked their packs of Camels down in them. Our bobby socks were white and so were our blouses. Women's bras, slips, and garter belts were mostly white.

Some of our long-sleeved, white shirts and blouses had slots on the sleeves for cufflinks. Boys' cufflinks typically had engraved designs of initials. My favorite pair had furry little animal faces. We often wore fake collars, which fastened around our necks over our sweaters or dresses. Most of these were furry, beaded, or lacy and added quite a different look to any outfit.

In high school, couples who were dating sometimes wore "date mate" clothes. This usually consisted of couples wearing identical shirts, but if they were real gung-ho about the idea, their entire outfits were exactly the same. That was one fad in which my boyfriends and I never participated.

We girls frequently wore scarab bracelets and gold or silver circle pins on the collars of our white blouses. Which side of the collar we placed the circle pin on was important. If it was worn on the right side, it supposedly meant that you weren't a virgin. We definitely didn't want to be accused of that.

For several years, my friend Barbara and I each wore a silver half heart necklace. Many best friends wore these. When the heart was held together it read, "Best Friends" (on the top line) and "For Ever" (on the bottom line.) The fad which still haunts me to this day is carrying around a real rabbit's foot as a token of good luck. During my junior high years, while shopping in the downtown Kresge's dime store, I picked out the hot pink rabbit's foot, which

I carried on my keychain for many years. I can't fathom doing that today.

Older girls were often given cedar hope chests. They were gradually filled with linens, dishes, and anything else that would be needed for housekeeping. These footlocker-shaped boxes were to be the girls' dowries, and what they would contribute to their future marriages. My sister's fiancé gave her a handsome one while they were dating.

One year, when we were in high school, almost everyone, boys and girls alike, received and gave ID bracelets for Christmas gifts. They were gold or silver and some resembled watch bands. All of them had a solid metal section, which had names or initials engraved on it. Girls' charm bracelets were popular for years. My bracelet never had a lot of charms compared to other girls' but my favorite one was the little black clarinet.

Another year, the popular Christmas gift for girls was beauty-shop-style hair dryers, with the big dome hoods. I can't believe we actually slept with a head full of hair curlers every single night, as practically all of us did. Makeup mirrors which folded out to make their own stands were popular another year. They had lights all around the mirrors and resembled the kind actresses use in their dressing rooms.

Hairdos certainly went through the changes. My sister and I got very short "ducktail" haircuts one summer when we were in grade school. The sides of our hair were brushed towards the back, with a duck tail on the bottom. In the early sixties, there were many tall, teased bangs and styles, the tallest being "the beehive." Sometimes girls wore a hair bow on their foreheads, right in the middle of their bangs. I always thought that looked pretty funny. Looking through my high school yearbooks, it is amusing to see how many of us girls had identical hairstyles. They were shoulder length with a perfect flip on the end, just like the one Jacqueline Kennedy made famous. Twiggy took the United States by storm in

1967 with her boyish haircut, large eyes, and skinny figure. She set the standard for thinking that we girls had to be thin like Twiggy, in order to be beautiful.

In high school, many girls wore coats with raccoon collars. Long, Chesterfield dress coats with lapel collars were popular too. These wool coats often had herringbone patterns and velvet collars. In the sixties, getting initials embroidered on our clothes was another popular trend. During that time, there was a thriving shop in town, on Hale Street, which specialized in monogramming. In the twelfth grade I gave my boyfriend Tom a monogrammed sweater for Christmas. It had a stylish design of his initials stitched on the front.

When we were in high school and college, it seemed like our country had an insatiable appetite for electronic gadgets. One year, most everyone received electric razors for Christmas gifts. Another year, the "hot" item was electric blankets. Electric hair curlers, which turned different colors on the ends when they heated up, were popular for a while. Electric carving knives became the next necessity. Then, finally, it seemed like practically every family had to have an electric can opener on their already overcrowded kitchen counter.

Almost every household had a deep fryer, and many had electric waffle irons. Most of our moms kept a large, standing electric food mixer on the counter, since it was used so frequently. Many families had a hand-cranked ice cream maker, which was a favorite thing to use when company came. Homemade ice cream always tasted so much better than the store-bought kind.

Metal ice trays which had a lever on the top were replaced by plastic ones. Trying to pull the lever on the metal trays to release the cubes could sometimes prove to be difficult. Usually, running a little warm water over the tray, could remedy the problem. Tripping the plastic trays with a slight twist of the wrist seemed to be so much easier. Everyday lightweight plastic Melmac dishes gave way to break-resistant china Corelle and heavy Pfaltzgraff stoneware.

In the late sixties, when I was in college, most of us had long, straight hair. Many of us wore mood rings and dresses with empire waistlines, and carried Aigner purses, if we could afford them. I saved money from my summer playground director's job to buy a fairly expensive one for college. It was on display at Embee's department store and caught my eye every time I walked by it. That purse was probably the most lavish purchase I ever made. To me, it was a real splurge.

During my first two years at college, female students were not allowed to wear slacks to class. We solved that problem by wearing plaid wool shorts with knee socks under tan trench coats. Thankfully, the administrators became liberated and did away with such an outdated rule.

One-piece jumpsuits were popular for a while, when I was in college. I remember making and wearing a long, zip-up one, which had green and brown geometric designs. Big bell-bottom pants, and long knee-length vests were popular in the late sixties and early seventies. Purses and belts with leather tooling and clunky brass belt buckles were popular, too. I made a cool macramé belt with a big brass peace sign belt buckle which I wore for many years.

Hot pants and miniskirts were the huge new trends when I started teaching in 1971. While looking at pictures of myself in miniskirts, I am surprised that I wore them to teach in, as short as they were. My favorite one was made of brown suede. We wore extremely short dresses, too. One of my students jokingly asked me one morning if I had forgotten to put on my skirt, since my dress was so short, it looked like I was wearing a long blouse.

Pretty Boy Pete, Little Lost Skipper, and Kitty the Turtle

Our toy fox terrier, Skipper, with me at Granny's house, 1957.

It seems like back in the fifties, almost every household had a pet parakeet and an aquarium full of guppies or goldfish. Ours was no exception. For years, we were thoroughly entertained by our perky, blue parakeet, Pete. He literally ruled the roost at our house. Being quite the socialite, he enjoyed our company as much as we did his.

Knowing how my parents used to be such clean freaks, it's hard for me to imagine how much they let their guard down when it came to our parakeets, especially Pete. This behavior on their part seems completely incongruous with how tidy and particular they were about keeping the house immaculate and germ-free.

All of the parakeets we owned throughout the years spent most of the time in their cage. It was located in the dining room between a window and the dining room table. The birds were often let out of their cage to fly around the house. Pete, however, had special privileges. During meals, while we were seated at the table, he was frequently allowed out of his cage to visit with us as we ate.

This funny blue parakeet liked to perch on the top of the dark, thick rim of my father's eyeglasses. He would lean over, upside down, and look into Dad's glasses, pecking on the lens. I'm not exactly sure, but I guess he could see his own reflection on the glassy surface, and was pecking at the "other bird" he saw.

He also liked to perch on the brim of my father's coffee cup and take a gulp of coffee. I don't think Dad ever actually drank after him, but it still baffles me that Pete was permitted to even come near the dining table, much less participate in the meals, and perch on Dad's cup.

Mom spent quite a lot of time working with Pete and trained him to do a few tricks. He could nod and turn around on command. She taught him to say, "Pete's a pretty boy," which he announced repeatedly, with somewhat impressive clarity and recognizable words.

One green parakeet didn't survive an episode of eating some of the garland on our Christmas tree. Another flew to his fate as he escaped out the front door, over our mom's head, as she opened the door to answer it.

I don't remember a time when we didn't own some kind of pet. One year we got baby ducks as Easter presents. Those precious little yellow peepers were so tiny and cute, for a while. Then they grew to be big, noisy, quacking, solid white ducks. We delivered them to a family who lived down the road from our camp. They had a nice farm and were delighted to get them for their pond.

One of my pets whom I was quite fond of was Kitty. She was a little turtle I had back in grade school for what seemed like a long time. I remember picking Kitty out from the multitude of tiny turtles on display in the basement of Young's Department Store. Each turtle's shell couldn't have been much larger than the size of a fifty-cent piece. Most of their shells were decorated with paintings of colorful cartoon animals.

The turtle I chose had a hot pink kitty painted on its shell, hence the name "Kitty." I loved that turtle. She never grew any larger and lived comfortably in her shallow, aquarium home. It had a curved ramp, which she often crawled down, allowing her to get into the water whenever she so desired. When the weather was warm, I liked to take Kitty outside and let her walk around the yard. The bright pink kitty on her shell made it easier for me to keep track of her as she walked through the green grass.

I could hardly contain myself one morning when I woke up and found Kitty lifeless. This was my first encounter with the uncertainties of death. So distraught with sorrow, I was sobbing uncontrollably. My parents had a difficult time trying to decipher my words as I attempted to tell them of her demise. Kitty was buried in a cardboard matchbox in our backyard. I offered profound words of gratitude during her eulogy, as her friends and family gathered around for the burial. She was sent off to turtle heaven in style, getting the proper funeral she deserved.

One day, when I was in my early years of grade school, Mom announced that she and Dad had decided to purchase a toy fox terrier for our family pet. An ad in the newspaper, from a breeder in South Carolina, had caught her attention. She called and placed her order, and mailed the breeder the asking price of twenty-five dollars. We anxiously awaited our new family member.

After several days, we received the phone call, saying our dog had arrived. Mom, my sister, and I excitedly hopped in the car and drove across town to the train depot. A man in the office instructed us to go to the loading dock. We drove up to the dock and walked through the large opening into the dimly-lit, nearly empty warehouse.

A gentleman had our mother sign a piece of paper, then walked over and picked up a wooden crate, which sat all by itself next to the front wall. He handed over the crate to us, and we peeped inside to get a glimpse of one precious, tiny, scared, shivering puppy. He appeared to be quite relieved and happy to have some company at last. We made a bed for him in a cardboard box that night and tucked a clock under the blanket to sound like his mother's heartbeat.

My mom's intuition of knowing that this particular breed of dog would make a perfect pet has always intrigued me. Perhaps the ad was convincing. Time would tell that he truly was a perfect match for us.

We named our new member of the family "Skipper." His short-haired coat was white, with large brown and black markings. Tri-angular ears, a black nose on a pointed snout, and extremely large brown eyes adorned his small face. Being the toy variety that he was, he never got very big. He had such a good personality, getting along with every human and animal he met. He ran the neighbor-hood freely, as dogs were allowed to do back then. Everyone loved

Skipper and made such a fuss over him. He thrived on getting all of that attention.

Shortly after we got Skipper, we took him on his first long car ride. During that trip, he began having convulsions. He was stricken with a severe case of distemper. The vet criticized Mom for buying a pet "sight unseen." He gave us a discouraging prognosis, saying that Skipper probably wouldn't make it. We were all so glum after receiving such horrible news. Against all odds, and much to our relief, Skipper survived the disease. Impressive dedication, genuine concern about him, and constant caregiving on the part of our vet and mother had paid off. He was to enjoy a long, full life after all.

Skipper and I literally grew up with one another, spending many hours together. I took him practically everywhere I went, often pushing him around our hill in a red and white doll carriage. I don't know if, or how much, he liked that, but he never squirmed or attempted to get away. In our neighborhood, Skipper reached celebrity status, often performing with our mom. He was billed as the "Singing Dog" and was a real hit with the kids. He and my mother performed at our grade school's talent shows and for our church's Vacation Bible School. Mom sang "Happy Birthday to You" and Skipper tilted his head back and "sang" along with her, howling at the sound of her voice.

On Saturday, July 8, 1961, our family headed out to the "Dam dedication," as everyone in my family jokingly called it. This was the official grand opening of the Sutton Dam in the little town of the same name. The dam was built across the Elk River for the main purpose of flood control.

People all across the state were excited about the centrally located dam. The beautiful large lake it created covered 1,440 acres and stretched fourteen miles along the Elk River. Swimming, skiing, boating, fishing, and camping, which the lake was to provide, were much-needed and anticipated recreational opportunities. All of those benefits were expected to deliver an enormous boost to the local economy.

The opening of the dam was an event of tremendous importance. Many people in the massive crowd were dressed to the hilt, decked out in their Sunday-go-to-meetin' clothes. Dignitaries and politicians were present and our governor, W.W. Barron, conducted the ribbon-cutting ceremony. The politicians walked along the edge of the crowd, shaking hands with those in attendance. We watched as Mom leaned over the security fence and shook hands with United States Senator Jennings Randolph.

Skipper had been traveling with us that day, as he did practically everywhere we went. Unbeknown to us, he had jumped out of our car on the way to the ceremony. As we were traveling up Route 4, we had pulled off the road to check on a carload of relatives who had stopped beside the highway.

It wasn't until we had been at the ceremony for a while when it finally dawned on someone in our group that Skipper was no longer with us. We could easily put two and two together and realize where we had lost him. All of us were sickened, thinking of what might be the outcome of this situation. We were so worried that he would get hit or run over by a speeding car on the busy road. Although he ran the neighborhood at home, he didn't have the street smarts or experience of dealing with so much traffic, traveling at highway speeds.

We immediately left the ceremony and started backtracking our steps. The forty-minute drive back to where we thought he had jumped out seemed to take forever. I'm sure there was a lot of silent praying going on in that car. We pulled up to the exact place where we had stopped beside the road, but to our dismay... no Skipper. With a lump in our throats and dwindling hope, we took out on foot, uncertain if we were on a rescue or recovery mission.

Dad knocked on the door of one family who lived beside the highway, fairly close to where we had stopped. The man who answered the door said they had witnessed the saddest, most heartbreaking scene. For a long time, they had watched the forlorn puppy. Once we had driven off and unwittingly left him behind, Skipper began pacing up and down the highway. They said he would sit at the exact place where our car had been, tilt his head back, and let out the most heart-wrenching howl they had ever heard.

Then he would run down the road, "thirty yards or so," do the same thing down there, then run back up to his original place. He repeated this over and over again. Having somewhat renewed hope, we all started loudly calling out his name. With a collective sigh of relief, and to our elation, someone excitedly pointed out a little white and black speck in the far distance. It was flying towards us at the speed of light.

I'm not sure who was more ecstatic, Skipper or us. We were all so thankful that this horrifying ordeal had a happy ending. One can only appreciate and imagine the angst, sadness, and confusion our buddy had endured during that exhausting afternoon.

Skipper lived to be nearly twenty years old. Like many aging dogs, he became both blind and deaf. That never slowed him down, and for several more years, he somehow continued to make his daily rounds throughout the neighborhood. After I had moved away from home, his long, full life eventually came to an end. He was hit by a most apologetic driver, who, ironically, said he couldn't see Skipper because he was so small. Of course, Skipper couldn't see him either, even though his car was so large.

Hamsters were the other animals we frequently had as pets. My sister recently reminded me of her favorite hamster episode. Our family had taken one hamster in the car with us as we picked up my sister from summer camp. When we left her camp, we traveled to Elkins to visit relatives. We left the hamster in the car overnight, in his cage, on the floor of the back seat. When my mother walked out to the car the next morning, she had quite a surprise.

She opened the car door to get her dress, which was hanging in the car. It was what she was planning on wearing that day.

The hamster had reached through the bars of his cage, grabbed the dress, and pulled some of it inside the cage. Such a large hole was chewed through the front of the dress in this escapade that the dress was completely ruined and could never be worn again. The hamster may have destroyed Mom's dress, but in doing so, he sure was successful at making himself the largest, fluffiest king-size bed any hamster could ever dream of having.

Another hamster, who had escaped from her cage without our realizing it, stirred up quite a ruckus one night at our home. She made an unexpected appearance during what was probably the most important event of the year for my mother. Our church had a large network of women's "circles." Each circle had around fifteen members and met once a month in different people's homes. The women had devotions and various programs, as they sat around in a large circle. I guess that's how the name originated.

Mom hosted a meeting once every year. We always teased her about it, saying we could tell it must be time for a circle meeting. This was such a big to-do for her that the house had to be flawless. She usually bought new throw pillows, washed the curtains in the living room and dining room, and had us help her clean every single window in the house. For weeks, she toiled over what to serve the visiting church ladies then carefully planned out and prepared the food for them.

When the big night finally arrived for this momentous occasion, we were shipped off to someplace out of the house. This was my mother's moment. It was her night to shine. Everything was meticulously prepared and had been planned out to the nth degree. What could possibly go wrong? Absolutely nothing...or so she thought.

Our escapee hamster dashed across the floor of the living room just as the speaker was giving her devotion and the room was perfectly quiet. The sight of a rodent running around their feet scared the ladies so much, they screamed hysterically. For all they knew, it could have been a rat. Most of them didn't know we owned a hamster. Oh, well. As the saying goes: "The best laid plans of hamsters and women often go awry."

The Magic of Christmas

Christmas at our house, 1951.

When we were children, Christmas was such a magical time, full of deep-rooted traditions. Every year, my sister, Jean, and I helped our mom bake and decorate sugar cookies. We used a set of red plastic cookie cutters that pressed embossed designs into the dough. After they were baked, we decorated them with different colors of icing. I'm sure we had more than these, but the

Santa face, Christmas tree, hanging stocking, and star are the ones I remember.

As a family, we drove to the local corner tree stand and picked out a handsome, nicely-shaped tree. My parents usually positioned the tree in a corner of our living room. Decorating it was an exciting time and an important event for the entire family. We used long, colored lights, resembling thin candles, which bubbled when they heated up. All kinds of glass bulbs and ornaments of different shapes, designs, and colors were hung on the tree. Finally, for the finishing touch, we meticulously covered the entire tree with heavy, silver icicles, hung one at a time.

On its circular track, my father's heavy-duty Lionel train tirelessly circled the tree. Around and around it went. Upon demand, the loud whistle blew and puffs of white smoke flowed from the engine's smokestack. The train was such a special treat for visiting children and our cats. Frequently, one of the cats hid nearby and stalked the moving train. After crouching down and shimmying back and forth for a few seconds, the cat lunged at the train, ambushing it and knocking it off the tracks.

To assemble the train each year, we carefully took the cars out of their small orange boxes, one at a time. After the holidays were over, we gingerly tucked them back into their boxes to be stored away until they were summoned for their next performance. It was always so much more special and fun to put up the tree and all of the trimmings than it was to take everything down. As we stored the tree ornaments and other decorations under the eaves until the next Christmas, there was a slight feeling of sadness. For several weeks after the tree was taken down, a huge void was left where it had stood.

Every year in the living room, we hung up our little toy bear on its tightrope. He traveled from one side of the room to the other. With the tug of a string, he skillfully rode backwards and forwards on his small unicycle. A horizontal bar with weights on the ends helped him to stay balanced. We had so much fun with him, having him "perform" for our visitors.

Our close friends, the Haynes family, took great pride every year in having a beautifully-decorated Christmas tree. One year, they woke up to a real shock. Their decorated, short-needle tree, standing in the living room, was practically completely bare, with only a few pine needles left hanging. Christmas trees went through a few short-lived fads and trends. For several years when we were in grade school, artificial metal tinsel trees were the fad. They were bright and shiny and most unrealistic looking. I recall seeing white, blue, pink, and silver ones in people's homes. Another popular trend was to have your tree flocked with artificial snow. One year we tried having a flocked tree, but it became a little problematic when the "snow" kept coming off all over the carpet.

On Christmas Day, one important tradition for our family was to have my dad read the nativity story from the Bible. His voice had such a presence about it. He had a soothing, deep, commanding voice, similar to that of a talented radio announcer or persuasive preacher. Visiting my grandmother's house on Christmas afternoon was another tradition. Her house was just a few blocks below ours. In the deep snow, when we were little, Dad often pulled us to her house on our big wooden sled made from rough-hewn boards. I remember walking to her house on one enchanted Christmas Eve. It was such a magical night. From the black sky, falling snowflakes the size of fifty-cent pieces glistened in the light shining down from the streetlights. Looking up into the dark sky, we wondered if we might see Santa's sled or the bright star, which once shone over the baby Jesus.

The last year I believed in Santa Claus, a young married missionary couple from the Philippines was visiting with us in our home on Christmas Eve. I told the lady that I was so eager to see which gift Santa might bring me, since I couldn't make up my mind between two choices. I wanted a chemistry set and the realistic-looking Baby Dear doll, but knew I couldn't have both.

To my delight and surprise, Santa brought me both gifts. I had fun experimenting with the chemistry set, and enjoyed dressing up Baby Dear in real babies' clothes. I immediately cut off her rather long hair, which I thought didn't fit the otherwise perfectly-sculpted newborn face. My Baby Dear is still at my mom's house, where many visiting children have enjoyed playing with her over the years.

Every year on Christmas morning, my sister and I were so excited about seeing what Santa brought us that we got up before the crack of dawn. To our disappointment, Mom and Dad never allowed us to go into the living room right away. They insisted that we take out our hair curlers and brush our hair before coming into the living room. Their girls had to look presentable for photographs. Our gifts from Santa were never wrapped, but we could tell whose were whose by what each of us had asked for. One of my favorite things to do was to reach down into my stocking to find hidden surprises. One year, down in the bottom, I found wooden pencils in a rainbow of colors with my name engraved on them. When I was in grade school, I discovered one of my favorite stuffed animals hiding among the branches of our Christmas tree. It was a chimpanzee with a great molded plastic face and long, curled tail. Our family always made the rounds on Christmas Day to visit close friends and relatives. The day after Christmas, we usually visited our neighbors to see what Santa had brought them.

As kids, we were always a little disappointed to open our presents from two of my father's sisters. They were very good at crocheting and tatting. Typically, they sent us crocheted slippers, tabletop doilies, or pillowcases. Those weren't very exciting gifts to children. As an adult, though, and one who has made plenty of crafts, I have a completely different perspective. Now I can appreciate the incredible amount of time they spent and the mastery of their skills. Those presents were real labors of love. I still use the crocheted doilies and pillowcases, which have beautiful, intricate designs made from tatting along the edge. The amount of time my aunts invested in our gifts still is amazing to me.

Some of my most treasured Christmas gifts as a child were from my friend Margie. She lived across the street and a few houses up from us. Her father, Harold, was a fine woodworker, and made gifts for Margie to give us. One was a small cedar chest, three inches deep and seven inches wide, and about three inches tall. It has a gold clasp on the front and is perfect for storing jewelry. The handwritten message on the bottom reads: "Merry Christmas to Nancy from Margie, 1956." Another year, he made us small, beautifully-crafted cherry chests of drawers. They were ten inches high and had three drawers, about six inches wide and four inches deep. He left no detail out, as the top and bottom were trimmed with molding, and the drawers had cut-off gold pop beads for knobs. These wooden treasures were so sturdily constructed, they could last forever.

Our family often made the presents we gave to one another and to friends. For two different years, my parents made plaster plaques as gifts. One year, they gave everyone a set of large decorative keys to hang on their walls. The keys were finished with a wood tone stain and actually looked like wood. Another year, they gave four season plaques as gifts. These were popular as well and were also stained a wood tone. The real deluxe sets were painted in color, showing all of the details.

I gave presents of paintings on wooden plaques and canvases, and drew animal portraits with pastels. My most ambitious gifts were pantsuits I sewed when I was in college for my mom and sister. Some of the most creative gifts were the padded stools which my first husband and I made. We bought small wooden barrels, which we sanded, stained, and varnished. The thick padded tops were covered with a heavy, red, textured velvety fabric. We lined the inside of the barrels with green burlap. My mom still uses hers in the den as a magazine holder.

One Christmas season after I was married, my parents' black poodle, Pepper, nearly became the Grinch who stole Christmas. While they attended an evening church service, he became quite mischievous. Upon arriving back home, they opened their front door to discover a shocking surprise. Pepper had filled the living room with shredded bows and ribbons and chewed-up pieces of wrapping paper. He had ruined the wrapping on every single present, which my mom had so painstakingly decorated to perfection.

Going Christmas caroling was always one of my favorite traditions. Every year our Scout troop and church youth group went caroling on frigid nights, with frozen hands cupped over our candles. We were grateful for the slightest amount of warmth coming from their flames. Caroling from house to house, we received warm welcomes and heartfelt words of appreciation. When we were finished, we always went to someone's home or back to the church to enjoy a delicious batch of steaming hot chocolate.

When my sons were in grade school, they insisted on going caroling at my parents' home on one extremely chilly Christmas Eve. I was sick and couldn't go, but the rest of my family took them around the neighborhood. They stopped to sing for the families they knew. I was so touched to see my young sons carrying on a tradition which has always been so dear to my heart.

TVs, TV Trays, and TV Dinners

Our family had the first television set in the neighborhood, and a few years later, we had the first color television. In both cases, there was a steady stream of children and adults alike, coming to our house to marvel at such an incredible and intriguing innovation. Those first models were boxy, awkward, and not very attractive. They took several minutes to warm up. In the early sixties, those were replaced by the larger console television/radio/phonograph units, which were meant to look like fine pieces of furniture.

The six-foot-wide Magnavox unit, which my parents bought in the early 1960s, still sits in my mother's living room. The two sliding doors on the front are simulated wood, made of molded plastic. The doors are permanently closed these days, since the TV hasn't worked for years. Mom's functional, flat-screen TV sits on top of the cabinet. On the top of the console unit, a sliding door covers the old phonograph, which served us well for many years. These days, a modern CD/DVD player sits atop the door.

I don't recall sitting in front of the TV for days at a time during my childhood. I do remember watching some shows regularly, especially after school and on Saturdays. *Popeye and Olive Oyl*, *The Howdy Doody Show*, *The Mickey Mouse Club* with Annette Funicello, *Lassie*, *The Lone Ranger*, *The Andy Griffith Show*, and *American Bandstand* were personal favorites of mine. I became an official member of the Steamboat Bill Fan Club. *Steamboat Bill* was a local show, filmed at WSAZ. It was hosted by George Lewis and featured Merlin the Sea Monster.

Those of us who watched the masked Lone Ranger will always remember his horse, Silver, and his buddy, Tonto. We grew up with Opie on *The Andy Griffith Show* and Timmy on *Lassie*. All of us followed our dancing idols on Dick Clark's *American Bandstand*. The teenyboppers on *Bandstand* captivated us so much that we knew each of their names. They were our trendsetters on how to look and dance.

I could definitely relate to Beaver on *Leave It to Beaver*. Like me, he was the younger sibling. The Cleavers were pretty similar to our family: two kids, a dressed-up, stay-at-home mom, and a father who went off to work every weekday. One of my favorite characters on the show was Wally's friend, the obnoxious, Goody Two-shoes, Eddie Haskell. He was always sucking up to June and Ward. Shelley Fabares, the daughter on *The Donna Reed Show*, was one of our teenage idols. Bob Denver's character, the sloppy Maynard G. Krebs, on *The Many Loves of Dobie Gillis*, was so goofy and pitiful, everybody loved him.

Of course, no one could resist keeping up with the shenanigans of *The Little Rascals*. The characters managed to get themselves into such dire, funny predicaments. My favorites were Alfalfa, Buckwheat, and their dog, Petey. He had a big black spot surrounding one eye, and a big black circle around the other. Eddie Murphy's portrayal of Buckwheat on *Saturday Night Live* was performed to perfection.

The show I was most dedicated to, by far, was *Sergeant Preston of the Yukon*. His devoted followers bought Quaker Puffed Wheat and Puffed Rice cereal so they could become the proud and excited owners of one-inch parcels of Gold Rush territory. "Get FREE Gold Rush Land Today!" was the teaser on the outside of the cereal boxes. Inside each box was a very authentic-looking deed to a one-square-inch parcel of land.

This promotion, called "The Great Klondike Big Inch Land Caper," was perhaps the most brilliant marketing campaign of all time. In 1955 alone, twenty-one million of these one-inch parcels were sold to baby boomers. Typically, the prizes in cereal boxes had been flimsy plastic toys, marbles, or little submarines which were powered by baking soda. The official-looking deeds to an inch of Sergeant Preston's stomping grounds were much more appealing than the typical prizes.

The much-publicized *Edsel Show*, in 1957, certainly lived up to its expectations. Unfortunately, the show itself proved to be more of a success than the ill-fated car it showcased and introduced. With a cast of such superstars as Bing Crosby, Rosemary Clooney, Frank Sinatra, Louis Armstrong, and Bob Hope, the show was destined to be a hit.

As a family, we faithfully watched Dinah Shore, Lawrence Welk, and Ed Sullivan and their weekly shows. Dinah's lively, dramatic rendition of the tune "See the USA in Your Chevrolet" will probably be engrained in our minds forever. The popular Lennon Sisters, with their soft, melodic harmonies, were my favorite act on Lawrence Welk's show. Out of the lovely quartet members, the one I could relate to the most was Janet. She was the youngest and was closest to my age.

In the 1960s, like many households, we gathered around the television and sang along with Mitch Miller on his *Sing Along with Mitch* show. He was so enthusiastic that his love of the music wore off on his viewers. With his encouragement and persistence, it was hard to not join in. He only played the classic, familiar tunes which everyone knew and loved.

Millions of us who were lucky enough to watch the Beatles' U.S. début on February 9, 1964, witnessed one of the most important events in music history. As a ninth grader, I tuned in to *The Ed Sullivan Show* and watched with great anticipation. With his typical very serious demeanor, Ed Sullivan introduced the much-anticipated act, as he spun around and pointed to the curtains. We were glued to the TV as the four young guys from Liverpool with the funny-looking hairdos belted out "She Loves You" and four other tunes. I especially remember them shaking their heads, as they sang the lively hit, "I Want to Hold Your Hand."

Game shows such as *To Tell the Truth, Beat the Clock, I've Got a Secret,* and *What's My Line?* kept us in suspense and forced our speculations. We hardly ever missed *The Honeymooners, I Love Lucy,* or *Gunsmoke.* Lucy and Ethel were so funny together. The perfect combination of the upstanding Marshal Dillon, beautiful Miss Kitty, wise old Doc, limping Chester, and bumbling Festus was such a wonderful blend of *Gunsmoke* characters.

Sometimes we watched *Dragnet.* I liked the no-nonsense approach of the serious, likeable Detective Sergeant Joe Friday. As he interviewed witnesses on leads, he often used his signature saying: "All we want are the facts, ma'am." Every episode began with the same words, in his deadpan voice: "This is the city, Los Angeles, California. I work here. I carry a badge."

One of my favorite memories about TV and my childhood is of Jon Gnagy's *Learn to Draw* show. My parents bought me his kit, which came with special pens and pencils and a clear sheet of plastic. The plastic film stuck to our TV screen, allowing me to draw right along with him, line by line. He was an excellent, methodic teacher. I used his step-by-step approach many times in teaching perspective to my middle school students.

In junior high school, I enjoyed watching Elly Mae, Jethro, Granny, and Jed Clampett on *The Beverly Hillbillies.* The antics of Mary Tyler Moore and Dick Van Dyke on their shows kept us thoroughly amused. My entire family got hooked on watching *Peyton Place.* When I came home in the afternoons in high school, I often stretched out on the couch and watched *That Girl,* with Marlo Thomas, or *I Dream of Jeannie,* with Barbara Eden and Larry Hagman.

We used to love watching Art Linkletter interview children in his "Kids Say the Darndest Things" segment of *House Party*. I always enjoyed watching the contestants on *The Newlywed Game*. So many times, the wives and husbands had such differing takes on the same questions. It was pretty fun to hear the creative questions and answers the contestants came up with on *The Dating Game*.

In the late sixties and early seventies, one of everybody's favorites was Martin and Rowan's classic comedy variety show, *Laugh-In*. Lily Tomlin's characters of Edith Ann, the little girl in the oversized rocking chair, and Ernestine, the smug telephone switchboard operator, were priceless. Ruth Buzzi was hilarious in her portrayal of Gladys, the little old lady on the park bench with the purse and hairnet.

I can still see Arte Johnson squinting his eyes, with his pensive expression, as he pondered, "Verly Interlesting." The jokes segment was always a favorite of mine. Cast members and guests yelled out questions or punch lines while popping their heads out of oddly-shaped doors. The little doors were scattered up and down the colorful wall decorated with mod motifs.

Richard Nixon appeared on *Laugh-In* in September of 1968, while he was running for president. He repeated one of the show's signature phrases, "Sock it to me," more in the form of a question than a statement. The eccentric Tiny Tim was introduced to us on *Laugh-In* with his singing of "Tiptoe Through the Tulips." On December 17, 1969, many of us watched as he and Miss Vicki tied the knot on *The Tonight Show* with Johnny Carson.

The seventies brought us many noteworthy programs. How could anyone forget the cantankerous, racist Archie Bunker and his somewhat ditzy, but loveable wife, Edith, in *All in the Family*? Their son-in-law, "Meathead," and daughter, Gloria, captured our sympathies in trying to deal with Archie.

The Bob Newhart Show kept us in stitches with his dry sense of humor. A very young Robin Williams, on *Mork and Mindy*, introduced us to his uncanny ability to gyrate and make strange noises that only he is capable of. The hilarious scenes on *The Carol Burnette Show*, with Carol, Tim Conway, Vicki Lawrence, Lyle Waggoner, and Harvey Korman, were irresistible.

The show which ranks at the top of my television greats list is the wartime comedy *M*A*S*H*. It ran for eleven seasons and delivered the full gamut of human experiences. The successful mix of episodes had us crying tears of both laughter and sadness. The *M*A*S*H* cast members, Hawkeye, BJ, Hot Lips Houlihan, Frank, Radar, Klinger, Colonel Potter, and Father Mulcahy were as funny and ridiculous as life itself. The two-and-a-half hour finale, "Goodbye, Farewell, and Amen," aired February 28, 1983. It was the most-watched American broadcast in television history until the 2010 Super Bowl. Millions of us will remember the message spelled out in the rocks, which Hawkeye looked down upon as he rode away in a helicopter.

When I was in grade school, Chet Huntley and David Brinkley brought us the national news every night after supper on their *Huntley Brinkley Report*. When Walter Cronkite began anchoring the CBS nightly news in 1962, we became a Cronkite household. When he passed away in 2009, I'm sure many people felt the same as I, like we had lost a relative or close friend. He had been such a constant presence in our homes for nineteen years.

Of course, this phenomenal new invention, the television, brought us the spectacular sight of watching Neil Armstrong take his first steps on the moon in 1969. We will always remember the words he spoke as he took that historic walk: "That's one small step for man, one giant leap for mankind." Walter Cronkite's enthusiasm and pride brought him to tears during his coverage of this historic event.

Television brought us terribly sad memories, too. The repeated images of the motorcade in Dallas, on November 22, 1963, when our beloved JFK was assassinated will remain in our memories forever. We will always remember the heart-wrenching image of the funeral procession, when three-year-old John-John, standing by his mother and his sister, Caroline, saluted his father's flag-draped coffin as it rolled by.

The mood was eerily somber in the dimly-lit halls of our junior high school after Cronkite's announcement of Kennedy's assassination. The usual sounds of talking and laughter were silenced by an unfamiliar atmosphere of hysterical crying, sadness, and shock. Charles, a popular black student, burst out loudly, with an angry and tearful, "I just know one of our people did this."

The year 1968 was a troublesome time for our country. On April 4, the girls in my college dorm gathered around the television in the laundry room in the basement. We stood in disbelief and sorrow as we watched the repeated images of the assassination of Martin Luther King, Jr. The revered civil rights leader was gunned down on the balcony of the Lorraine Motel in Memphis. Just a few short months later, on June 6, the entire country was dumbfounded and appalled to witness yet another tragedy. During his campaign for the Democratic presidential nomination, Bobby Kennedy was assassinated in the kitchen of the Ambassador Hotel in Los Angeles. Both men were in the prime of their lives, had so much to offer, and were true champions for justice. All across the country, there was such a palpable feeling of grief, bewilderment, angst, and uncertainty.

Naturally, the introduction of television brought us many memorable jingles and commercials. Every baby boomer can probably hum the long-running jingle in the Alka-Seltzer ads: "Plop, plop, fizz, fizz, oh, what a relief it is." In the Rice Krispies commercials, the cartoon characters Snap, Crackle, and Pop played their instruments, danced, and sang: "Snap, Crackle, Pop, makes the world go round." The little cartoon character in the Maypo commercials who repeated, "I want my Maypo," will forever help us remember one of our favorite oatmeal cereals.

In 1969, an ad campaign was launched to help offset the increase of venereal disease resulting from the sexual revolution. The American Social Health Association came out with a most unique public service ad, "VD is for Everybody." It featured beautiful actresses and handsome actors going about their everyday lives while a heavenly rendition of "VD is for Everybody" was sung in the background. The ads themselves were contagious and seemed more like a promotional campaign for a product.

Along with TVs came TV dinners and TV trays. On rare occasions, we had Banquet or Swanson TV dinners for supper. This only occurred when our mom was unable to cook or be home. The newfangled dinners were packaged in heat-and-serve aluminum trays resembling a smaller version of a school cafeteria tray. My favorites were the turkey and roast beef entrées.

We usually ate these dinners on TV trays in the living room, allowing us to watch our favorite shows while we ate. The earlier TV trays were metal and somewhat flimsy, usually decorated with decals of flowers or birds. Later, those were replaced with the stronger fake wood ones. Now, the only TV trays I see for sale are thick, light colored, solid oak ones.

Some foods seemed particularly suited, for watching television. Pizza was one of them. After school one afternoon in the third grade, I was visiting my friend Judy at her house. Just returning from the grocery store, her mother asked us if we wanted to try this new item she had just seen at the store. She read the box and pronounced it the way it looked, "pie-za" pie. Little did we know then what a profound impact pizza pie would have on our country's eating habits.

For years, when my sister or I had friends over to spend the night, we frequently fixed ourselves a Chef Boy-Ar-Dee pizza from the "Complete Pizza" boxed kits. I think we liked fixing them because it gave us something to do. The dough had to be made from scratch, which took a while. Looking back on it, we weren't very creative for the longest time making these pizzas. At first, we didn't even consider adding extra toppings. Eventually, we experimented with all kinds of toppings, which made for some pretty delicious pizzas.

Another food we liked to fix for TV snacks was popcorn. After many years of standing at the stove, shaking the kernels of corn in hot oil, a new way of making popcorn was introduced. It was an enclosed foil pan already filled with oil and popcorn kernels. As you held the wire looped handle and shook the pan over a hot burner, the foil twisted and expanded. By the time all of the kernels were popped, the pan had become quite tall. We often bought these for camping trips since they were so convenient. This product was sold under the names of E-Z Pop and Jiffy Pop.

I doubt that we would have ever believed anyone if they had told us how effortless it would be to fix popcorn in fifty years. It would have been outlandish to suggest that one day, at the touch of a button, we would get perfectly-popped popcorn in five minutes.

I'm closing this chapter the same way Walter Cronkite ended his nightly news broadcasts, with his signature signoff: "That's the way it is."

Gone but Not Forgotten

Rock Lake swimming pool, 1940s. Photo from the collection of Jerry Waters.

One of our city's fallen institutions, which enjoyed tremendous popularity during our youth but no longer exists, is Barlow's Roller Skating Rink, or Skateland, as it was later called. It was a modest, short and wide wooden structure running parallel to the railroad tracks near Park Avenue, on the West Side. Our church rented the rink one night a month during most of my grade school and junior high school years. Sometimes we skated there on Saturday afternoons, when it was open to the public.

No one could have ever imagined, from looking at its simple exterior, that the interior of this building had one of the most enchanted atmospheres in town. The place had such an aura about it. A distinctive smell of leather filled the air, coming from the rink's sizable inventory of worn, lace-up skates. Hundreds of pairs, neatly arranged by size, were tidily tucked in their slots on the wooden shelves behind the skate rental counter. They had black skates for the guys and white ones for us girls.

A young man in a wheelchair worked behind the counter. Two rather serious-looking men in their late twenties who were very accomplished skaters ran the joint. They patrolled the place as they sped through the crowd on their skates. Constantly circling the rink and the sideline viewing areas, they often stopped and offered help to skaters who had taken a tumble.

Hanging close to the low ceiling, above the middle of the concrete floor, was a rotating sphere covered with tiny squares of mirror. When the lights were dimmed and colored lights were shone on it, the globe filled the rink with swirling specks of colored lights. The lights were only dimmed when the soft-spoken man on the microphone announced, "ladies' choice," or "couples only." The swirling lights and darkened rink produced such a romantic atmosphere, that it heightened the desire to be a part of the action on the floor.

I usually nabbed my childhood heartthrob, Jamie, for the "ladies' choice" skates. Most of the time, I was delighted when a guy asked me to be his partner during the "couples only" skates. Sometimes I hid out in the bathroom, which had black rubber floor mats, to avoid a little pesky boy who always wanted me to skate with him. It was fascinating to watch how well some couples could skate so closely together, with their arms around their partner's waist. Each stride they took was perfectly executed in sync with one another.

I recently spoke with Jim Thomas, an eighty-five-year-old skating enthusiast who frequented Barlow's for many years. He said as a young man, he always liked it when they announced during "couples only," that they were starting "advance skating." When that began, every time the whistle was blown, the men advanced up to the next girl. He said, "All of us guys loved that, because we got to skate with every girl on the floor."

Loud, calliope-type music came streaming out of the impressive Hammond organ, which sat near the front entrance in a glass enclosure. The rink's owner, Margaret Barlow, played the organ and was very talented at it. She was an older, attractive and most distinguished-looking, petite blonde, with Gibson-style bangs.

It invariably threw me off for a while when the announcer instructed us to "reverse directions." Getting used to going the opposite direction took a few trips around the floor until it felt right. During the "all skate" time, which was most of the time, I envied the showoffs who could skate backwards with such a smooth flow of speed and style. My attempts at skating backwards consisted of lots of clumsy, jerky moves and were anything but graceful. Sometimes the rink employees threw tickets on the floor, and when the music stopped, everyone would dive to get one. The tickets were for one free admission to the rink.

I was never very good at doing the Limbo, either, but I marveled at those who were. How could they get as low as they did without falling backwards? Like everyone else, I loved doing the Hokey Pokey. Practically every person in the joint skated out to the middle of the floor to join in on the fun. The Hokey Pokey was easy, completely nonthreatening, there were no winners or losers, and it was simply fun to do. "You put your right hand in, you put your right hand out, you put your right hand in, and you shake it all about. You do the Hokey Pokey, and you turn yourself around, that's what it's all about." Clap, clap. You just can't lose with those lyrics, and there were many more verses to follow. Some people got a little carried away with their "shaking" and gyrations.

Recently, an African American friend of mine, Terry, and I were reminiscing about our grade school days. He volunteered an entirely different experience he had from Barlow's. He said that he and another black student from our fourth grade class were invited to attend a birthday party at the skating rink for Robert, another student in our class, who was white. The two boys walked down to the party, laid their presents on the counter with everyone else's, and proceeded to put on their skates. As they were leaned over on the bench, lacing up their skates, Mrs. Barlow came over to them, and said: "We don't allow coloreds in here. You'll have to leave." Terry said they were so shocked and in disbelief. That was his first experience of being discriminated against because of the color of his skin. As a child, I never noticed that Barlow's didn't have any black skaters. Back then, we were so used to places in Charleston being segregated, we didn't pay any attention to it. The skating rink was closed in 1967, when the owner refused to integrate.

Similar to the fate of the roller skating rink was the demise of the Putt-Putt miniature golf courses. In their heyday, they popped up all over the place. They were scattered throughout the Kanawha Valley, with one in practically every neighborhood. The Putt-Putt was a fun place to go on dates, or as a family, or just to hang out with friends. We often got so slaphappy, laughing hysterically, when someone made an embarrassing, misguided swing or putt. For a brief period of time, beside the Putt-Putt near us was a trampoline court, Mister John's Jump-Away. The public could rent trampolines for half an hour at a time. Jumping on those was a lot of fun, even though we weren't very good at it. The tops of the trampolines were ground level and covered the deep pits that had been dug underneath them. This eliminated the danger of someone falling off. Still, the place was very short-lived. We always suspected that this was due to liability issues.

During our youth, other popular hangouts were the go-cart race tracks. There was one off of Sissonvile Road and another on the West Side at Patrick Street, beside the railroad tracks. The Haynes girls and my sister and I often walked over to the noisy track on Patrick Street to watch their older brother, Bobby, and his friends race. They could race ten laps for fifty cents.

Another extremely popular hangout during our youth, Rock Lake Swimming Pool, is no longer around. In 2006, a church purchased it, filled it with dirt, and converted it into a playground. For many decades and for thousands of people, Rock Lake was the "happening" place. I was thrilled to find several Websites about it which had great photographs of the crowded pool on a typical summer afternoon. The Wilan brothers owned and operated the pool from 1942 through 1985. They could often be seen patrolling the grounds and buildings in their gray work outfits. The place was so grandiose, that it had a beach resort feel to it. The pool, which was 550 feet long, was touted as "the largest and most beautiful pool in the East." It certainly lived up to its description. Built in an old Spring Hill rock quarry, tall, majestic, natural stone cliffs surrounded much of the pool.

The enormous dance floor was similar to those at beach pavilions and was crowded every time we walked up to it. It was on the mezzanine floor of the huge white bathhouse-snack bar complex. On Saturdays, Dick Reid of WCHS-TV hosted *Record Hop*, a local version of *American Bandstand*. In the fifties and sixties it was broadcast live from Rock Lake. The show's sponsors were Pepsi, Henry's Men's and Boys' Shop, and Valley Bell Dairy. Swimmers could venture out to several platforms in the crystal clear water or sunbathe on colorful benches lined up along the sandy beach. For the not-so-faint-of-heart, there were trapezes to jump off, platforms on the rock cliffs to dive from, and a monster-size slicky slide to ride down.

I remember the day I chickened out of going down the bigger, fifty-foot slide. It was my very first attempt. With much trepidation,

I had climbed to the top of the tall ladder, but when I looked down at what a frightening, long, steep drop there was, I froze. After frantic deliberation, I opted to back down the intimidating ladder, one scary rung at a time. I held on for dear life as I descended back to safety. Many loud moans and groans came from the annoyed, disgruntled swimmers, who had to precariously step aside for me on the tall ladder. Eventually, I overcame my fear of going down the gigantic slide, enjoying the rush from the fast, long, downward ride. The strong force of landing in the water at such a fast speed inevitably managed to force the top of my two-piece bathing suit out of place and under my chin. There seemed to be quite a bit of suit adjusting going on in the water at the end of the slide, for boys and girls alike.

While we were taking a lunch break one day, I found a dollar bill on the grounds of the grassy picnic area. Especially to a young child, a dollar was a lot of money back then. I was so excited about finding it. On our way home, we stopped by Young's Department Store on the West Side. I proudly purchased, with my new wealth, an iridized, aqua, see-through inner tube. It was my swimming companion for many years, until I could swim on my own.

In those days, no one was ever allowed to swim or step a foot into the water until precisely one hour was up from the time we had finished eating. There were no exceptions to this rule. Thankfully, Rock Lake offered many other activities to keep us entertained during this mandatory "no swimming" period. We spent a lot of time playing on the seesaws, swings, and jungle gym. Sometimes, we watched the teenage boys show off their muscles on the gym bars or the dancers do their thing on the packed dance floor.

I was completely taken aback when I read that Rock Lake was segregated. In the sixties, civil rights leaders held protest marches in the street outside of the pool. What surprises me about this is not so much that it was segregated, but, like with Barlow's, I was completely oblivious to the reality that there were no black swimmers. That's how accustomed we were to segregation during our youth.

Shortly after the closing of the pool in 1985, the facility was reopened as Putt-Putt Golf and Games. For around twenty years, it was booked for many children's birthday parties and school field trips. A large laser-tag course was one of the most exciting indoor attractions. Outside, there were miniature golf courses, bumper boats, and a playground. Part of the original swimming pool was converted into the course for bumper boat rides. It was an entertaining place for families and people of all ages. Our family went there for several fun birthday parties, and just to hang out for an afternoon. We were so disappointed to see it close.

Christmas Carol

Jean with me on Easter Sunday, in our front yard, 1954.

My only sibling was born in 1946, three years before I came along. She was part of the first wave of baby boomers. Since she was born near Christmas, my parents named her "Carol," like a Christmas carol. When she started school, there were three "Carols" in her first grade class, so she volunteered to use her middle name and become a "Jean."

When we were very young, my mother liked to dress Jean and me in identical outfits. Sometimes Aunt Virginia dressed our cousin Joyce exactly like us, too. Joyce was Jean's age, and although she is our height these days, when we were young, she was much taller than my sister. Several times, the three of us wore identical outfits, but in three different colors.

One of my favorite photographs of us sisters is in our front yard on Easter morning. We were wearing identical dresses, hats, shoes, and purses. Our shoes and little purses were white leather, our hats were covered with pink and white silk flowers, and our dresses were pink taffeta. The top layer of fabric was sheer pink tulle, with small black and white designs. During the winter months, Jean and I wore white furry padded muffs, to keep our hands warm.

Back in those days, our mom purchased Toni home permanent kits at the local Cohen drugstore and gave us perms at the dining room table. I can still smell the pungent odor from the milky setting solution. Most of the time she pin-curled our hair with small, ridged bobby pins. We seldom used hair dryers at our house. When we held our heads upside down over the big floor furnace, our hair dried in a matter of minutes.

Before the upstairs to our house was built, Jean and I shared a bedroom and a double bed. Every night we recited together the bedtime prayer, "Now I Lay Me Down To Sleep." Recently, she reminded me of how I drove her crazy every night. After we went to bed, I started rubbing her arm while simultaneously sucking my thumb. Each time, she had to yell out to my parents, who were just across the hall, and ask them to please come and make me stop.

During that same era, when we were watching a movie at a local theater, I had given a man sitting in front of us the same treatment. He turned around and said to my mother: "Lady, will you please make your little girl stop rubbing my ear?" I was standing up in front of my family, and had latched onto his earlobe, rubbing it, while I sucked my thumb.

Most of the families we visited with had children Jean's age. I was usually the odd kid out. Frequently, the older kids chose me for things like standing in front of our closet door while they shot rubber darts around me. Jean had two close friends, Georgette and Betsey, who lived near us, and the three of them spent a lot of time playing together.

Whenever our family went on vacations, Jean had a horrible case of car sickness. My parents let her ride up in the front seat to help alleviate the problem. In those days, we had to travel through the Narrows in Virginia to go to the southern beaches. That stretch had many steep, hairpin curves and was especially hard on her. During one vacation in Florida, Jean picked up a colorful jelly-fish-looking creature along the surf. As she took it up to show our parents, she felt a severe, stinging sensation from it. What she had picked up was a Portuguese man-of-war, notorious for the excruciating pain it can inflict on humans.

Jean and I had chores to do every week. Sometimes we got an allowance for this, and other times we didn't. We eventually figured out that we were better off not getting an allowance and simply asking for money when we needed it. Every Saturday morning, we pulled various chores out of a jar. "Run the sweeper in the living room" and "Dust the furniture with Pledge" were examples of such assignments. No matter what chores we did on Saturdays, every night after supper, it was our job to do the dishes. For a while, we alternated washing or drying them every other night. That system wasn't very successful. Since Jean was three years older, she was faster than I. When it was my turn to wash the dishes, I couldn't keep up with her pace of drying them so quickly.

She would get antsy and tease me about being so slow. We finally agreed that she would wash and I would dry, all of the time. That seemed to make both of us happy.

Dad and Uncle Ralph finished the attic to our house when I was in the third grade. That gave both Jean and me a good-size bedroom of our own. We also had a nice, big bathroom upstairs, which we shared. Jean's favorite color was lavender, and she had the most lavender room anyone could imagine. She had lavender walls, a bedspread and ruffled curtains with lavender flowers, lavender throw rugs, and lavender toss pillows on the bed. Everyone admired her beautiful "purple room."

Our bedrooms had spacious closets with double sliding doors. One of the most frightening episodes I ever had was the night Jean hid in my closet and scared me half to death. I had no idea she was hiding there as I was getting ready for bed. When I slid my closet door open, she yelled and jumped out at me. I stood there, in shock, letting out the loudest, longest, blood-curdling scream. After that incident, I remained a little apprehensive, about what might be behind the closet doors.

As a kid, I was jealous of my sister for having cut her own record. We had a 78 record of her singing "Poor Little Robin, Walking, Walking, Walking to Missouri." My parents had it made at the local school carnival. The only real sibling rivalry we ever experienced had to do with wearing each other's clothes. We wore the same dress size when I was in junior high and she was in high school. On several occasions, we got so angry at one another for wearing each other's sweaters or blouses, without permission. Most of the time, we went our separate ways, since each of us had friends who were our own age.

When I was in junior high school and Jean was in high school, my parents let me go along with her to the "snake dance" celebration before the big Stonewall and Charleston High football game. She and I and several of her friends crammed into a classmate's car. We were following the line of vehicles driving around town. As we pulled out at an intersection near the Civic Center, another car slammed into us. I had never been in a car wreck before, and the sound of metal colliding is one I'll never forget. Three of our friends were hospitalized for several days. I received a pretty bad cut on the top of my head, but didn't tell my parents since I didn't want to get stitches. Once I got home, I was in the bathtub washing the dried blood out of my hair. At that very moment, my mom walked in on me. This sparked one of her rare, hysterical, "Where did I go wrong as a parent?" frenzies.

While I was in high school and Jean had graduated but was still living at home, the two of us became partners in crime. We loved to shop in the big department stores of downtown Huntington. Since it was only an hour away, we decided to drive down there one Saturday, just the two of us. We knew that our parents would never allow us to go on our own, so we didn't ask for their permission. It was such a fun day, shopping together and just enjoying each other's company. We thought we were pretty slick, pulling off such a feat. Getting busted was never even a consideration or worry. After church the next morning, our mom went into yet another one of her hysterical, "Where did I go wrong as a parent?" outbursts.

Apparently, one of the members of the congregation had been in Huntington, too, on the same day. At church, she casually mentioned to Mom that she had seen us. "No, my daughters were not in Huntington yesterday," our mother emphatically told the lady, who soon set her straight. I'm sure that was humiliating for Mom, and I know she was extremely disappointed in us.

After graduating from high school in 1964, Jean attended a local business school, Center College, where she learned keyboarding. Her first job was working the night shift at the phone company. She would come home after midnight, while I was sound asleep. I often sat up when she came upstairs, and the two of us carried on fairly lengthy conversations. The next day, I never remembered a single word from any of those visits. One afternoon, Jean and I had to go check out the first fifteen-cent hamburger joint in town, BBF, or Burger Boy Food-a-rama. We will never forget the twelve-inch hair I found in my bun when I bit into it.

One summer evening in 1965, at the DuPont Hunting and Fishing Club, my sister first met her future husband, Larry. Our family had gone there for years to swim and picnic. In those days, when we drove across the Poca River going to the club, we could see what color the water would be in the swimming pool. The old pool was made from damming up the river, and it had little minnows in it, nibbling at our feet. We had just finished swimming and were hanging out at the pavilion. Larry was there with a couple of his buddies. After he and Jean were introduced to each other, he kept telling me, over and over again: "I just met the most beautiful girl in the world."

During my tenth grade, Larry and Jean double-dated with my boyfriend, Johnny, and me on a fun trip to Camden Park. It was a local amusement park about an hour away. Johnny and Larry sometimes went to our family's camp with us. They both seemed a little bit uneasy about the rough living conditions. For a prank one night, my dad threw some small object into the bedroom where they were sleeping. Both guys jumped out of bed and raced into the main room, not knowing what they had heard.

Larry drove a little square-shaped gray Hillman and taught me how to drive a stick shift. During one such lesson, we pulled up to a four-way stop. As I attempted to take off, I made the car hop a couple of times, just like a rabbit. We nearly died laughing, as the driver of the other car at the intersection did the exact same thing. All we could do was hop at each other before the engines stalled.

Jean and Larry dated a few years while he was finishing college. They were married in 1968 in a private little ceremony at Emmanuel church. Their best friends, Patty and Donnie Cooney, stood up for them at the wedding. As was the reward in those days for men who had recently graduated from college, Larry was immediately drafted into the Army. He went to boot camp, and then was to be stationed in Germany for a few years. Jean quit her job and flew over to Mannheim to join him in Germany. They seemed to be having the time of their lives, making new friends and, practically every week, traveling to different countries. Much to their disappointment and astonishment, Larry soon received orders to report to Vietnam, cutting their stay in Germany drastically.

Jean came to my rescue several times when I was in college and while I was taking graduate classes. I was a "hunt and peck" typist, and she could type so incredibly fast. She breezed through ten pages in the amount of time it would take me to type one. Many of my terms papers were often more than twenty pages long. Of course, those were the days when we were still using typewriters, so accuracy was critical.

My first husband, Doug, and I visited a lot with Jean and Larry when we first got married. We often fixed hot dogs and french fries. Back then, everyone used deep fryers and made homemade fries. My Ronco Veg-O-Matic was an invaluable tool to have in the kitchen for cutting up the potatoes. At that time, Doug's alma mater, Marshall University, had an outstanding basketball team, so the four of us watched some pretty exciting games together.

Jean and Larry never had children, but they always had pets who were like children to them. They had three white toy poodles, then two precious Peek-a-poos. Now they have two identical, solid black cats who adopted them. My two sons got to spend a lot of time sleeping over at "Aunt Jeanie's and Uncle Larry's" house. Their house always looked like a photograph out of a *House Beautiful* magazine. I'm sure it was quite a contrast to the boys, from our primitive little farmhouse. All of us enjoyed going out with Jean and Larry on their pontoon and fancy fishing boats.

Larry has been a real inspiration to many people with his dedication to exercising. Before he retired, he got up at three o'clock every morning to run on the treadmill for ninety minutes before leaving for work, by five-thirty. By maintaining this grueling exercise routine, he was able to stay in great shape.

Jean and I don't see a lot of each other these days, except for holidays, because, as when we were younger, she has her friends, and I have mine. Practically every day we e-mail one another several times. She has been a tremendous wealth of knowledge about incidents from our youth. Since she was three years older than I, she can remember many more details about some of our experiences.

It is so good to see that she and her husband are finally getting to enjoy the fruits of their labor. They are both retired now and seem to be enjoying each other's company, taking a lot of day trips. To exercise, they frequently go on long walks together. Working outside in their beautifully-groomed flowerbeds is an activity they both enjoy.

Jean and I try to share the responsibility of taking care of our eighty-seven-year-old mother. We have to push her in a wheelchair everywhere we go. Slinging that wheelchair in and out of the car trunk five or six times a day is pretty hard on the back for two gals in their sixties. Yet, we fully understand how fortunate we are to still have Mom with us.

School Daze II

Our band director, Joseph Gasper with his wife, Brenda, at our band dance, in Woodrow Wilson's gymnasium, my ninth grade year, 1964.

Photo courtesy of Brenda Gasper.

When it was time for my classmates and me to start junior high school in 1961, it was difficult to be separated from many of our good friends from grade school. The majority of us had been with each other since the first grade. Most of the children on our hill, like me, who attended Robins, went to Woodrow Wilson Junior High. Some of the students who lived in the Edgewood district went to Lincoln Junior High School. For many of us, this wasn't a complete hiatus from our close friends, since we went to church together and were still in the same Scout troops. We also visited and played with each other at slumber parties and, during the summers, at the neighborhood swimming pool and at the Robins playground. In the seventh grade, all of our parents took us down to the old North Charleston recreation center to get our Sabin polio sugar cube vaccines.

Big slumber parties were very popular back then, usually with ten to twelve girls. I went to a slumber party that a friend of mine from Scouts had. She went to Lincoln, so it was a mixed group of girls from both schools. At the party, a girl from Lincoln, Nan, who had the gift of making everyone crack up, jokingly made an astute observation: "If you go to Wilson, you say, 'I attend Woodrow Wilson.' Think how strange it would sound for us to say, 'I attend Abraham Lincoln.' Saying, 'I attend Jackson High School' doesn't sound right either. You have to say 'Stonewall' or 'Stonewall Jackson High School,' because no one would know what 'Jackson High School' meant."

My sister had a big slumber party at our home while I was in junior high school. Every girl brought her own sleeping bag, pillow, and blanket. I hung out on the couch with the older girls for a while before going upstairs to bed. The main activities going on were styling each other's hair and making up each other's faces. Rouge, lipstick, eye shadow, eyeliner, makeup, and mascara were being applied. Some girls curled another person's eyelashes with the metal, squeeze-handle eyelash curler. This went on for hours, long after I went to my bedroom. In the wee hours of the night, my parents finally made the girls turn off the lights and go to bed. Sometime in the middle of the night, one of the girls unwittingly stepped on a tube of lipstick and smeared it all over the carpet, leaving a smudge with each step.

When the girls finally discovered what had happened, everyone in the house was awakened by their loud remarks of "Oh no" and "Your parents are going to kill us." No one tried to expose a single culprit, since it was unintentional, and it wouldn't have mattered anyway. All of the girls pitched in, scrubbing the stains from the carpet as best they could. The stains didn't completely come out, so soon after the party, we got new carpet. In reality, I think Mom was actually happy to finally have a reason to get rid of the old brown sculpted carpet that we'd had for so many years.

I often had my own slumber parties when I was in junior high school. For breakfast, I liked to fix my guests cinnamon toast and hot chocolate. My crowd wasn't into makeup yet, so we usually entertained ourselves by played group games. Some of our favorites were "Rhythm," "Black Magic," and "Apples, Apples." Another fun thing to do was to put common household items and kitchen gadgets on a tray and make each girl, while wearing a blindfold, feel them with her feet. Then everyone had to write down what they thought the objects were.

"Rhythm" was a game we played while sitting in a circle. Everyone did the movements simultaneously, while the chant worked around the circle. If you couldn't think of a word in the chosen category, then you were "out." The movements consisted of: slap both hands on your legs, then clap, then snap your right hand, then the left. The slap, clap, click, click, continued repeatedly. The words were said while clicking the fingers. The leader started out a category by saying, "Cata-gory (click, click) of States (click, click)," or whatever topic she chose. Then each person chimed in with a state while she and everyone else were snapping their fingers. This could prove to be difficult once it had gone around the circle several times and everyone was running out of names of states, candy, countries... whatever the category was.

"Black Magic" and "Apples, Apples," were similar "trick" games. My dad used to start out the "Apples, Apples" game. He held a yardstick in his hand and tapped it on the floor as he repeated, "Apples, apples, fine red apples, five cents apiece." Then the girls would try to get the saying and motions just right, as they attempted it. The ones who knew the answer to the game, chimed in to say they got it wrong. Clearing your throat before you started reciting the saying was the trick. It had nothing to do with how the yardstick was tapped, or how the words were spoken.

"Black Magic" was a real fun game, too. One person left the room, and together, everyone else picked out one object, anywhere in the room. When given the OK, the person returned to the room and tried to guess which item had been picked. Someone who was in on the secret pointed to different objects with a yardstick, asking, "Is it this?" The trick to the game was: the person who was pointing to objects always knew the secret and pointed to something black right before she or he pointed to the chosen object. To those who weren't in on the secret, it seemed impossible that people could guess the chosen object.

Junior high school was an awkward time for me. I was what you call a "late bloomer," not really "blossoming" until my ninth grade year. Since I was so skinny, my doctor put me on a special diet to help me gain weight. I had to drink a can of Metracal, a liquid meal-replacement drink, with every meal, plus drink a milkshake each day. Probably because I was on the majorette corps, I was invited to several boy-and-girl parties. Those were pretty painful, too. I was definitely the wallflower who was more of an onlooker than anything else. At that time, "Spin the Bottle" was the game that was played at pre-dating, adolescent parties. I remember walking out of the room to kiss a friend, Darrin, who had spun the bottle, and it pointed to me when it stopped. He was extremely kind and gentle as he kissed me on the lips. I'm certain he could sense my apprehension and awkwardness.

At Wilson, most students had pretty disrespectful nicknames for teachers. "Cough Syrup Sam" and "Bull Dog Davis," were such examples. What I remember most about being in junior high is how frequently we girls passed notes to one another. My best friend, Barbara, and I were in almost every class together, yet we wrote notes to each other constantly. We could hardly wait to read the notes, which had been passed to us in the halls between classes. At that time, I was diligent about keeping a scrapbook. Not long ago, I came across one of those nonsensical notes in my old scrapbook. I had written it to Barbara, and she had answered me back. The note showed just how boy-crazy we were at the time: "Guess who turned around in his seat, and was staring at me in math class?" I used to sit in class and doodle, usually drawing girls' faces. Sometimes I filled an entire sheet of notebook paper by writing my name as "Mrs." in front of the name of the boy I had a crush on...that particular day.

Another thing that I think is hilarious about our behavior in junior high school is, girls would "be sweet on" a certain boy for quite a long time, without the guy even knowing it. During baseball season, Barbara and I faithfully walked a good distance, once a week, to Cabell field to watch a boy named Buddy play. He was a lefty who pitched for Mac McClure's TV Service's team. Buddy was completely oblivious to the fact that I liked him. I thought he was "tuff," which was what we called cute guys back then. I had a mad crush for a while on Johnny Kirby, a handsome football standout, who had no idea I liked him.

We also walked several blocks down from Barbara's house to the large Patrick Street open air market. Her aunt and grandmother sent us there to buy fresh produce for dinner. They were such good cooks. At the foot of her hill, on Washington Street, were three drug stores, Lowman's, Thaxton's, and Gordon's, which all had soda fountains. She and I spent quite a bit of time in those places, swiveling back and forth on the tall chrome stools, sipping on vanilla and chocolate Cokes. Sometimes we stopped in the Wurlitzer jukebox and pinball store to buy used 45 records for a quarter. Barbara and I often spent the night with each other. I had trundle beds, and we pulled out the bottom one for her to sleep on. At her house, we shared her twin bed. The mattress was so soft, that we were each trying to sleep on a downslope all night. I thought her grandmother's little white eyewash cup was the most ingenious invention. It seemed like back then, I was always getting something in my eyes.

At Wilson, we had quite a few sock hops on school time. More often than not, girls danced with other girls, and most of the boys either looked on or ran around the gym. "The Stroll" always brought out a nice crowd of participants. Everybody had fun with it as they strutted their stuff, dancing in between the two lines. I always envied the couples who could jitterbug real well. Some of the best times we had were decorating for the annual band dances. These were more formal dances. A professional photographer was always set up at one end of the gym, with an elaborate display which went along with the theme of the dance. During the dance, he took portraits of the couples in their formal attire. Not long ago, I came across two black and white portraits from those dances. One was of me and my friend, Jamie, in the eighth grade. We were all decked out in our fancy clothes, posing under an arched trellis with a three-tiered fountain in front of us. Three leprechauns were positioned around us to go with the St. Patrick's Day theme.

The other photo was of Jerry, a boyfriend in the ninth grade, and me. We were under an arched trellis too, but surrounded by snowmen and a snow-covered village, to go along with the winter theme. The inside of the snowman invitation read: "Do you want to hear the #1 record spin? Then come to the Winter Whirl at Wilson's gym." For several dances, I went to get my hair styled at a beauty parlor in O. J. Morrison's, a downtown department store. Each time, I was so displeased with how my hair looked that

I immediately hurried down to the ladies' restroom in the basement and brushed it out. I clearly remember this happening at least twice, with identical results.

As majorettes, we used to perform at the annual talent shows. Barbara, who was also a majorette, and I practiced our routines over and over again in my living room. For one show, we wore red satin Santa outfits with white fake-fur trim around the short skirts, long sleeves, and collars. Santa hats and slippers with jingle bells completed our outfits. My parents took me to a professional photographer to get a formal portrait taken in my majorette uniform. That was a real big deal back then. Sometimes after majorette practices, we walked down to get a snack at the Kozy Corner. In the fall of our ninth grade, after we had practiced on Stonewall's dirt field, we walked down to Sid's to get milkshakes. It was a breezy afternoon. On Stonewall's front lawn, we had such fun, running around, catching the colorful, swirling leaves as they fell from the gigantic trees.

My friends and I liked to shop at Wilson's bookstore during breaks, at lunchtime, and before or after school. The printmaking class ran off editions of the *Woodrow Wilson News*, our weekly newspaper. The paper was an impressive piece of journalism for a junior high staff. We bought our Woodrow Wilson Wolverines maroon and white notebooks, with the vicious image of a wolverine on the front. For homecoming football games, most of us purchased white mum corsages, with a maroon and white bow, and a little plastic football dangling from the bow.

In junior high school, we attended numerous football and basketball games during school time. We watched many exciting ballgames in the gymnasium and on the football field. Those were real bonding experiences. I was so disappointed when the powers that be decided to disallow games on school time. What happened outside of the classroom was just as important as our school lessons. It was the total experience, which helped us to develop into well-rounded individuals.

One of my greatest fears I had in junior high school was getting hit by snowballs walking home from Wilson. The school was about six blocks away from my house, so there was plenty of opportunity for this to happen. It was always the same group of older boys, who hung out on the corner of Beech and Garvin, ambushing their selected targets. There weren't many places to hide or ways to avoid them.

Although Woodrow Wilson was an extremely old building, I think most of us were pleased with the quality of education we received. Many excellent teachers took an interest in us and were a major influence in our lives. We girls had crushes on several of the younger, good-looking male teachers. Mrs. Doll, an older math teacher, was such an inspiration to me. She had a genuine love of her subject, used a no-nonsense approach with her students, and was such an effective teacher. I am certain that she was instrumental in my decision to pursue teaching. A few years ago, I decided to send her a note, thanking her for having such an impact on me and the choices I made. I was so saddened and disappointed to hear that she had just passed, the year before.

My homeroom teacher for all three years was Miss Hall, who also was my sewing teacher. She came to our parades to watch the band and majorettes perform. When I was in high school, she continued to follow what I was doing. Having her as a sewing teacher laid the foundation for my becoming an enthusiastic seamstress. Always so kind and soft-spoken, she was such a patient instructor. Our homeroom was held in a regular classroom, across the hall from the sewing lab. On one occasion, we were having a party, and Miss Hall had given us bottles of pop and ice cream. One boy was showing off, and put some ice cream in his pop bottle. He put his thumb over the top of the bottle, and shook it real hard. I am still surprised at this, but his concoction squirted straight up, like Old Faithful. That was the only time I ever saw Miss Hall get upset or raise her voice. Understandably, she was so mad, her face turned red. She made the boy get a mop and ladder and clean up the mess he had made on the ceiling.

One of everybody's favorite classes was Mrs. Ferguson's music class. She was a bubbly, vivacious singer and pianist, somewhat resembling Ella Fitzgerald. Her enthusiasm was so infectious to all of us students. She truly made her classroom feel as though it was a fun place to be. I liked Mr. Morris's West Virginia history class too. One of my favorite assignments was making a small map of West Virginia out of bubble gum. He gave us little three-by-three-inch squares of poster board, and a few pieces of gum. After chewing it a while, we took the gum and made the irregular shape of our state, detailed with the Appalachian Mountains built up. I came across the one I made a few years ago.

In world geography class my seventh grade year, we were given the assignment of writing a report on any foreign country. Switzerland was the country I chose, since my grandmother grew up there. Sitting on the floor of my bedroom, I pored through our thick red encyclopedias, writing copious notes and researching information on Switzerland. I decided to format my report as a day in the life of a Swiss girl who was my age. I was so proud of the finished product.

Our teacher's reaction to my report was completely disheartening. He walked up to me in class, after he had graded our papers, and asked: "Did you have a lot of help from your parents on this assignment?" What an insult to my intelligence! He certainly had no basis for his accusation, as this assignment was the only one which had required any originality. All of our previous assignments had been coloring in maps, or simply answering questions at the end of a chapter. I was tremendously disturbed and offended by his questioning my ability, or lack thereof.

Mrs. Maness' earth science class was a highly-charged, motivational learning environment. She was a very strict yet inspiring teacher. Her high level of standards and expectations of us made up for her diminutive stature. I was in her advanced class. As was the case with all "major classes" in those days, students were grouped according to IQ test scores. Every time she passed out graded tests, she seated us according to our test scores. It was very prestigious to have the highest grade and to be seated last. This created an air of extreme suspense and competition. Those who had the lowest scores were seated in the front of the room. Of course, arranging students by their test scores would violate the students' privacy rules of today. For us, it was an extremely effective means of motivation.

In May of our ninth grade, Mrs. Maness took a busload of us students around the state on what she called the "West Virginia Tour." We toured the campuses of West Virginia Wesleyan College, Davis and Elkins College, and West Virginia University. Other sights we took in were the Sutton Dam, Blackwater Falls, Seneca Caverns, Greenbank Observatory, and Seneca Forest. I was always so touched and appreciative of her taking that much interest in us. To organize an overnight trip for a group of junior high school students was an extremely admirable undertaking. It was definitely beyond the call of duty.

How we behaved on that trip was anything but admirable. Our chaperones had a hard time getting us to settle down and stop running the halls in our old, stately hotel. Remembering how rowdy we were has always been a deterrent for me when I considered taking my own students on overnight trips. When another teacher and I took a group of Natural Helpers on an overnight retreat, we were up practically all night long trying to get the kids settled down and to stay in their rooms. I think the saying, "What goes around, comes around," is most appropriate here.

The Band Played On

All decked out in my junior high majorette uniform, 1963.

Being in the school band in junior high and high school was a perfect fit for me. I loved everything about it and credit having been in the band for helping me to be more confident about myself. During our youth, the bands in our local schools were so much larger than those of today. In the seventh grade, I started out in the prep band with a black Bundy clarinet (in a plaid case) which I didn't know how to play. With the instruction and patience of my talented band director, Joseph Gasper, at Woodrow Wilson Junior High School, I progressively became a fairly proficient instrumentalist. By my senior year at Stonewall Jackson High School, I had worked my way up to third chair in our large clarinet section, with forty-three members. I can still recall the taste of the wood from sucking on my thin clarinet reeds, and the distinctive smell of the wax I rubbed on the cork tenons.

In junior high, our band director held practices in the mornings, before school started. My friend Barbara and I frequently missed those early morning sessions. The punishment for being late or missing practice was working off demerits by walking laps around the gym after school. We spent a tremendous amount of time walking around the enormous gym's old wooden floor. I didn't mind the morning practices, I just hated walking six blocks to school by myself, in the dark. Extremely cold weather was a deterrent, too. We were almost better off missing the entire practice, because walking in late was so embarrassing.

I was surprised when I ran into Mr. Gasper recently at a local restaurant. He immediately said, "Williams, clarinet section." He was probably actually thinking: "Williams, too many demerits and absences from practices." I was amazed that he hadn't changed in appearance one bit, other than his black hair is now white. The fact that he could recall what instrument I played some fifty years later is incredible.

At Wilson, I was a band member for the first two years, and then became a full-time majorette for the last year. During my eighth grade year, I was what was called an "alternate" majorette, performing in talent shows and at concerts. Of course, all of us majorettes were also band members, playing with the band during concert season. Our band uniforms were maroon, and our majorette uniforms were white, with maroon citation cords.

My favorite remembrance of junior high band is performing at our spring concert in the ninth grade as part of a clarinet sextet. We played a composition from *Hansel and Gretel*, by the nineteenth-century composer Engelbert Humperdinck. It was a beautiful blend of harmonizing. In my scrapbook, I still have the program from that 1964 concert, brown and brittle from age. Our junior high had a lot of athletic events on school time. The band, as well as the entire student body, walked over to our football games at Cabell field, several blocks away. Frequently these treks were in pretty uncomfortably hot conditions. We majorettes performed at halftime, and the thick leg makeup we wore would run down our legs when we got so hot and sweaty.

Being a majorette and in the band at our high school was not for the faint of heart. Practices were grueling on the big, dusty, dirt field on the hill behind our school. Senior band members were in charge of younger or new ones and were pretty demanding and strict on us. Everything was approached in a no-nonsense manner, especially by our very competent and serious band director, Al Frey. One evening after practice, he walked up to address us majorettes. He matter-of-factly said: "It looks like a few of you need to lose some baby fat." We were so taken aback by that, because all of us thought we were in pretty good shape. One night on the practice field, Mr. Frey was addressing our entire band while we were still standing in formal formation. At that precise moment, a bird flew over him and splattered droppings on the top of his head. Even he had to laugh about that.

At Stonewall, I was a majorette for my junior and senior years. I was so honored to have made it as a Stonewall majorette. Our majorette corps started practicing in the summer, several weeks before the entire band came. By the end of the morning practices, it was miserably hot. Girls frequently overheated and had to run to the side of the field to throw up. In those days, being a Stonewall majorette carried a tremendous amount of prestige. People who I went to school with often tell others that I was a majorette, as if that still carried some clout.

Our high-stepping drum majors led the band with their long batons in parades and at football games. They wore tall white fur hats, black boots up to their knees, and handsome uniforms with a big breastplate design. During football pregame performances, our band made the traditional SJ formation.

Our majorette corps wore sharp-looking red velvet uniforms, with gray satin lining and gray citation cords. The head and assistant head majorette wore gray uniforms with red lining and cords. Our military-style hats had huge ostrich feather plumes. I can so clearly remember running the hot water in our shower and hanging my plume upside down in the steam. Fluffing out our plumes to perfection was a real art, and we were the envy of the other majorettes if we had one of the biggest plumes. Our tall, thick, white leather boots were hot, especially in parades, and had the distinctive smell of worn leather. We twirled silver batons, with large, heavy metal ends which screwed on for formal performances. During practices, we used lighter, rubber ends.

The *Charleston Daily Mail*'s annual Kanawha County Majorette Festival was our most serious competition. It was a time-honored tradition, held at the beginning of every school year, since 1947. Stonewall had the reputation of doing well in the festival, and both our band and majorette corps were expected to place in every category. We hired an older, very talented dance instructor, Charlotte Abbott, to teach us routines for the festival. She coached several corps across the county. In the Originality category of the competition during my junior year, we performed to "Supercalifragilisticexpialidocious," a lively tune from the popular *Mary Poppins* movie. The Mary Poppins outfits had a short red dress with a white ruffled apron. We danced across the field to the music, opening and closing and twirling our red umbrellas, which also had white ruffles.

During my senior year, we performed to the Herb Alpert and the Tijuana Brass' hit "A Taste of Honey." Our bee costumes were black satin, with wide, bright yellow-orange satin horizontal stripes and big, black mesh wings, with sequins and orange fake fur trim. Antennas attached to our heads, black slippers, and fishnet hose completed the costumes. Our head majorette, Donna Tickle, was crowned the prestigious "Miss Kanawha Majorette" of 1966.

Our formal corps routines at the festival were always performed to John Phillip Sousa's "The National Emblem" march. The band did such a great job with all of the tunes we performed to, but they really knew how to play a spirited version of that march. It was a perfect selection to accompany a marching and twirling routine. The crescendos and variety of tempo accommodated our various twirls and formations.

At football games during halftime, one of my favorite things we did was to perform our fire baton routines. It was quite a spectacle. The stadium became pitch black, then simultaneously our batons were magically ignited. The fire from our batons was the only light to be seen. We wore beautiful costumes of black leotards, with one gigantic blue, red and gold sequin flame on the front. The sequins glistened with the reflections from the fire on our batons. One night, the entire entourage of buses carrying our band to an away football game was held up for at least half an hour because I forgot my fire baton. The buses full of impatient band members were lined up beside the interstate, while my parents hurriedly brought me the baton. I was relieved at how calmly our band director reacted to the situation, but you can believe that several of my friends never let me live down that blunder.

During some of the frigid football games in the latter part of the season, my fingers became so completely numb, that I could hardly tell whether or not I was twirling the baton. The same was

true for me as a band member, not being able to tell if I was playing the notes on my clarinet. Little metal, palm-size hand warmers
were our saviors during those wicked, cold games.

All of the band bus trips we took were such exciting times.
Since Mr. Frey was very proficient in getting trips organized, we
traveled to many away football games, the Cherry Blossom Festival in Washington, D.C., and the World's Fair in Montreal. During
my sophomore year, our head majorette, Stephanie, used the bus
driver's microphone and serenaded us with her angelic voice. A lot
of flirting and unlikely pairing up occurred on those trips. During
our D.C. trip, we marched in the Cherry Blossom Parade and that
night partied and danced aboard a sternwheeler on the Potomac
River. Kids in other bands, who were from all over the country,
partied with us. At the World's Fair, we performed on the stage in
an outdoor amphitheater. "The Shadow of Your Smile" was my
favorite tune we played. That trip to Canada was the first time
many of our band members had traveled to a different country.

One year, our band director was out on an extended leave. In a
gesture unprecedented by an administrator, our principal, George
Steadman, took over the band. Some of the students misbehaved
pretty badly while he was there, and he ended up giving us a lecture which I will remember forever. "No one likes to feel like they
are being taken advantage of," he told us. Then he proceeded to
read us the riot act. He explained that he thought he was doing
us a favor, during our director's absence, by enabling us to continue with some normalcy. No doubt, after his heartfelt lecture, the
behavior improved tremendously.

By far, the best perk about being in the band was the great
group of friends we had. There was, and still is, a special kind
of camaraderie among our band members. I have always thought
that there was simply something uniquely interesting about people
who like to play music. As fellow band members, we enjoyed a
great, common interest in music. We spent so much time with one
another, suffering alongside each other at exhausting practices and

performances. There were many shared moments of victories and accomplishments, and sometimes at competitions, of defeats and disappointments. My recollections, from all of those meaningful experiences from being in the band, still conjure up some of the fondest memories I have from my youth.

Our band had many stellar musicians who organized their own bands. They became quite popular, performing at local dances and concerts. The Esquires and Soul Survivors were two bands formed by some of our band members. It always pleases me to see or hear of fellow band members who continue to enjoy playing music. Occasionally I catch a glimpse of one former band member, Richard Stockton, high-stepping it down Capitol Street, marching in the local Metropolitan Band. Al Frey serves as that band's director these days.

I sold my clarinet to a younger cousin when I was in college. Several years ago, the band director of the school where I was teaching at the time walked by my art room and saw the old brass French horn that I had purchased at a yard sale. It was part of my still life display I had set up for my students. Understandably, he wanted to trade me something for that horn. I ended up trading it for a white clarinet, which looked so odd to me, since I wasn't aware they even made clarinets in any other color except black. I couldn't wait to go home and play it.

I was so disappointed, but not surprised, when I could barely get a squeak out of it. Playing a clarinet, with all of its complex finger placements, is not like swimming: "Once you learn how to do it, it will stay with you forever." Now that I'm retired, I think I'll give it a more serious attempt. Or, maybe I'll try playing a flute… or guitar…or hammered dulcimer…or saxophone…who knows? The possibilities are endless.

Be Prepared

That's me standing in front of the campfire at Wheelgate Girl Scout camp, 1955.

When we were in grade school, my mom was my sister's Girl Scout leader. Dad and I tagged along when her troop went on overnight camping trips. One year, when we were camping at Camp Wheelgate in April, it snowed on us. No one was prepared for snow. Wheelgate was a local Scout camp on Dutch Ridge, about half an hour from Charleston.

My favorite thing I got to do with their troop was to make my own "sit-upon." They were made from two squares, each two feet by two feet, cut out of oilcloth. We punched holes along the sides of the squares, then stitched them together with yarn. These were real handy to have on camping trips to sit upon wherever we needed a seat. They folded up into a small, flat square, which easily fit into a pocket or could be hung from a belt.

In the summertime, I used to go to day camp with my mom's troop. We caught a school bus at our school every morning which took us to Kanawha State Forest. "Catalina Matalina" was one of my favorite campfire songs we learned. The silly lyrics have stayed with me for a long time: "She had two teeth up in her mouth. One pointed north and the other pointed south."

When I was in second grade, two of my friends' mothers, Mrs. Dalton and Mrs. Harrison, started a Brownie troop for us at Robins. I loved our little brown uniforms, which we wore to school on the days of our meetings. My brown-haired Terri Lee doll had her own Brownie uniform, identical to mine. I thought that was pretty special. Terri Lee dolls had hard plastic molded faces, with enormous eyes and beautiful features which somewhat resembled Oprah's. Our troop embroidered tea towels, made various craft projects, and helped serve food at a local soup kitchen. For a special trip, we went to WCHS's studio to be on the television show, *Lucky 8 Ranch*, hosted by Dick Reid. We couldn't have been more excited as we sat in the corral on the show's set. Being on television was a real big deal to us grade school kids.

After a few years, Katherine Shelton took over the leadership of the troop. "Shelley," as she was called, had just moved into the neighborhood with her husband and niece, Laura, who was our age. I think the other leaders were more than happy to let her be in charge. She was excited about being our leader and had a perfect room in her basement for our weekly meetings. Mrs. Dalton continued to be our co-leader, and the two of them took us on frequent camping trips, often to Camp Wheelgate.

When we went camping, we were divided into groups, and each group was assigned chores. Cooking a meal, digging the latrine, gathering kindling wood for the campfire, washing pots and pans, and walking to the pump house to get water were typical chores. There was always something so fascinating about sitting around a campfire. Listening to the wood snap and pop, watching the golden embers fly up into the night sky, and enjoying the warmth from the flickering flames could be so comforting. Occasionally someone told ghost stories, like the standard, "I Want My Tailypo."

All of us loved to fix S'mores around the campfire. These tasty snacks, with a roasted marshmallow, Hershey bar, and graham crackers, were everyone's favorites. Roasting marshmallows to perfection required some skill. Just one fraction of an inch too close to the fire would cause the marshmallow to go up in flames. This always resulted in a gooey, charred, black ball on the end of your stick. If the marshmallow wasn't held closely enough to the flames, it never got done.

Ears of corn on the cob, which we wrapped in foil and grilled over the campfire, tasted so much better than what our moms boiled at home. One of my favorite meals was Ring-Tum-Ditty. It was a concoction of a little bit of everything: bacon, corn, tomatoes, onions, green pepper, and cheese. Actually, anything tasted better when prepared outdoors over a campfire. All of us ate out of our metal Scout dinnerware. Each piece conveniently nested into another. We drank out of our accordion-style, folding metal cups, which flattened to the size of a chewing tobacco tin. Most of us carried drinking water with us on hikes in flat metal canteens covered with green canvas or plaid flannel.

In early spring one year, we went camping in a wooded area near Blue Creek, about forty-five minutes from Charleston. It got so cold, that we shivered in our sleeping bags all night long. When we got up the next morning and began to prepare breakfast, all of our food was frozen: the eggs, bacon, juice, bread, and water. For that trip, I guess it would have been more appropriate if our motto had been, "Be Prepared for the Unexpected," instead of simply, "Be Prepared."

In the summertime, our troop joined many other area troops for a day camp at Coonskin Park. We hiked around the nature trail loop, beside the waterfall and rocky cliffs, as we sang popular Scout tunes, such as, "I'm Happy When I'm Hiking." That was always a fun time, to be able to interact with girls from other troops all over the county.

I liked all of the little round badges we could earn and display on our sashes. They had such intricate, colorful, symbolic images stitched on them. After fulfilling all of the requirements for the badges, it was a real reward to wear them proudly. There was such a nice variety of badges, so it was easy to find something that suited everyone's interests.

Since all of the girls in our troop had such a keen fascination with horses, we decided to travel to Calumet Horse Farm in Lexington, Kentucky. To reach this goal, we stepped up our efforts of selling Girl Scout cookies. My friend Barbara asked her mom to drive the two of us around the East End of Charleston to all of the large apartment buildings. We went door to door, from apartment to apartment, taking orders. It was never too difficult to peddle Girl Scout cookies. Like myself, practically everyone had a fetish for Thin Mints. By far, those were our best-sellers.

I still have the newspaper article which featured Barbara, Becky, Teresa, and me as the top sellers in our region that year.

Everyone else in our troop did well at selling cookies, and with all of our profits, we were off to Kentucky. Practically for all of our lives, we had played either like we were horses or like we were riding them. We were nuts about horses and all fourteen of us were fired up for the trip. My dad bought a new white Chevrolet station wagon, so we would have a reliable vehicle for the trip. It had a red interior with an extra seat in the very back, facing backwards. We were so excited to be riding in style.

Calumet Farm personnel were very cordial and accommodating. We were taken on a guided tour around the 762-acre farm's pastures, training facilities, and barns. It was worth the trip just to see the handsome Triple Crown winner, Citation. Miles of green pastures lined with white wooden fences surrounding hundreds of magnificent thoroughbreds was an awe-inspiring sight.

In Charleston, one of the most memorable community services our troop did was to help prepare the grounds at Sunrise. The residence of a former governor, the stately, old MacCorkle mansion, was to be transformed into a new museum. In 1961, we started going there every Saturday morning and worked for most of the morning and afternoon. We tended to the grounds along the carriage trail and the lower yard, which faced the Kanawha River. The adult volunteers had us clear brush, pull weeds, rearrange stones, and anything else that needed to be done.

When we were in junior high school, the last big trip we went on before the troop dispersed was to Watoga State Park. We stayed in a huge log cabin with a large barracks-style bedroom. It had plenty of bunk beds, which accommodated all of us girls. Our chaperones had private bedrooms.

During the days, we went swimming at their pool, hiking on the many wooded trails, and horseback riding. At the pool, one of their handsome lifeguards, Nate, had a crush on one of our girls, Teresa. Of course, we all got a kick out of that. We went on several long horseback rides through the park's extensive trail system.

On Saturday night, we attended the weekly barn dance on the top floor of their barn. Local musicians played, and boys from a nearby Boy Scout camp were there. That was a fun time for everyone. We got along so well that the boys invited us to visit them. On Monday, we rode over to their camp, Dilley's Mill. We spent several hours at the beautiful reservation, visiting with our new friends and riding in canoes on its pristine lake.

During the last year of our troop, I earned the God and Community Award. My focus was community service, and I put in a lot of hours working with younger children at church. My friend Becky earned the Curved Bar Award. That was the equivalent to the Boy Scouts' Eagle Award. We were all so proud of her receiving such a distinguished honor.

Charley West

Snow-covered Capitol dome, 1978.

I'm proud to say that Charleston, West Virginia, is my home-town. Just like in the *Goldilocks and the Three Bears* story, it wasn't too small, not too big, but "just right." Charleston used to be referred to as "Charley West" by pilots, air traffic controllers, and navigators. It is also the name of Pat Schell's long-standing newspaper caricature on the front page of the *Charleston Daily*

Mail. His popular cartoon character has been offering his witty commentary on local events since 1958.

We had many relatives scattered all across the state, so our home was somewhat of a boarding house. Since they lived in much smaller towns or rural communities, Charleston seemed like a big city to them. It was the hub of retail shopping, and many relatives came to Charleston specifically to shop for Christmas gifts and school clothes. Other times they just came to visit us and see the capital city with all of its attractions. Sometimes they came to celebrate the Fourth of July and enjoy the impressive fireworks show. When necessary, many of them stayed with us while their loved ones were in local hospitals.

We frequently took our visitors to see the beautiful capitol grounds and building, designed by architect Cass Gilbert. Everyone marveled at the marble rotunda with the spectacular, enormous glass chandelier. The small museum in the basement of the capitol building wasn't very impressive, but I was always intrigued with the flea circus display. Just recently, a new, incredible state museum was opened in the basement of the Culture Center. Many times we took our visitors up to the Kanawha Airport to watch the big planes come in and take off. We usually stood on the viewing platform, outside of the airport or watched from the tall windows inside. I loved watching the colorful blinking lights on the runways as planes arrived and departed.

Sometimes we took a picnic to the scenic Hawk's Nest State Park, about a forty-minute drive from Charleston. We walked out to the popular overlook area, made of huge slabs of flagstone and a stone wall topped with wrought iron pickets. It offered a spectacular, panoramic view of the New River Gorge. Dad fed the tall, silver viewing scopes a quarter and held us up so we could look through them. We watched the long coal trains, which seemed to stretch for miles on the other side of the river. They crept at such a slow pace, meandering around the horseshoe-shaped track. During the fall foliage extravaganza, the brilliant color diversity of the deciduous forest was breathtaking. We often drove over to Babcock State Park, not far from Hawk's Nest, to visit the much-photographed Glade Creek Grist Mill and hike in the dense woods on their rocky trails.

*Aunt Glenna and Dad with Jean and me in front of
the Glass House on the turnpike, 1954.*

Other times, we took our guests on a little drive down the West Virginia turnpike to the Glass House. It was a swanky restaurant on the turnpike which offered fine dining and the famous "Mile-High Pies," with deep layers of delicious meringue. Occasionally, our relatives bought us enormous "All Day Suckers," from the tall Lollipop Tree displayed near the cash register. These were as big as a 45 record, with bright, colorful, swirled designs. We literally sucked on them all day long.

One year, some of our relatives from Gassaway came down for one of the big circuses coming through town. They bought us front-row tickets. We were thoroughly enjoying the performance, and then the tigers were brought in. Right before their act, one of the male tigers backed up to the edge of the big cage and raised his tail. Before we knew what was happening, he started urinating all over our section of the audience, with the force of a garden hose turned on full blast. A bevy of circus employees showed up in a heartbeat. They were very apologetic and gave us towels, wet washcloths, and vouchers to get our clothes dry-cleaned. Then, they immediately mopped up the urine.

My sister and I used to beg our parents to drive us by the West Side croquet court, on the corner of Stockton Street and Sixth Avenue. We felt like we were getting a glimpse of a bygone era. The flat, dirt court was a gathering place for elderly gentlemen. There were never any women or children present. We liked to park and watch them play. Two sides of the court were lined with weathered wooden benches full of older men wearing dark suits, large brimmed hats, and white dress shirts. They used big mallets with cutoff handles. Every time we drove by, the place was buzzing with activity.

As a family, and with Scout and church groups, we frequently had huge day-long picnics at Coonskin Park, Kanawha State Forest, and the DuPont Hunting and Fishing Club. Horseback riding trips on the trails of Kanawha Forest or in the ring at Coonskin were always exciting adventures. During extremely cold winters, the pond at Coonskin froze over. We joined other ice skating enthusiasts and spent the day circling the frozen surface. Those were carefree, fun days. It was such a community event. Many people gathered around the gigantic bonfire to get some welcomed relief from the painfully cold air. Mom brought a Thermos full of hot chocolate, which helped to counter the chill.

During our youth, we often had very deep snows. Living on the West Side hill offered plenty of thrilling sleigh rides down the steeper streets. In the snowy weather, people from all over town came to sleigh ride at Edgewood Country Club's golf course, where the public Cato Park course is today. There was always a huge, rip-roaring bonfire there too. It provided a nice warm break in between downhill runs. I got my first taste of skiing and the art of snowplowing on the slopes of the old golf driving range at Coonskin. In the wintertime, when we had deep snows, the driving range turned into ski slopes. A primitive-looking, mechanized rope-pull dragged us back up the hill. These days, that property which is located to the left of the park entrance, is occupied by the West Virginia Air National Guard.

Intersection of Capitol and Quarrier Streets, downtown Charleston, 1970s.
Photo courtesy of Jerry Waters.

One of my favorite remembrances about living in Charleston was shopping downtown. It was the center of the city, where we ran into everyone we knew. There was such a difference in shopping downtown compared to shopping in a mall. Braving the elements, walking from one store to another, certainly was part of that difference. Back in those days, we didn't have parking garages. There were enormous parking lots peppered all over downtown. My brother-in-law put himself through college by working as a parking lot attendant for Charleston's parking lot tycoon, Spyro Stanley.

Jean with Santa and me at The Diamond, 1951.

My very favorite thing to do was shopping downtown at Christmastime. Every tall streetlight was decorated with a lantern, hanging in a garland wreath. The sound of the Salvation Army bell ringers, and seeing all of the window decorations, put everyone in such a festive mood. The enchanted, marvelously-detailed, animated Christmas scenes in the windows of The Diamond and Stone and Thomas department stores were captivating. The Diamond's facade was draped with beautiful vertical strands of clear Christmas lights. Our parents took us to The Diamond to have a picture taken with Santa. When the snow was falling, everyone got into the holiday spirit of giving. Perhaps even the poor beggar with no legs got an extra coin or two. He was usually sitting in front of the bank next to the Diamond, on his wooden platform with wheels on it, and a tin cup in his hand.

All of the larger department stores downtown with multiple floors had full-time employees operating their elevators. For many of these "elevator ladies," this was their lifetime profession. We became so familiar with a few of them, that they felt like friends to us. At The Diamond, we often ate lunch at the snack bar on the first floor, or waited in line on the fifth floor to eat in their cafeteria. Frequently, we stopped by Federal Bakery, on Capitol Street, for some chocolate chip cookies or salt-rising bread for our Cheese Squares recipe.

The beautiful Louise Corey offered classes at Stone and Thomas in etiquette, fashion, and grooming. She was a Charleston icon who epitomized grace and beauty. When I was in junior high school, most of the girls in my Scout troop and I attended her classes. In the late summer, before school started, Mom took my sister and me to back-to-school fashion shows, held at the Scottish Rite Temple. The Diamond hosted the popular shows and featured young models from the county's high schools.

Thinking back to all of the stores in downtown Charleston, I can't get over how many there were. I so vividly remember looking at Poor Pitiful Pearl dolls in the toy department of Coyle and

Richardson. It was right before Christmas, and our parents had taken us shopping to look at ideas for Santa gifts. For many years, I could find clothes that I liked at Frankenberger's, Embee's, The Diamond, and Stone and Thomas. We usually bought our school shoes in the shoe department of The Diamond, and dress shoes at John Lee's or Palmer's. There were so many places to buy shoes. In addition to specialized shoe shops, all of the larger department stores had their own shoe departments.

One day, Mom and my sister and I were shopping on the second floor of The Diamond. We were exchanging a training bra Mom had bought for me. Our next-door neighbor Juanita was working in that department, as she had for many years. She thought it was hilarious that the store's undercover security guards were following us. We were completely oblivious to the fact that we were being followed. They must have thought we looked suspicious, walking in with our bags of items to return. After that incident, we frequently saw the two women closely following other unsuspecting shoppers everywhere they went.

We bought books and picked up our developed photographs, in little yellow or gray booklets, at the S. Spencer Moore Company on Capitol Street. At Maynard's pet store, we often replenished our guppy population. Sometimes my friends and I were allowed to shop in the big dime stores by ourselves. We loved to put a quarter in the slot of the photo booth at Woolworth's and get a strip of pictures made as we tried to look as silly as we could. Sometimes we got milkshakes on the mezzanine floor. One holiday season, I purchased fancy, white lace-trimmed handkerchiefs with colorful embroidered flowers at Kresge's dime store. Those were Christmas presents for my grandmother.

Two downtown institutions which I miss are The Sterling Restaurant and the stately, old, stone, public library. It was originally built as the Capitol Annex. Many times, after dances or dates, we went to The Sterling because it was still opened and was known for its excellent food. I loved the old library and was sad to see it torn down in 1966. It was a significant and beloved landmark in downtown Charleston, having such character, with its two sets of curved steps leading up to the front doors. I spent many hours poring through the card catalogues, working on high school research papers.

During the days of our youth, there were many movie theaters around town. The Virginian, Kearse, Capitol, Rialto, Lyric, State, and Village were the ones I remember. Most of these places had such lavishly-decorated interiors, resembling fancy opera houses. We liked to sit in their balconies. Our parents often dropped us kids off to watch the movies without any adult chaperones. That's how safe we felt. Sadly, all of those theaters closed, once the mega-theaters moved into town. The Capitol, now owned by West Virginia State University, is still used for special film festivals and theatrical performances.

When the Town Center mall opened in 1983, several of the downtown stores relocated there. Some store owners tried to stay in their downtown locations and make a go of it. Their demise was similar to the independent theaters. It was heartbreaking, to see businesses which had flourished for so long be forced to close their doors, one slow death at a time. Two downtown stores which beat the odds and are still around today are The Peanut Shoppe on Capitol Street and Fife Street Shoe Shop. The interior of each of these places looks like it did fifty years ago. Walking into the Fife Street Shoe Shop definitely feels like stepping back in time to 1920, when the shoe repair shop first opened.

In junior high school, my friend Becky and I were hanging out with two of our classmates, Sam and Ronnie. We were at her home, close to the Boulevard, and decided to walk over to the mysterious Magic Island for a little adventure. All of us had ridden by the island in Kanawha River many times, but none of us had explored it before. To our disappointment, the island, which looked so appealing from a distance, was a rat-infested eyesore, littered with debris from the river. The old island was transformed several years ago, into a beautiful, well-groomed, popular multi-purpose park.

There were two interesting, iconic characters who became household names to those of us who grew up or resided in Charleston. Earl Harvey, or "Lightning," as he was fondly called, was a short, pleasant, elderly, African American gentleman. He stood on the street corners downtown or at the capitol complex and directed traffic by whistling and waving on the cars, with a bundle of outdated newspapers under his arm. When we rode by him, he was usually talking to himself. We called out his name and waved, as one would do to any good friend. He always returned the gesture. Everyone knew the familiar story that Lightning was a mathematical genius. According to the legend, he could guess how many bricks there were on a side of any building, with some accuracy.

Bill Dunn, or "Aqualung," as he was called, was Charleston's famous street person. He resembled the figure on the *Aqualung* album, by Jethro Tull. When he first came to town, he had a lady friend with him, but that was short-lived. He scavenged the streets and alleys of downtown Charleston for decades, with his grocery cart crammed full and overflowing with treasured possessions. Taylor Books' art gallery, in downtown Charleston, recently had several remarkable portraits of him on display, by local artist Rob Cleland. Earl Harvey died decades ago, and Bill Dunn disappeared several years ago. I miss seeing those two intriguing individuals.

Charleston had its share of soda fountains scattered all over town. In the fifties, Mom and Dad frequently treated my Scout troop to sundaes at the Valley Bell ice cream shop, on West Washington Street, where the Fountain Hobby Center is located. The hot fudge sundaes and banana splits were my favorites. For many years, I stopped by the Valley Bell store, across from Lincoln Junior High, to purchase a toasted almond ice cream cone. A few weeks ago, I stopped at the store to get another cone. As I walked by the table on the sidewalk in front of the place, a gentleman sitting there said: "Lady, the ice cream shop closed a few years ago." What a surprise and disappointment that was.

The Fountain Hobby Center has certainly withstood the test of time. The family-run business originally opened in North Charleston in 1947 and was actually a soda fountain, too, hence the name. In 1960, it moved into its current West Side location. The hobby store has always carried many of those hard-to-find items needed for hobbies or craft projects. When I taught craft classes, I spent quite a lot of time there, getting ideas and buying supplies. For many years, Tandy Leather was down the street from the hobby shop. That was another place I often frequented as an art teacher. While I was teaching in the seventies, my students were into making and wearing tooled leather wristbands and belts. Those were popular and trendy fashion accessories during that era.

Sunrise museum opened its doors to the public when we were in junior high school. It offered many interesting exhibits and art shows. Its "Christmas Trees around the World," was a popular annual attraction. The small zoo in the basement was a big hit too. In 2003, Sunrise was replaced by the Clay Center for the Arts and Sciences of West Virginia. It offers art exhibits and classes, concerts, symphony and theatrical performances, movies in the round, a planetarium, and a science discovery center.

In 1971, Charleston began its long-running Sternwheel Regatta Festival over Labor Day weekends. My grandmother used to love watching the sternwheeler races on the Kanawha River. The Taste of Charleston was a popular event and one of my favorites. It offered a sampling of many of the city's finest restaurants and was such a culinary feast. A few years ago, the Regatta was replaced with FestivALL, where "A City Becomes a Work of Art." One year, the incredible, world-renown sidewalk artist Julian Beever was commissioned to create an amazing mural of a whitewater rafting scene. Entertaining street acts, like the hilarious Mutts Gone Nuts, are performed throughout the ten-day event. Concerts are ongoing in several locations, and art shows and colorful exhibits are scattered all over town.

The long-standing Vandalia Gathering is one of Charleston's most popular annual events. Since 1977, musicians from all over have come with their instruments in hand to gather on the capitol grounds to play old time and bluegrass music. It is quite a sight to behold. Impromptu concerts pop up all over the place, as musicians join in with others. The three-day Memorial Day weekend event offers ethnic dance performances, music competitions and concerts, liars' contests, storytelling, art and crafts exhibits, clogging, and square dancing. Of course, the food vendors are a major attraction. They offer delicious, mouth-watering treats such as barbeque, roasted ears of corn, Greek salads, baklava, homemade ice cream, and strawberry shortcake.

A similar festival, Multifest, has attracted huge crowds with its multicultural concerts on the capitol grounds for over twenty years. One of the most romantic events I have ever witnessed was at Multifest one year. At a real wedding, held during the festival, a popular, local black disc jockey sang the Delfonics' hit, "La La Means I Love You," to his beautiful bride.

During our youth, one of the biggest events in Charleston every year was the football game between the two high schools in town, Charleston High and Stonewall Jackson. They were such rivals, and the city was divided into two groups of fans. Before the game every year, students from Stonewall had huge "snake dances," which meandered through the city streets. It seemed like the entire population of Charleston showed up for the ball game at Laidley Field. In 1989, the two schools were consolidated into a new school, Capital High. The long-standing East Side-West Side rivalry came to a screeching halt. These days, Charlestonians join together in rooting on Capital High whenever it faces competitors from all over the county and state.

One of the most anticipated events in our city's history was our state's one hundredth birthday party. Many people and dignitaries poured into Charleston to celebrate West Virginia's centennial on June 20, 1963. Numerous women, including my mother and grandmother, had sewn authentic-looking nineteenth-century dresses and hats to wear for the momentous occasion. My family and I were part of the crowd which stood out in the rain for hours, on the grounds of the state capitol, to hear President Kennedy's speech. He told the onlookers: "The sun does not always shine in West Virginia, but the people do." We were up on top of a set of steps and could look over the throng of people. The sea of umbrellas was such an unforgettable, peculiar-looking sight. No one could have predicted that only five months later, our beloved president would be assassinated.

The crowd at our capitol, waiting to hear JFK's speech at the centennial celebration.

Photo from the West Virginia archives collection.

I met my second husband, Peter, in 1979. He came to Charleston from New Hampshire as part of a crew of New England carpenters hired to build an authentic eighteenth-century Colonial reproduction house. Peter started doing carpentry work for a family on Newton Road, in South Hills. Over a few months, he brought their leaded glass windows to me so I could repair them. While I was installing several windows, the owner pointed out a garage apartment on their property which had once served as the caretakers' residence. Recently, I spoke with an interesting black gentleman, Tom Toliver, who grew up in that apartment. His parents had been the caretakers of the estate for the Thomas family. Last year, Tom was honored with the prestigious Jefferson Award for his ongoing work in mentoring children whose parents are incarcerated.

Tom had an intriguing story about Charleston's history, from his youth. In the 1940s, he often rode his horse over to Bedford Road, off of Connell Road in South Hills. There, he watched the drop-off and pick-up of the mail courier service. This was before the Kanawha Airport opened in 1947. Huge sacks of mail were dropped from a Stinson aircraft at the end of the road. Then, the pilot circled around and, with a gigantic hook dangling from the plane, he or she snatched up a large cable extending between two mounds. The cable had bags of mail attached to it. After it was pulled up to the plane and the bags were taken off, the cable was dropped back down to the mound. His story gave me a new visual for the term "air mail."

School Daze III

Stonewall Jackson High School, Charleston, West Virginia, 1960s.
Photo from the collection of Jerry Waters, courtesy of David Waugh.

My years at Stonewall Jackson High School were some of the best times of my life. I met my first true love, Johnny, in the summer of 1964, between my ninth and tenth grades. We met in his neighborhood, at Faulkner's corner drugstore. It was a teenage hangout in the flat district of the West Side. I had spent the night with my close friend Becky, who lived a few blocks away. We were sitting at the soda fountain when he and a friend of his walked through the door. I think it was pretty much love at first sight for both of us. At that time, I had my traditional blonde streak on the front of my hair from peroxide and sun exposure.

When I was a sophomore, he was a senior, and he always owned a vehicle. I had never dated anyone who had a car before, so this was new and exciting to me. We double-dated with another couple, Harry and Connie, who became our close friends. The four of us spent so much time together and enjoyed each other's company tremendously. Connie and I were both in the band, so the two guys had someone to hang out with while she and I sat with the band and performed at our football games.

John always had some pretty cool muscle cars. He took a lot of pride in taking care of his cars, frequently washing them and buffing the chrome bumpers. Over the years, he owned a custom Impala and a cool souped-up black Ford Galaxy, which had previously been a police car. By far, my favorite vehicle he had was a copper-colored '57 Chevy. He picked up my friend Nancy and me for school every morning in it, and drove us home at the end of the day. He and I both loved that car. It was in great shape, and we enjoyed cruising around town in style.

He was a happy-go-lucky guy and liked to play practical jokes sometimes. One day we were driving down Park Avenue, and he saw a buddy of his walking along the sidewalk. He called the guy over to his window, and as they were talking, John pushed the button to release the windshield wiper fluid. The stream of liquid was so forceful that it squirted all over his friend. Although the guy had been caught completely off guard, he was still a good sport about it. They both laughed so hard, knowing he had been tricked. John thought it was hilarious to stop the car in front of the notorious stone brothel at the foot of Capitol Hill. He would toot the horn, and an elderly lady sitting at a window would open it, and yell out, "Two dollars."

I will never forget the day when someone crashed into the Chevy. Johnny told me about the wreck, and he was so nonchalant about it, especially for someone who just had his prized vehicle totaled. He shrugged his shoulders and said, "It's just a car." At that point, I knew how special he was. One reason I always thought he had such a good personality, was because he was the middle child in his family. His beautiful mom and laid-back dad had four kids. John was in between an older brother and younger twins.

On dates, we usually went out to eat at Shoney's restaurant, before going bowling or to a movie. In warm weather, we often went to play miniature golf at one of the local Putt-Putts. Sometimes we went to the drive-ins at A&W or Shoney's, where we were waited on by their carhops. We liked the hot dogs and the slushy tops on the root beer at A&W, and the onion rings and Slim Jims at Shoney's. It was fun watching the constant show of loud muscle cars, parading nonstop through the drive-ins. Sometimes on Saturdays, we went to Rock Lake swimming pool. We played around in the water and sunbathed on the decks. He liked to dunk me and splash me as I slowly inched my way into the icy cold water. Since he was so good at it, I loved watching him work out on the tall gym bars, where many of the older teenage boys liked to show off their muscles.

At the end of our dates, we drove up to the top of the West Side hill, where there was a popular parking spot, along an undeveloped road. To quote David Clayman, a revered Charleston psychologist: "Ours was a generation of good kissers." We were all great make-out artists, because for the overwhelming majority of us, having sex was not even a consideration. We did have some steamy make-out sessions in the front seat of his car, where, unlike today, we could sit side by side, not divided by bucket seats.

One of my parents' friends from church came to our house on a Saturday morning. I heard him tell my mom that he had seen Johnny and me parked along the road the night before. He lived up in that neighborhood. We had actually waved to him, mistaking his car for a friend's from school. When Mom approached me about it after he left, I jokingly told her she should be happy that we were sitting up and he was able to see us. Most weekend nights, I had a curfew of being home at eleven. After a while, when we had come in from a date, if it got to be too late, my father would toss his house shoes out into the hallway across from their bedroom. This usually happened around midnight. It was his subtle way of hinting that it was time for Johnny to go home.

I like John Mellencamp's description of how our generation was in his hit, "Cherry Bomb." The lyrics, "Dancing was everything" and, "Holding hands meant something, baby," are great descriptors of how we were. Slow dancing was about as sexy and intimate as anything we did, and we had such a good time dancing to the fast songs. We held hands everywhere we went.

Johnny's mom worked at a record distributorship and brought home sample 45s. I ended up with an extensive record collection, many with the famous blue Motown label on them. The familiar labels had the word "Motown" at the top, in bold, color-blended letters, juxtaposed over part of a Michigan map. Detroit was marked with a red star beside it.

On school days, while we dated, Johnny and I went to my home every day at lunchtime. Mom always had lunch ready for us. Most of the time, it was some variety of Campbell's soup with a sandwich, on white bread, of course. Usually the sandwiches were peanut butter and jelly, bologna, or tuna salad. Sometimes we also had peanut butter or pineapple cream cheese on celery stalks. Occasionally we had potato chips or Fritos with French onion dip. Frequently Mom baked brownies or chocolate chip cookies for dessert. My favorite lunch she fixed was her delicious homemade potato soup, served with oyster crackers. One of the last times John and I talked with one another, he said that he felt like my mom was practically a second mother to him, since he spent so much time at our house.

As far as boyfriends go, Johnny pretty much spoiled me. He treated me like a princess, always opening doors for me, surprising me with lavish gifts, and going with me to church services and our camp. Like Forrest Gump said about himself and Jenny: "We were like two peas in a pod." One of our most exciting dates was in 1965, when we drove to Veterans Memorial Field House in Huntington to watch our outstanding basketball team play in the state regionals. During the last few seconds, Maurice Pendleton threw the ball halfway down the court to score the winning basket at the sound of the buzzer. That same year, during the summer after my tenth grade, the seventeen-year cicadas showed up in Charleston. Everywhere we went, the sound from the insects was so deafening.

During my junior year in high school, and after he had graduated, John was drafted to serve in Vietnam. I lost my best friend and constant companion. We saw one another a few times after he was drafted, but his family moved to Florida, I went off to college, and we went our separate ways. The last time I saw him was when I was in college. I called him one day, and the next day he drove up from Florida. At that time, he was driving the coolest little yellow car, a fancy Triumph gt6.

When Johnny left for boot camp, he insisted that I date other guys. I did go out with some other boys, but it felt pretty strange, since he and I had been so close. To everyone's amusement, including his, one of the busybodies in my neighborhood called his house to tattle on me for dating other boys. I went to a Cotillion dance one evening with Gary, a friend of mine from our school band. Thankfully, he was a patient person. When he showed up at our house to pick me up, my mom was still sewing iridescent sequin trim on my dress. After waiting for what seemed like an eternity, the fancy dress was finally finished. He and I took off and had a great time, dancing the night away.

I don't know what it is about a girl's psyche that finds extremely handsome boys to be unattractive. At least for me, if they were too perfect, in their looks or behavior, I was completely turned off. I had a few suitors after Johnny left who fell into this category. We dated for several weeks or even months before "the curse of the pretty boy" took over. The only reason I could give myself for not being interested in these guys was simply that they were a little too perfect. Maybe they seemed too much like a Goody Two-shoes to me. Whatever it was, it sounds pretty unfair to them.

At Stonewall, there were plenty of activities to occupy my time. Since I was on the majorette corps, I hung out a lot with other majorettes. Most of us drove, and during breaks from practices, we usually loaded up in someone's car and went to nearby drive-ins. When we were driving back to practice one day, one girl was dissing a junior high school friend of mine, who was dating her ex-boyfriend. Just by standing up for that girl, for better or worse, I immediately gained the reputation of not going along with the crowd.

Pep assemblies were always an exciting time for us majorettes. We waited in the big foyer outside the auditorium, to be introduced. An enormous Stonewall Jackson looked down upon us from a painted canvas overhead. "Here comes the Stonewall Jackson majorettes," the announcer yelled into the microphone, before the band struck up the school fight song. The auditorium was packed with the entire student body, standing and clapping to the music. It was an emotionally-charged atmosphere.

We divided into two groups as we strutted down the outside aisles of the auditorium. Dressed in full uniform, we took long strides and swung our arms back and forth. Sometimes we performed in front of the stage, and other times on the stage. The cheerleaders formed a circle with us, and together we performed our routine to the familiar fight song. During the talent show our senior year, we performed our majorette festival routine to "A Taste of Honey."

Stonewall only had four varsity cheerleaders during my senior year. They wore saddle oxfords, wool pleated skirts down to their knees, and sweaters with a megaphone on the front. White turtle-necks, bobby socks, and gloves were the final details. The round, gray and red pom-poms they used during most cheers were enormous. The biggest difference between those cheerleaders and the ones of today, other than fewer numbers, was that our cheerleaders mostly led cheers. The entire crowd in the football stadium used to stand up and cheer with them on the old standard, "Two Bits, Four Bits." At basketball games, the cheering from the crowd could rock the house.

During my senior year, our school drama club put on a production of the musical *Brigadoon*. I helped with the stage props. It was so much fun, staying after school and making the backdrops for the various scenes. I helped other students paint a huge stone wall, which ended up looking pretty authentic. The performances were so good, they looked very professional. Another fun activity was decorating for our proms. In those days, proms were held in our school's gymnasium. We spent several days transforming it into a beautiful party atmosphere.

Being a staff member of *The Jacksonian*, our yearbook, and working with its sponsor, Mrs. Elliott, was another memorable experience from high school. Her room number was 208, my lucky number. Our staff members enjoyed driving around town to various sponsors, posing for and taking pictures to be used in their yearbook ads. Several of us *Jacksonian* staff members attended a summer seminar at Ohio University. We learned valuable, new and improved techniques on how to produce a better yearbook. The accomplishment which I was most proud of, as editor of the advertising section, was getting a photograph I had wanted for the opening two-page spread of that section. It was a sepia-tone image of the Charleston skyline at nighttime. The light reflections from the city and streetlights were shining on the waters of the Kanawha River. I was very pleased with how it looked.

I had many good teachers at Stonewall, but I especially liked Mr. Armstrong's senior English class. "Mr. A," as everyone called him, was an eccentric character who was a talented pianist and loved the color purple. It was very prestigious to be placed in his class and I was thrilled when I found out that he would be my senior English teacher. While I was working on a research paper on Stonehenge for his class, I got introduced to and hooked on researching and writing. Every time I walked up the curved steps to the old stone library in downtown Charleston, an unusual excitement came over me. I couldn't wait to work on the assignment and became completely engrossed in the process. Using my little three-by-five-inch index cards, I took copious notes. Then I organized and arranged my cards, preparing to write the paper.

To my delight, I got a good grade on my written report. After he returned our papers, we were required to present an oral report on the topic. As I was giving my speech, I thought I could sense that my classmates were staring at me in a peculiar way. When I finished speaking, I returned to my desk, and several people asked me if I felt all right. They were worried because, unbeknown to me, as I spoke, red hives crawled up my neck and onto my face.

Everyone was required to take a life science class at Stonewall. Our parents were a little uneasy about this "sex education" class, which is what they called it. After all, they didn't want us to have sex, so they certainly didn't see the need for us to learn about "the birds and the bees." Our gym teacher taught the all-girl class in the auditorium. Much of the subject was a real eye opener for me, especially the part on human reproduction.

In high school, I finally decided to have a keloid scar on my left shoulder removed. It was from a smallpox vaccine I was given as a child. I had always been extremely self-conscious about it. My parents took me to a surgeon, who said there were no guarantees with the operation, but he felt confident that he could leave only a hairline scar. As I lay on my stomach on the operating table, I could look up and watch the entire procedure in the reflection of the doctor's glasses. Since I was squeamish at the sight of blood to begin with, I only glanced up occasionally. Although the operation went well, the outcome was a complete failure. I was left with a much larger keloid scar, approximately four times the length of the original one. Of course I was disappointed in the results, but took it in stride, knowing that the outcome had always been unpredictable.

During the last semester of my senior year, I got wiped out with the debilitating disease mononucleosis. I had such a wicked case of mono, it was nearly impossible for me to do any kind of catching up on my schoolwork. My teachers were extremely understanding and accommodating. They extended deadlines and postponed tests so I could still graduate.

I'm not sure why, but I jokingly started telling my parents that I wanted a 1967 pink Mustang convertible for a graduation gift. The likelihood of that happening was slim to none. There was just something about those rare pink Mustangs that was so appealing. Needless to say, I never got the coveted car, but it remains to be a long-standing family joke.

The last Cotillion dance I went to during my senior year was on the first-floor roof of the modern Heart O' Town motel, in downtown Charleston. It was a beautiful, warm spring evening. Romance was in the air as we danced to the tunes of the Esquires. One of the guys in our school band brought some booze into the dance in a flask. Back then, drinking was such unthinkable behavior, so everyone got real stirred up about it.

My senior year had a perfect ending. Our band took a bus trip to perform at Expo '67, the World's Fair in Montreal. It was a bittersweet time for all of us seniors. We knew this would be the last time for us to be together, before going off in different directions to college. Eating in Canadian restaurants was somewhat frustrating, but still an interesting experience. None of the restaurant employees spoke English, and they had no clue what we were trying to order. We didn't appreciate their culinary preferences when it came to hot dogs. They served theirs with pickle relish only, not like the ones we were used to, with chili and slaw.

Traveling Back in Time through Music

Practically our entire lives can be defined by music. Nothing can take us back to a particular place and time as quickly and as perfectly as music does. Music can rejuvenate the heart and soul like nothing else.

In the 1950s, my sister and her friends liked listening to the McGuire Sisters, so their music is what I remember the most from that era. Their two hits, "Sincerely" and "Sugartime," are the ones that have stayed in my memory. My first real infatuation with a song was back in grade school in 1960, when I was listening to "Alley Oop" by the Hollywood Argyles. I recall so vividly hearing it play over my palm-size, red and silver, hand-held transistor radio. As my friends and I walked around our summer playground, we listened to the top 40 hits. I liked the raspy voice of the lead singer on "Alley Oop," and thought the lyrics were pretty cool: "Like, Hipsville." I saved my money and bought it on a 45 record. That was the first of what would be many purchases of music over the years. To this day, I am most content when I have music playing in the background.

For most of us, the first few notes of any song can send us back to a moment from the past in a matter of nanoseconds. The late fifties and early sixties were dominated by the handsome teen idols, such as Fabian, Bobby Vee, and Bobby Vinton. I remember listening many times to Vinton's "Roses are Red," Fabian's "Tiger," and Vee's "Take Good Care of My Baby."

In 1960, the combination of the movie "Where the Boys Are" and Connie Francis's hit by the same name was such a romantic feeling. Francis's crystal-clear voice helped convince us girls that Prince Charming would someday come and sweep us off our feet. In junior high school I was, like most girls, totally in love with and completely enthralled with the Beatles. In 1962, "Love Me Do" was one of our favorite hits to dance to at our sock hops, which were often scheduled in the afternoons during school. In 1963, we fast danced to "I Want to Hold Your Hand" and slow danced to one of our favorites, "This Boy." I still melt whenever I hear the Fab Four harmonize in that song. At school dances, no one could resist dancing to "Do You Love Me?" by the Contours. Everyone was able to follow the simple lyrics that told us what to do: "I can Mash Potatoes," and "I can do The Twist."

The lyrics from Dionne Warwick's 1962 hit "Don't Make Me Over" and her 1963 hit "Anyone Who Had a Heart" resonated with us, as we could relate them to our schoolgirl puppy loves. Both of those songs were around for years, continuing to be popular when we were in high school. When I hear Martha and the Vandella's 1964 hit "Dancing in the Street," I go back in a heartbeat to those romantic street dances which were held in our neighborhood every summer. That same year, Betty Everett told us what to look for in a guy in her "Shoop Shoop Song" with the lyrics: "If you want to know if he loves you so, it's in his kiss." Most of us took that for gospel. I certainly remember believing it.

Nothing takes me back to 1965, running around with my boyfriend, in his '57 Chevy, like the Four Tops' hits "Baby, I Need Your Loving" and "I Can't Help Myself (Sugar Pie Honey Bunch)." Listening to the 1966 Righteous Brothers' hit "You're My Soul and My Heart's Inspiration" sends me back into my high school date's arms as we slow danced so very closely. Percy Sledge's "When a

Man Loves a Woman" whirlwinds me right back to the front seat of my boyfriend's car, where we made out until our lips were sore.

The sultry, pleading voice of Lorraine Ellison in her 1966 hit "Stay with Me (Baby)" brings me back to a moment where my boyfriend and I were having a difficult time staying together. I remember calling WKAZ, my favorite local radio station, and making several requests to hear that song. To us girls especially, music meant so much. What wonderful, romantic times those were. Especially when we were in high school, there was such an abundance of awesome, talented musicians. The ones I have named here are just a fraction of the talent. I'm sure many of you have your own favorites that I haven't even mentioned.

At soda fountains or restaurants where we hung out, some of the standards on the jukeboxes were:

Smokey Robinson and the Miracles—"More Love"

The Supremes—"Stop in the Name of Love"

Chuck Jackson—"I Wake Up Crying"

Mary Wells—"My Guy"

The Temptations—"My Girl"

Roy Orbison—"Pretty Woman"

Van Morrison—"Brown Eyed Girl"

The Box Tops—"The Letter"

Herman's Hermits— "Mrs. Brown You've Got a Lovely Daughter"

Eric Burton and the Animals—"The House of the Rising Sun"

Tammy Terrell and Marvin Gaye—"Ain't No Mountain High Enough"

The Shirells—"Will You Love Me Tomorrow"

The Beatles—"And I Love Her"

Stevie Wonder—"Fingertips"

Sam and Dave—"Soul Man"

The Impressions—"It's Alright"

Barbara Lewis—"Make Me Your Baby"

Ben E. King—"Stand By Me"

Jimmy Ruffin—"What Becomes of the Brokenhearted"

Gladys Knight and the Pips—"Every Beat of My Heart"

Wilson Pickett—"The Midnight Hour"

Chubby Checker—"The Twist"

The Delfonics—"La La Means I Love You"

James Brown—"I Feel Good"

The Temptations' hit "Don't Look Back" sends me back to the sorority and fraternity dances and parties at Concord College. This is especially true for the lyrics: "If it's love that you're running from, there's no hiding place." "Cherish," by the Association, and "You've Made Me So Very Happy," by Blood, Sweat, and Tears, take me back to the days and times spent on Concord's campus. "Colour My World" and "Make Me Smile," by Chicago, remind me of listening to music in the dorm while I worked on my art assignments.

Two concerts which stand out in my memory from my college days are the ones performed by The Friends of Distinction and John Denver. When I hear their songs, "Grazing in the Grass" and "Take Me Home, Country Roads," I am once again sitting on the wooden parquet floor of the ballroom in the student union watching their performances. Concord did a good job of offering various programs for us students. I was completely mesmerized by a tall, folksy older student named Jane, who belted out "The September Song": "Try to remember the kind of September when life was slow and oh, so mellow." Equally enchanting was her version of "The Water is Wide": "I leaned my back against an oak, thinking it was a mighty tree, but then it cracked and then it broke, just as my love proved false to me."

After graduating from college in 1971, I immediately found myself in hippiedom. My boyfriend at the time, Doug, who was to become my first husband, had a head start on me with that. He introduced me to John Sebastian's "She's a Lady," and to the album by Neil Young and Crazy Horse, "Everybody Knows this is Nowhere." That album remains to be one of my favorites. Our signature song when we were in hot pursuit of one another, right before we got married, was the 1972 hit by the Delfonics, "Didn't I (Blow Your Mind This Time)." Every time I hear that tune, I am looking in Doug's face again, as he soulfully sings it to me.

Of course, part of the hippie ritual was listening to loud music as we sat around dark, incense-filled rooms with Janice Joplin, Bob Marley, and Jimi Hendrix posters glowing from blacklights. Hearing the Rolling Stones' hit "Give Me Shelter" ("It's just a shout away"), "Mean Mistreater" by Grand Funk Railroad, and "Long Haired Lady" by Quicksilver Messenger Service can send me right back to my bell-bottom, long-haired, hippie-chick days.

While Doug and I lived in Columbia, South Carolina, we had friends move in with us for most of our year-long stay. We listened to a lot of Pure Prairie League, Elton John, Rita Coolidge, Kris Kristofferson, and the Eagles. One day, at a local record store, I bought two different Rita Coolidge albums. When I got home and opened them, they were the exact same record. The store owner didn't believe me, when I went back to exchange one.

After we divorced, I dated a photographer on and off for five years in the late seventies and early eighties. I so vividly recall listening during that time to the Seals and Crofts 1976 hit "Get Closer": "Darlin', if you want me to be closer to you, get closer to me." That song summed up our on-again-off-again, uncertain relationship. The 1981 hit "Leather and Lace," by Stevie Nicks and Don Henley, became my theme song for when I was dating

Peter, my second husband. The lyrics, "Still I carry this feeling when you walked into my house that you won't be walking out the door," helped to define our courtship and can take me back to that time in a flash.

This chapter was by far one of the most fun to write. With the offerings available on the Internet, I was able to take a fantastic journey back in time. I pulled up most of these old favorites, listening to them on YouTube. I was especially thrilled to find Lorraine Ellison's "Stay with Me (Baby)." I hadn't heard it since my high school days.

I hope this chapter strikes a chord with you, too...pun fully intended.

The Campus Beautiful

Our graduation procession in May of 1971.

Concord College, now Concord University, in Athens, West Virginia, was where I chose to further my education after high school. I wanted to go somewhere away from home and was interested in attending a smaller school, not too big. Concord's slogan was "The Campus Beautiful." It certainly did live up to that description, having one of the most beautiful campuses in the state. The administrators and professors prided themselves on having a strict reputation, and the school was considered to be a stellar institution of higher learning.

I attended Concord at a perfect time. There was excitement in the air as the college was changing so rapidly. During my years there, the campus grew exponentially, with the completion of several new buildings. As an art major, during my last three years, I enjoyed the benefits of a brand new fine arts building and gallery. While I was a freshman, a new bowling alley and recreation complex opened up in the student union. Part of our gym class curriculum was learning to become better bowlers in the new facility.

During my last two years, I was fortunate enough to be one of the first residents in the Towers. It was a state-of-the-art dorm complex, with an open, spacious, glass lobby and its own cafeteria. The cafeteria manager was very progressive. Frequently, he visited with students during meals, asking us for ideas on how he could improve the food service. He was receptive to our suggestions, about what foods we would like to see offered.

During my freshman year, I lived in Sarvay Hall, the oldest dorm on campus. It was a stately red brick building with large white columns. The big front yard was adorned with tall, majestic, evergreen trees. On my first day there, after my parents left, I immediately ran downstairs, to the vending machines in the hallway. I couldn't wait to purchase my very first pack of cigarettes. After taking a long draw, I nearly choked to death. That was the end of my very short-lived, college smoking experiment.

Since I didn't know anyone else going to Concord, I was assigned to a third-floor suite with two complete strangers. Thankfully, my roommates, Marsha and Karen, were congenial, with extremely amiable personalities. Marsha was very tall and thin, with shoulder-length blonde hair. Karen was my height, with the deepest dimples and short, reddish hair. We looked like quite the motley crew. Although we hadn't known each other previously, the three of us got along well, sharing some fun times together.

On my second day there, over the loudspeaker, I was called to the front office. When I walked into the office, our elderly dorm mother told me I had a phone call. I held the receiver up to my ear, and said, "Hello," but no one answered. Finally, I heard an ever-so-faint reply from my sobbing mother, who was beside herself with grief. She was crushed because I hadn't called her. Since my older sister had never left home, Mom was having a real hard time losing one of her babies for the first time.

Most of the girls in our dorm didn't have a vehicle, so we spent many nights and weekends at the Sweet Shop. It was a popular little restaurant, right across the road from campus. As we hung out in the wooden booths, we devoured numerous milkshakes, root beer floats, hot dogs, fries, and burgers. The atmosphere was warm and friendly in the rustic interior, surrounded by thick, natural pine paneling. An eclectic mix of music filled the air by Joan Baez, Sam and Dave, Sly and the Family Stone, the Association, Chicago, the Beatles, the Temptations, Jefferson Airplane, Petula Clark, Bob Dylan, and many more musicians. Frequently, the music was drowned out by a rambunctious crowd. Three tunes for a quarter was a good deal, so the music continuously flowed from the jukebox.

A tradition every fall at Concord was a student-planned water shortage. The word spread that everyone was to run water and flush their toilets at a specified time. That prank worked our freshman year. We got a break from classes for a few days, allowing the enormous water tank to fill back up. I don't remember that happening any other year, but a friend of mine thinks it occurred every single year we were there.

I used to pierce people's ears back then. Once the word got out, there was a steady stream of girls coming up to our room who wanted their ears pierced. I got out my monster-size needle and sterilized it. Each girl numbed her own earlobes, one at a time, with ice cubes. The procedure was virtually painless. It often baffled me as to why these girls couldn't pierce their own ears. After a while, my free ear-piercing service became a real nuisance, and too time-consuming. I was compelled to finally put a stop to it.

Often on Saturday nights, a group of us girls went to school-sponsored dances. They were held in the lower level of the student union. What an unpleasant, painful experience that could be... waiting for someone to ask you to dance. To me, it felt as if we were on an auction block. Just like farm animals on display, the men looked over the selection to pick out the most desirable one. Of course, there were several nights when some of the wallflowers in the room were never invited to dance. That must have been extremely hurtful.

One of my favorite activities we did during our freshman year was travel on Greyhound buses to Campus Crusade for Christ rallies. They were hosted in Blacksburg, several hours away, on the campus of Virginia Tech. The meetings were held in a large conference center arena, with impressive crowds of several hundred young people. Students were in charge of the program, which included spirited worshipping through uplifting songs of praise, accompanied by talented musicians. Frequently, individuals from the audience volunteered to give moving, heartfelt testimonials. A powerful ambiance of verve filled the room. All of us came away from every rally inspired and touched by the experience.

During my freshman year, on Sunday mornings, I walked to the local Baptist church in downtown Athens. I enjoyed attending its morning worship services, and especially liked the church's old bell tower and informal architecture. The sanctuary had large, dark, wooden beams. The congregation members were extremely friendly and welcoming. I loved it when, while we were dating, one of my boyfriends accompanied me every week.

When I started college, I fully intended to become a math teacher. In high school, I had loved everything about my upper-level algebra, geometry, calculus, and trigonometry classes. They were challenging and exhilarating to me. I thrived on the competition among our class members, who were mostly boys. Being a tough competitor against the smartest guys in Stonewall was something I took seriously. At Concord, I was scheduled to have an eight o'clock math class three days a week during the first semester of my freshman year. I was having a difficult time trying to follow my professor. Obviously the man knew his subject matter, but I simply couldn't follow his soft, monotone voice.

I had the good fortune of being assigned to a wise and caring faculty advisor, Mr. Bard. After my first day of classes I went to him, explaining the difficulty I was having. He willingly found an opening for me in a design class. Although I had never taken an art class in high school, other than a lettering class, I snatched up the opportunity. As the saying goes, "The rest is history." I found my niche in Concord's art program.

For me, every studio class was a new challenge. Unlike other subjects, where you are given a book to read or problems to solve, with art assignments, you are faced with a blank paper or canvas. Everything has to come from your own imagination and creativity. A lack of dedication and originality are the biggest obstacles standing in the way between you and your ability to turn out awe-inspiring works of art.

My professor for the design class, Mr. Butcher, was the head of the art department. He proved to be one of the most enlightened individuals I ever met. Tall and lanky, with a gray flattop, he had a friendly and interesting tan face, deeply wrinkled with age. He grinned frequently as he lectured, with the widest smile, which stretched from one ear to the other.

On my first day of his class, he walked into the room and succinctly stated: "Design is one line or shape in relation to another." Ah ha! I immediately "got it." His clear introduction to design is what I ended up using many times, with my own students. I always had them do an exercise which so clearly proved his point. Mr. Butcher had met my parents a time or two. As he and I were walking across the campus one day, I was so surprised when he referred to my mother as having "a domineering personality." Those of us who love her and know her well realize what an astute observation he had made. I have always appreciated honest, intuitive people.

My previously-mentioned advisor proved to be equally as intuitive. He took such a sincere interest in my success. I never had liked any kind of history class in high school and really struggled as a college freshman with my Western Civilization class. The thickness of the textbook alone was intimidating. We were assigned hundreds of pages to read for each exam, with no idea of what would be on the test. Usually there were six to ten essay questions. Foolishly, I tried to pull several all-nighters before the exams. Of course, by the time class started, I was a complete zombie and couldn't remember anything.

Oddly enough, my advisor was also my professor for Western Civilization. I actually found his lectures to be interesting. The difficulty I had was not being able to retain what I read while studying for his tests. After class one day, he asked me to stop by his office. In an insightful move on his part, he told me that he thought I had a mental block about the subject. To my relief, he suggested that I drop his class. His advice was for me to reschedule the class for the upcoming semester. A young instructor with a more laid-back approach would be teaching that class. I gladly accepted his recommendation and was considerably more successful in the other professor's class.

Although I had excellent English teachers in high school, I fell in love with my freshman English class. I'm sure it didn't hurt that our young professor had beautiful blue eyes and Ivy League good looks. We dissected *Moby Dick* and *The Grapes of Wrath* in ways which I didn't know were possible. No symbolism, or possible symbol, was to be overlooked or unexamined. This was new and fresh to me, capturing my interest and participation with every discussion.

Swimming class was also very enjoyable for us students. For my entire life, I had loved to swim. It doesn't get any better than doing what you love and receiving college credits while doing so. After class, we often walked across the campus on frigid mornings with wet hair, which became frozen stiff.

Our geology professor was passionate about his subject. His genuine interest had a contagious effect on us students. That class proved to be one of the most interesting college experiences I had. My exuberance for the subject rubbed off on my entire family, turning my grandmother into an enthusiastic and obsessive "rockoholic." She insisted on my Dad frequently stopping the car whenever we went on trips. Then, like a giddy little girl, she excitedly searched through the rocks along the roadside for new treasures. Her rock collection became extremely impressive and popular. An energetic science teacher from a nearby school, Margaret Dennison, walked her students to Granny's house so they could see her outstanding collection.

My geology class went on many field trips, often traveling to unopened segments of a nearby interstate still under construction. We examined the strange, often diagonal striations of the massive banks of rock. They had just been exposed from blasts of dynamite and had never been seen before.

Our professor took us to the intriguing Sinks of Gandy, in Raleigh County. That was a memorable spelunking expedition. We studied the interesting and unusual rock formations inside the popular cave. Hundreds of bats hung upside down on the ceiling overhead as we explored the dark tunnel beneath them.

Of course, since I was an art major, most of my time was occupied by working on assignments for various art classes. Mr. Coiner, whom I greatly respected, was my professor for several classes. We developed a good working relationship. One day, he asked me if I thought taking drugs helped students to become more creative. I always wondered if he posed that question to me because he thought I would know the answer from my personal experience.

His lettering class was one of my greatest challenges. Everything had to be meticulously executed with perfection. I spent numerous hours in the lounge across from my dorm room working on assignments, often into the wee hours of the night. Frequently, I became so engrossed in the execution of the letters that I completely overlooked misspellings. Of course, when that happened, I would have to start all over again. A project I did for him, an Old English piece on tea-stained paper, hangs in my cousin's home. It has two angels on each side, and the verse is from the love chapter of the Bible, I Corinthians 13.

Mr. Casto's sculpture class, which I had my freshman year, was held on the back side of campus, in an old Quonset hut. That was an enjoyable experience. He gave us a tremendous amount of freedom, allowing us to sculpt whatever we wanted within assigned categories. The life-size bust I made of Mark Twain was chosen to be in my senior art exhibit. During his weaving class, I bought some special yarns from Lucy Quarrier at her family's famous Glenwood mansion on Charleston's West Side. She was such an inspirational weaver and gracious hostess, showing me all around the interesting estate. Although her home was right across the street from my high school, it remained somewhat mysterious to me. The main house was built in 1859. Behind it was a smaller house, once used for the slave quarters.

Watercolor class proved to be a fun and adventurous time. Our professor often told us, "Go paint." Fortunately, my friend Vicki, who was in the class, had her trusted vehicle, a little Vega which she fondly called "Vera." That gave us a tremendous advantage over most of the other students, who didn't have cars. They were limited to painting scenes of the campus, or whatever else was in walking distance. We spent productive afternoons at Camp Creek State Park and at a popular swimming hole, not far from campus, which had spectacular waterfalls. It was inspirational for me to paint with Vicki. She had such a natural talent for capturing rays of sunlight as they shone through the trunks and branches of the dense forest.

My family and I had some pretty horrendous trips on the West Virginia Turnpike going back and forth from home to Concord. On one such trip, when the Youngs were with us, a hard, unexpected snow came down quickly. The road was so snow- covered, we couldn't see the lines which separated the lanes. Occasionally, my parents had me ride the Greyhound bus back to school. Those trips were twice as long as traveling directly by car, since we stopped at every little town along the way. I always felt a little abandoned whenever they dropped me off at the bus depot.

During my freshman year, I decided to pledge into a sorority. I was inducted into a very prestigious sorority and became an officer my junior year. It proved to be a great, diverse group of girls. I developed close friendships with several of them, especially those who became my roommates or suitemates. Our sorority always had a good time decorating floats for homecoming at a Princeton fire station. Once a year, we hosted a nice banquet at a local motel for Parents' Weekend. My mom and dad came down every year for that. I loved it when they visited. We usually went shopping at Leggett department store in downtown Princeton, or at the new Hill's store on the outskirts of town. My father used to help me smuggle my black cat into the dorm, by hiding it under his trench coat. That was so out of character for my straight-laced dad.

Our sophomore year, several of my sorority sisters and I worked tirelessly at trying to increase our breast size. One girl had ordered a plastic gadget that resembled an old pump billow for fires. We spent so many hours pumping it between our palms, holding it precisely the right way, with elbows held high.... and with absolutely no success. Sororities and fraternities were assigned floors in the dorms so their members could room with one another and live close together. Our floor was pretty serious, with studying being the top priority. In cold weather, we got reprimanded frequently for hanging plastic bags full of food and drinks outside of our dorm windows.

One of the most exciting sorority experiences I had was participating in the annual singing competitions between all of the sororities and fraternities on campus. Our sorority had the reputation of consistently winning this event, and everyone took it very seriously. We walked over to our coach's home, in the residential part of Athens, and had numerous intensive practices. She was an extremely vivacious, competent coach, and her enthusiasm rubbed off on us. Her forte was arranging our voices to create such a wonderful blend of harmonizing. On the thrilling day of the competition, we took our places on the stage wearing identical dresses with stylish long ties. We wowed the audience and judges with a beautiful rendition of the popular Simon and Garfunkel tune "Bridge over Troubled Water." I think we surprised ourselves with how good we sounded. The intense practices and our coach's expertise had paid off. Once more, our sorority walked away with the prestigious first-place trophy.

Another year we performed a unique arrangement of the song "Hush, Little Baby, Don't You Cry." It had beautiful harmonization and sounded nothing like the common version. The experience was exactly like the first... grueling practices with our amazing coach. Holding on to the tradition, we walked away with another trophy. During my senior year, I shocked everyone by becoming a "sorority dropout." I remained friends with the girls, but simply didn't want to continue my membership.

During spring break my junior year, I went to Florida with a carload of students. We crammed into a little sports car, taking turns driving, so we could drive straight through. I vividly remember how fast everyone was traveling, and how many dead animals lined the interstate. My mother still reminds me of how offended she was, over the fact that I called to *tell* her I was going, instead of *asking* her if I could go.

The worst mayhem I ever witnessed was at a football game in Bluefield between Concord and Bluefield State. I don't remember what sparked the outburst, but I always thought it was a racial issue. Someone recently told me that it had to do with a cannon being shot off during the game. It seemed out of nowhere, men with hatred in their eyes started running through the stands and began beating one another with baseball bats. The motivation for the fight must have been brewing before the game, since all of the participants were armed with weapons.

Preparing for my senior art show was a grueling ordeal. I was living back in Charleston, doing my student teaching. My father and I set up shop in the den and started cranking out frames for all of my pieces. We picked up a variety of attractive, wooden framing stock at Evan's Lumber Yard. He and I couldn't have been more pleased with how all of the mitered corners turned out, and with the overall quality of the frames. I textured some frames with modeling plaster, then antiqued them.

Several of our friends from church attended the opening of my senior art show with us. Our drive from Charleston was one of the most treacherous rides of my life. For some reason, we had chosen to not travel the turnpike. None of us were familiar with the secondary road we were on, and near Spanishburg, the fog quickly settled in. My father was driving, and he just crept, as we made our way to Athens, trying to navigate in zero visibility. At the show, I was beaming with pride, to have many of my favorite works of art on display, hanging in the brand new gallery.

Overall, I was pleased with my college experience and am glad I went to Concord. My professors were right. They did have a more rigorous grading system than most colleges. Taking graduate classes at other colleges and universities verified their claim. One of our wise, prophetic professors kept warning us: "This is not the real world. Being in college is nothing similar to the real world." I felt very prepared after graduating from Concord as I began to face the challenges of stepping out into the "real world."

The Seventies

Cousin Joyce, sister Jean, friend Becky with me at my wedding in May of 1972.

For many baby boomers, the decade of the seventies was jammed full of multiple life-changing events. I graduated from college in 1971, immediately was hired to teach art at Spring Hill Junior High School, and married my first husband, Doug, the next year. In 1973, we moved to Columbia, South Carolina, for a year, and then returned to Charleston. I went back to teach at Spring Hill, and he and I divorced in 1977. By the end of the decade, I had become a stained glass artist.

Ironically, Doug and I met on a blind date at Marshall. My sorority from Concord went to spend the weekend in the enormous sorority house of our sister chapter at Marshall. One of the Marshall girls arranged a blind date for Doug and me. We went to a dance together, had a great time, and really hit it off. It was astonishing to us to see how much we had in common.

While Doug and I were dating, I spent most of my weekends in Huntington. He was still a student at Marshall, and I was teaching in Kanawha County. We had a close-knit group of friends and remained close to them throughout our marriage. Several of our friends had been Doug's close buddies for many years and were childhood friends from Boone County.

Our circle of friends did everything together and we were always there for each other. Continuously staying busy, we went to parties, concerts, movies, ball games, played Frisbee, and picnicked in the park, just hanging out together. We celebrated each other's weddings and new babies, and mourned together at friends' funerals.

Listening to good music was an important part of our lives. Great musicians like Bob Dylan, Bruce Springsteen, Carole King, Neil Young, Janice Joplin, Jimi Hendrix, and numerous others were always playing in the background. On many occasions, several of our friends sang and played their instruments.

Frequently, we moved each other from one house or apartment to another. We helped clean each other's new digs and often meandered through the alleys in Huntington, to see what great furniture finds there might be. Usually, at the end of each semester or summer session, departing students discarded much of their furniture. Some of the best antique chairs and other treasures were found during those alley excursions. Grocery shopping and cooking together took up much of our time. We shared some great meals at each other's homes or out at restaurants. One of our favorite places to eat was Frank's, a local sandwich shop near Marshall's campus. The owner took great pride in making the best sandwiches in town. It was one of those places where anything on the menu would taste scrumptious.

One time when there wasn't such a party atmosphere in Huntington was in November of 1971. I had driven down from Charleston for the weekend. It was the first anniversary of the horrid airplane wreck which killed most of Marshall's football team and coaching staff, as well as many prominent community members. Guys who were typically loud, rowdy party animals were silenced and grief-stricken. They were so saddened as they reminisced about friends they had lost that dreadful night. The mood was somber all weekend. There were lots of quiet reflections and heartfelt eulogizing of lost, beloved heroes.

Doug and I were the first couple in our circle of friends to get married. Several of our long-haired male friends were his groomsmen in the wedding. At the end of the rehearsal, Doug asked the guys if they all knew what they were doing. One of our close friends, Mike, who had beautiful long red hair and a great sense of humor, half-seriously and half-jokingly replied: "We were all wondering if you knew what *you* were doing." Sadly, like several other friends, he is no longer with us.

I loved our wedding ceremony. It was held in the church where I had grown up. Two white doves were released from a cage in the spacious sanctuary, when we kissed after repeating our vows. A talented flutist and student of mine played "The First Time Ever I Saw Your Face," by Roberta Flack, and "We've Only Just Begun," by the Carpenters. The church was full of family and friends. All of my bridesmaids wore identical dresses with long navy skirts which had a small floral design, and each had a different color bodice. They wore large-brimmed hats the color of their dresses and carried matching baskets of flowers. My flower girl wore a small version of their dresses. I made my Juliet-style dress and garnished it with blue pearls. The men in the wedding party wore matching black tuxedos with a subtle pattern of blue brushstrokes. Appropriately, Doug and I spent our honeymoon in the Honeymoon Cabin at Watonga State Park.

When we were newlyweds and first moved into our new home, we had a dishwasher but had forgotten to buy dishwasher soap. Being the novice housekeepers that we were, we decided it would be just fine to use laundry detergent instead. That was a huge mistake. The dishwasher immediately began spewing out soap bubbles, and in no time we had a deep layer of suds all over the kitchen floor.

The first winter after we were married, Doug and I went sleigh riding at a local golf course in my parents' neighborhood. While we were sledding, his wedding band came off. We scoured the hillside looking for it, but that was definitely like looking for a needle in a haystack. The next summer, he went back to the same course to go golfing. He decided to look over the area where he thought the ring had come off. He was shocked and in complete disbelief, when he found the missing ring. What a serendipitous moment that was.

Soon after Doug and I were married, we decided to get a pet, so we went to the local animal shelter. A beautiful, long-haired, tabby kitten, with unusually large eyes, captured our hearts. We proudly took her home and called our new baby "Missy." She immediately needed to have surgery on a hernia on her stomach. The vet had instructed us to not let her be active for a while. Before we knew it, when we arrived back home, she jumped away from us. Within seconds, she was scurrying up one of the tall pine trees in our front yard, stitches and all. Everyone loved Missy and commented on how beautiful she was and especially on how big her eyes were. For Doug's birthday one year, I drew a pastel portrait of her. He was so touched by that. We took her practically everywhere we went and were so protective of her that we often kept her on a leash. She was a perfect fit for us.

Doug and I spent quite a lot of time with his father, Hivens, who was such a patient, interesting character. He helped us refinish a rather dark and unattractive antique Victrola Talking Machine cabinet, which I had found at a local thrift shop. By the time we had finished with it, we had a handsome piece of fine furniture. The cabinet had claw feet and beautiful wood grain patterns, which were finally revealed when the thick, dark varnish was removed. Another project, which the three of us spent endless hours on, was completely overhauling an old Ford cargo van. Of course, my job was that of the official gofer and flashlight-holder. I marveled at the father's and son's uncanny ability to tackle such an overwhelming job. I certainly walked away from that experience with a new appreciation of a good mechanic, and a greater awareness of the internal parts of a vehicle.

Doug and I were notorious for being late for any occasion. With that in mind, our friends told us that their wedding in Huntington was an hour earlier than it actually was. To everyone's amusement, we still arrived late. It was such a beautiful outdoor ceremony. The highlight of their wedding was when the groom, Robbie, played and sang a beautiful rendition of the Allman Brothers' song "Sweet Melissa" to his glowing bride, Melissa.

Robbie and Melissa are one of the rare couples who have survived the test of time. We were so fortunate to have him and another friend, Steve, play their guitars and sing whenever we got together. To no one's surprise, Robbie is now a well-known, successful slide guitarist in a popular country singer's band. Steve still performs in Charleston with a local band.

One afternoon, traveling back from a Marshall football game in Ohio, Doug and I were having car trouble. We had pulled off of the highway, along the side of the interstate. It was overwhelming and heartwarming to see how many carloads of friends pulled over to offer assistance. When I was recovering from an operation after Doug and I were married, several friends drove over from Huntington to visit. One friend, Bill, brought a copy of Herman Hesse's *Siddhartha* for me to read while I was recuperating. That book remains to be one of my favorites.

In those days, most of us sported bell-bottom jeans, which often had brightly-colored patches sewn on them. Embroidered Peter Max-style designs were sometimes stitched on our jeans. We shopped for distinctive-looking clothes and accessories at local head shops. Pepperland in Charleston and the Joyful Alternative in Columbia were two of my favorites. I still have a brown linen blouse from India with wide, bell sleeves and fancy embroidered designs all over the front. Doug gave me that blouse for a Christmas gift, and I wore it for many years. Most of us had long hair, men and women alike. Our African American friends wore huge Afros. Frye boots and leather sandals were our preferred footwear. Most of us wore wide leather belts with big brass belt buckles. Many girls had tooled leather purses or suede handbags with long fringe.

One afternoon, several of my friends and I were in the large lobby of a bank in downtown Charleston. An older acquaintance of mine saw us and came up to me. He gave me the most unwarranted scolding for being dressed the way we were, in public. Although I'm sure his criticism was well-intended, we were somewhat dumbfounded by his remarks. My friends and I were confident that there was absolutely nothing wrong with the way we were dressed. To us, we were as hip and chic as anyone could possibly be.

Similarly, one of my pet peeves about some of our "hippie" colleagues was their unnecessary criticism of others. Many of these individuals literally walked around repeating their motto,

"Do your own thing." Yet, they were critical of others who didn't dress, look, or act like them. I always thought that to be so hypocritical. At a party one night, I blasted a young man who was making fun of people for wearing polyester clothing. Eventually, I convinced him that it wasn't cool to judge people by the fabric content of their clothes. Some people seemed to be so shallow in their thinking.

Like many boomers did in that era, even after we were married, Doug and I did our fair share of partying. Our friends in Huntington lived in apartments or rented older, stately homes in the residential districts. Many nights, we went party-hopping from one place to another. Their apartments were typically furnished with waterbeds, lava lamps, beaded doorways, blacklights, psychedelic posters, Indian print curtains and bedspreads, beanbag chairs, and lots of green plants. To cure the munchies in the wee hours of the morning, we frequently found our way to Ward's doughnut shop, which was open all night. When our friends from Huntington came to Charleston for concerts, they often ate dinner at our house, and then spent the night with us after the show.

At an indoor concert in the auditorium of Morris Harvey College in Charleston, a well-known man paced up and down the aisles during the concert, calling out, as one would in an emergency: "Does anyone have some speed?" A female member of the audience was crashing on too many Quaaludes. I guess his rationale was to find something to bring her back up. We never knew the outcome of that precarious situation. Sadly, during that era, so many remarkable musicians and acquaintances died from drug overdoses.

To everyone's surprise, Doug and I decided to move to Columbia, South Carolina, in 1973. Both of us had always liked going to the beach. We thought it would be great to live in closer proximity to the beaches, allowing us to take frequent trips. Ironically, after we moved, we took very few beach trips. The two of us did spend numerous Sunday afternoons swimming and rafting at beautiful

Lake Murray. We rented a nice brick house with tall pine trees in a great neighborhood.

We had a horrible experience buying a used car when we first got married. On the way home from the dealership, after we had purchased the yellow clunker, it broke down on us. The salesman couldn't have cared less. So, considering that unfortunate episode, Doug and I decided to treat ourselves in Columbia to a brand new truck...one that would be worry-free. To our dismay, our new pickup kept dying on us under any conditions, high or slow speed. Numerous times, we had to get it towed to the dealer where we purchased it. The dealer's mechanics never could find anything wrong. Finally, after many trials and tribulations, an elderly mechanic solved the mystery. Somehow, a frog had ended up in the gas tank. Every time the frog floated over and blocked the fuel line going to the engine, the engine would cut off. Once the frog was removed, we finally had ourselves a worry-free vehicle.

In Columbia, Doug had a well-paying job working for a large mortgage bank. I was unable to get a teaching job, so I worked for an unemployment office for a while. Soon after that, I got a job working in a popular art and craft store, The Dutch Door. I enjoyed working there, even though I was earning much less than my teaching salary. A regular customer at the store never did understand that I came from a separate state, not western Virginia.

One day, while I was working at the store, a young girl walked in holding the cutest little fluffy puppy with huge paws. "Does anyone want a dog?" she asked, with a pleading tone to her voice. I was sucked in immediately. The golden pup was a wonderful blend of collie and German shepherd. Doug and I called him "Opie," after the TV character. He proved to be one of the best pets anyone could possibly have. Doug taught him how to fetch a Frisbee. It was amazing to watch him catch it in midair. After he leapt so high and caught it, he immediately turned around and brought it back, eagerly awaiting the next throw. Wherever we went, Opie drew a large crowd with his impressive Frisbee-playing skills.

On a hot afternoon, while we were still in South Carolina, Doug and I attended a huge outdoor concert at a nearby college campus. Pure Prairie League was the headliner, and the main reason we wanted to go. We were a few years older than the college students who made up the vast majority of the audience. I can so vividly recall the scene. What a horrendous sight we witnessed as we looked across the grounds and maneuvered our way through the young crowd. Everyone was sitting shoulder to shoulder on spread-out blankets. We saw several kids shooting up drugs in broad daylight. Some were passed out. It was a horrible, sad scene of a human wasteland. Doug and I were both taken aback by the experience.

Two of our close friends and their beautiful Afghan Hound lived with us in Columbia for the better part of our year-long stay. The four of us enjoyed each other's company and shared a lot of good times. We usually traveled together, going back and forth from West Virginia to Columbia. As a group, we were very organized with shopping and meal preparation. Everything was precisely planned out to the most minute detail. Together, we waited out long lines at service station gas pumps during the 1973 gasoline crisis. On weekends, we often worked together, securing low-income houses which had been abandoned. The houses were part of the federal Section 235 housing program. We boarded up windows, changed door locks, and cleaned up the interiors of the houses, which had often been trashed and ransacked.

When Doug and I moved back to West Virginia from Columbia, we first lived in a little house his parents owned in Boone County. My most embarrassing moment from the seventies happened there. We had hosted a big party at our house on a Saturday night. The next morning we were sleeping in, worn out from staying up so late and entertaining guests. To our utter shock, a straight-laced, very proper relative of mine knocked on the door. She and her husband had stopped by for a surprise visit. Oh no! What were we going to do? The place was a wreck, with scattered remnants and leftovers from the party. I quickly put on some clothes, brushed my hair, then stepped out on the front porch to visit with them. There was no way I was going to let her see our house in that condition.

In the mid-seventies, through an adult education program, Doug, a friend of ours, and I got involved in a pottery class. We became close friends with our teacher, Lynn, and another student, Bob, who was quite an accomplished potter himself. We frequently got together and made delicious homemade manicotti. I became so involved in pottery that I bought myself an electric Robert Brent potter's wheel. We were living in my deceased grandparents' house at that time. My grandfather's former woodworking shop made a perfect pottery studio. As fate would have it, I got involved with stained glass by going to a pottery workshop. On the first day, it became obvious that the instructor wasn't going to do much instructing. He walked into the room and, in his burned-out hippie voice, said, "OK, man... throw pots." The next day, I switched classes and attended a stained glass session. I fell in love with that medium. The panel which I designed for that class ended up being one of my favorites and was my best-seller for many years.

The Rashid brothers gave me my first breakthrough stained glass commission. I worked with Claudette Rashid, coming up with a period design for their Chilton House restaurant. We decided upon an ivy motif which was inspired from a layer of old wallpaper she had uncovered during the building's renovation.

Doug and I divorced in 1977. Like us, most of the couples we visited with in the seventies are no longer together. On rare occasions, and in public places, I'll run into one of these old friends. Doug lives in Maryland now with his wife of many years. The last time I saw him, at a local restaurant, we greeted each other with a big hug, like old friends do. Doug and I had one of the most amicable divorces anyone could ever have. We painstakingly tried to split up our album collection. There were a lot of comments like: "No, you take that record. It was always one of your favorites."

Both of us still respected and cared about each other. As so many married couples do, we simply found ourselves going in different directions, growing apart from one another. We didn't have children, but I'm sure Doug missed our pets. Without a doubt, they missed him, too. Every time Doug came by, Opie started yelping and barking. He was as excited as any puppy gets, whenever his owner returns from a long trip.

After our divorce, becoming a single person again, I found being thrown back into the dating scene to be pretty awkward. One of the most fun times was when I dated a photographer on and off for five years. Living in rural Clay County was a welcomed change for him, from being in New York City. He enjoyed traveling the back roads of West Virginia, taking pictures of the landscapes and portraits of the locals. We shared a lot of adventurous road trips. On one trip to Pocahontas County, we happened upon Marlinton's Pioneer Days. That was a lucky find. We had the best home-cooked meal in the basement of an old red brick church.

On another trip, while we were sleeping under the stars in an old cemetery, I watched the full moon cross over the night sky. For one Fourth of July, we went to a big barn dance at the Jackson County Livestock Auction. It was at Fairplain, near Cedar Lakes, where both of us were exhibiting at the art and craft show. We were so surprised when the music started. People of all ages rose up from their seats and started dancing up and down the aisles of the bleachers. They clanged two spoons together in their palms, as they danced and kept time to the music. Everyone looked like they were having the time of their lives.

Here's to You, Dad

Dad washing his car in front of our house, while I look on, circa 1952.

My father, Russell Lee Williams, was born on September 26, 1919. He was the eleventh child born to Flora and Alfred Williams of Gassaway, West Virginia. The year 2008 marked the tenth anniversary of my father's passing. I still miss that character. He was the breadwinner and symbol of rock-solid strength in our family. At the beginning of every meal, it was my father who said grace. He was the protector who, armed with a baseball bat, bravely inched his way into the den one night when we heard a noise back there. My dad and I didn't have a lot of interaction with one another during my childhood. We had a pretty typical "Leave It to Beaver" household. He went off to work five days a week, with his bag lunch in hand, and Mom stayed home and tended to us children. Dad bowled once a week in a league from his workplace, and on very rare occasions went squirrel hunting or frog gigging with my Uncle Ralph. He was a tee-totaler, but liked his Pall Malls. I used to crack the window to get a whiff of fresh air whenever he smoked in the car.

I do remember Dad spanking me at the end of our standoffs we had practically every night after dinner. I hated white milk and refused to drink it. Nearly every night, he set the timer for thirty minutes. When the timer went off and the milk was untouched, he carried out his Gestapo routine of putting me over his lap and spanking me with the back side of a hairbrush. Every time he said: "This hurts me more than it hurts you." Of course, I never bought that. It was always a blessing to me when the Haynes family came to our house for dinner. One of their daughters, Mary, deliberately sat beside me at the table so she could do me a favor and drink my milk. I got some temporary relief with chocolate-flavored paper straws. The same was true for Nestle's powder and malt-flavored Ovaltine. No spankings took place when we had those items in stock, or if we had company.

Upon reading this, my sister, who is three years older than I, reminded me of my most frequently-used trick to win this standoff. I acted like I was drinking the milk, and held it in my mouth until I carried my dishes into the kitchen. Then, with no one watching, as I rinsed off my dishes, I spit the milk into the sink. I don't think my parents ever caught on to that one. They did eventually discover, however, that I was hiding my milk behind the toaster, which sat on a little side table within reach of where I sat at the dining table.

I only remember hearing my dad cry one time. Back when we were young, men weren't supposed to cry. My parents were serving on a pulpit committee, which was scouting for a new minister. The committee members had traveled to hear one potential candidate preach at his home church. They were impressed with him and his style of preaching. The committee voted to invite him to come to Emmanuel for a trial sermon. The congregation members weren't pleased with the preaching candidate and voted him down. As chairman of the pulpit committee, it fell on Dad's shoulders to tell him the outcome of the vote. I can only imagine how painful that must have been for both men.

While we were in grade school, our dad did two things in particular which made my sister and me feel special. On the day before Easter one year, he drove down to the nearby florist, Valley Cut Flower, by Litton's Shoe Shop at the foot of our hill. He bought us pink carnation corsages with decorative little bees on them. We were so honored with his surprise and felt like little princesses wearing them. When our family was vacationing in Florida one summer, we were looking in a nice Oriental gift shop. Dad walked over to the glass showcase where my sister and I were and said: "Both of you can pick out anything in this showcase for a souvenir." That was so out of character for our dad. Jean and I looked at each other in disbelief. My little porcelain Japanese figurine which I picked out still sits upon his cushion in his colorful silk kimono. He is on display in my china cabinet and reminds me of how special I felt that day. We always hit up Dad for change when we stopped for gas on trips. He carried a white, rubber, football-shaped coin holder in his pocket, which he squeezed open, then dug out some coins for us.

While my sister and I were in grade school, for a Christmas present one year, Mom gave our dad a paint-by-number set of two birds on two separate canvases. He spent endless hours at the dining room table, painting the intricate little sections of the pictures. I can still smell the tiny plastic jars of oil paints, which came with the kit. We never knew if he enjoyed painting the bird pictures or if he even liked how they looked. Nevertheless, he kept at it until he finally finished them. They hung in our living room for many decades. Mom was going to throw them out several years ago, and for nostalgic purposes, I took one of them.

When I came home for visits from college, Dad frequently told my mom to get him more coffee. Women usually waited on men back then, so that was pretty typical behavior. The newly- liberated gal that I had become suggested that he get it himself. I bet he regretted sending me off to school many times, with that kind of changed attitude and behavior.

One of the most difficult situations for Dad to deal with was when my mother's aunt moved in with them. It was a long and difficult year. She had lived out of state most of her adult life, so we rarely heard from her. As a woman in her seventies, she was getting too old to continue working. She didn't have children or the wherewithal to get her own place. I had offered for her to live with me, but Mom didn't think that was a good idea. So, in no time, my parents had given up their bedroom for a relative, whom of course they loved, but didn't really know very well.

Accustomed to working as a live-in nanny for wealthy families in California, she was used to a ritzy lifestyle. She could be pretty persnickety at times, too. For instance, she insisted that her cold drinks be served with three ice cubes, no more, no less. Understandably, my parents were overwhelmed with the situation, especially Dad. To have their privacy completely taken away was simply too much. Dad would say: "I can't believe she calls our house her home." One afternoon, he showed up at my front door, saying he just needed to get away. After my aunt had lived with them for about a year, Mom was able to secure a nice low-income apartment for her in a senior housing development.

Dad retired after working as an accountant at the DuPont chemical plant for more than forty years. I threw a big surprise retirement party at my house for him. Many of our close family friends and relatives came. When he and Mom came through the back door to my kitchen, we excitedly yelled out, "Surprise!" In a somewhat displeased tone he said: "You're not supposed to give parties for people just for retiring." Eventually he calmed down and enjoyed himself. He was never comfortable being in the limelight.

Dad soldering on a glass commission at the Williams Stained Glass Studio, 1983.

The timing for his retirement couldn't have been more perfect. He was bored and needed something to do. I was taking a break from teaching to open a stained glass studio. So, in the early eighties, for six years, we worked together at the shop. Every day, he sat at the table in the kitchen area, spending much of the day consumed with paperwork. He was the real stalwart of the shop, mowing grass, shoveling snow, waiting on customers, cutting and soldering glass panels, making bank deposits, helping to teach students, and anything else that needed to be done. A person really gets to know someone, working so closely together. What a remarkable work ethic he had.

He loved it when I had my infant sons at the shop with us. When they were newborns, I kept them in padded laundry basket "cribs" on the countertop right beside us. Eventually, they were moved into a playpen, where they became quite the main attraction for many of our customers. I'm positive several people stopped by regularly just to see the babies. Over the years at the studio, we constructed hundreds of glass panels for homes, restaurants, churches, and hospitals. We hired several talented local glass artists to help with our workload when we had more than we could handle. One of our employees, Evelisse, was from Puerto Rico and occasionally treated us to delicious homemade flan. These days, I like to swing by Saint Francis hospital, to see the two large panels of tranquil landscapes we created for their chapel, out of Blenko glass. Other times I like to eat at the Little India restaurant and look at another favorite commission in their stairwell, of a fireman climbing a ladder. I designed that for the former Firehouse #4 restaurant.

My dad was a deacon at the church I grew up in and was pretty straight-laced. I was shocked when I found *Playboy* magazines he had bought at a yard sale and had stashed in the back room of the studio. His eyes nearly popped out of his head one afternoon when a friend of mine, Janet, was visiting us at the shop. She pulled down the back of her shorts to show off her new, beautiful butterfly tattoo on her behind. Dad didn't know how to handle that one.

I can hardly believe we did this, but when we had the shop, Dad and I flew to a world-wide stained glass convention in New York City. We were bursting with pride to hear some of the most famous glass artists in the world praising the rich colors, superb quality, and unique texture of Blenko sheet glass. The Blenko family and their workers have hand-blown this incredible glass for generations. Their world-renowned factory is in Milton, West Virginia, and was only thirty minutes from our studio. We bought a lot of Blenko glass for commissions, when clients requested it and were interested in quality, without having to be restricted by a tight budget.

The New York City convention ran for several days. One day we played hooky from the sessions and went on a sightseeing tour. Since it was the first trip to the Big Apple for both of us, we couldn't resist the temptation. We took in the usual sightseeing stops, such as the Statue of Liberty and the Empire State Building, and my favorite, Chinatown. Dad had always been extremely frugal, so it surprised me when he took me to an upscale restaurant one night for dinner. He said: "Order anything you want off of the menu." To justify this quirky behavior, he shrugged his shoulders and said: "You only live once." On our own, we walked around town and shopped at Macy's. We witnessed what were probably typical scenes for New York, but still strange to us. An angry cop was screaming at the group of onlookers gathered around a cyclist who had just been hit by a car. No one would admit that he or she witnessed the accident, and that outraged the policeman. We were shocked to see an elderly homeless lady squat down in the middle of a bustling downtown street and relieve herself.

One of the funniest incidents at the shop with my dad involved a pizza delivery guy. We taught evening stained glass classes at the studio. I always suggested to our students that they carry their glass projects back and forth from their homes to the shop in pizza boxes. One night, a young man walked in the front door with a pizza box in his hand. Dad instructed him to set up at one of the work tables. The baffled man's confused expression was priceless. He was simply trying to deliver a pizza to one of our students. We had a good time teaching hundreds of students and seeing what fine glass panels they constructed.

Dad had Alzheimer's for about five years before he died. The best thing about that was he developed a sense of humor like we had never seen before. He frequently laughed at himself when he bungled his speech, although I'm sure he was really frustrated over it. We still laugh about how he puffed on his french fries in public, as if they were cigarettes. One year, my eldest son ended up in a hospital in Charlotte, North Carolina, for an emergency appendectomy. We had been on our way to vacation at Myrtle Beach. Dad walked up to the lady at the information desk in the lobby of the hospital and asked to check into a room. He thought he was in a motel lobby. Sometimes at restaurants, he would go to the restroom, and then sit back down in a completely different area, far from where we were.

The worst thing about his Alzheimer's was the realization that we could never again have a meaningful, coherent conversation with the old Dad we once knew. He would converse with us, but most of his words came from anything he could read at the time, such as magazines, billboards, and signs. Dealing with Alzheimer's is so very difficult, because the person is physically with you, but not with you emotionally or mentally.

Mom had her hands full in dealing with Dad for a number of years. She often called to solicit help from my sister and me. Frequently he pilfered around the house, trying to pack up various items so he could "go home." I think those were the hardest days, because he couldn't be calmed down and was into everything. Dad died after a short bout with pneumonia. He had been nonresponsive in the hospital and nursing home for more than a month. I always thought that was God's way of preparing us for his death. Even though he has been gone for more than twelve years, I still think about him every day. Here's to you, Dad. Miss you.

"Go to Class."

I was destined to be a teacher. There were many teachers on both sides of my family. After high school, I went to college with the intention of becoming a teacher, and never considered any other profession. When I first started teaching, one of my students said: "My father told me, 'Those who can, do, and those who can't, teach.' " What nonsense! I have always believed that teachers hold one of the most significant roles in our society. Many great teachers have had a tremendous influence on me. A plaque, which one of my students gave me, hangs in my home. It reads: "The influence of a good teacher can never be erased."

Right after graduating from college in 1971, I went for my first job interview. It was for an art teacher position at Spring Hill Junior High in Kanawha County. Walking down the hallway towards the office, the vice principal said to me, "Go to class." That's how young I looked. With hair down to my waist, a short navy skirt, and a red, white, and blue striped top, I probably did look just like another student. To my delight, I got the job, which paid a little over $7,000 a year. Like many new teachers do, I thought if I were nice to the students, they would be nice to me. It simply doesn't work that way. Once my students got out of control, there was no turning it around. Riding out the first semester and trying to survive it was the only option I had. When the second semester finally began, I was ready for it. I started out with a very strict regimen in my classes, which worked wonders. During that time, I was shopping with a boyfriend and we ran into one of my students. "She's a drill sergeant," he complained to my date, as if he were tattling on me. That was one of the best compliments I could have received.

The worst problem during my first year was students arguing over an Elvis Presley record. I had brought in a small record player to play music during class. It never dawned on me that it would be the source of such heated emotions. The boy who had brought in the Elvis record was a big, rugged-looking "creeker." He was ready to punch out another student who didn't want to hear his music. A similar problem which I didn't anticipate was having vigilante students. One boy in particular, J. D., was very protective and confronted anyone who he thought was being disrespectful towards me. Looking back on it, this probably helped me gain acceptance by some of the rougher kids, because J. D. was so revered by them.

Even though I didn't have the greatest classroom control my first semester, overall, teaching in those days was so very different than it is today. If students misbehaved, teachers simply had to threaten them with being sent to the office. They had heard the loud, intimidating crack of the vice principal's paddle too many times to know they didn't want to feel it. Nowadays, there aren't really any effective consequences for bad behavior. There is such irony in suspending students for skipping school. That's exactly what they wanted in the first place.

One year at Spring Hill, the worst problem I had all year was a student saying, "This sucks," about an assignment I had given him. In retrospect, that's pretty remarkable, compared to all of the problems teachers face today. In recent years, at several schools where I taught, teachers were physically assaulted by students. At one school, a student who had shoved a teacher ended up being honored on the "Superlatives" page in the yearbook as "Class Clown." I never understood why we honored students with unacceptable behavior.

Teachers deal with so many issues today: having to defend every word or action in front of belligerent parents, inappropriate student attire, kids wanting to text on their cell phones, apathetic student attitudes, students running the halls or skipping classes, truancy, and blatant disrespect from students and parents. None of those issues were commonplace when I began teaching in the 1970s. Now, they are so prevalent. Sometimes it is nearly impossible for teachers to teach the students who want to learn, because they are too busy browbeating disruptive students.

Before I retired, I was exhausted from telling girls to pull up their tops, which were revealing too much cleavage. The problems with boys' attire were drooping pants which showed their boxer shorts and T-shirts with inappropriate, offensive pictures and sayings about women, drugs, or alcohol. At one school, all of the male self-proclaimed rednecks carried camouflage baseball hats in their hands all day. They tried to put them on whenever no one was looking. At another school, "bling" was big. Boys swaggered down the hallways wearing expensive, flashy necklaces. For several years, at that same school, boys tried to wear one pants leg rolled up, to indicate they were gang members.

Since Spring Hill was my first school, I didn't realize how fortunate we were to have a staff which got along so well and worked so effectively together. After teaching at several other schools, I appreciated how special our faculty was. At a few of those schools, colleagues would often remark: "I can tell you have taught at a school where everyone got along." Spring Hill had a teachers' lunchroom, which was packed every day. I believe that contributed to the staff's cohesiveness and camaraderie. A staff which ate together also proved to be unique. At my other schools, teachers mostly ate in their rooms or in little cliques.

Many of us at Spring Hill were young teachers, close in age. We shared an enthusiasm for teaching which sometimes dwindles over the years. I spent many weekends working in my classroom. Some friends and I spent several nights building two wooden potter's wheels for my students. My fellow art teacher and I drove to

Cedar Heights clay factory in Ohio on our personal days to purchase inexpensive dry clay for our classes.

Some of my best friends are from Spring Hill. One friend, Jesse, frequently stopped by my room after school. He and I philosophized about religion and other weighty topics. Mary Lou offered words of wisdom with her refreshing approach to life. Occasionally another friend, Sally, would come by my room at lunchtime, and say: "Let's go out to eat. I just need to get out of here a while." Three of us, Martha, Nancy, and I, became very close and shared similar life-changing experiences. Our classrooms were across the hall from each other. We were a source of strength for one another, and a shoulder to cry on. In a short period of time, all three of us went through divorces. On weekends and over the summers, we visited in each other's homes and went on trips together. They both moved out of state, but we still keep in touch.

Our vice principal, Dick, wanted me to teach him how to sew. We stayed after school, and he was an eager student. He made a handsome, pastel yellow, polyester leisure suit, which he proudly wore to school. In those days, wearing leisure suits was the newest, hot fad. During that time, I taught evening adult education sewing classes. One year, in addition to teaching art, I taught a cooking class. My students teased me about teaching nutrition to them, yet walking in every morning with my breakfast of a Dr. Pepper and a package of Nabs. I had students make their favorite recipes for the class. Bobby Plants' cobbler recipe is still one of my favorites.

I have fond memories of many Spring Hill students. Since I was so young, there was quite a bit of hero worshiping going on. One student, Connie, came up to me after Christmas break my first year. She excitedly said: "Look, Miss Williams, I got a purse for Christmas exactly like yours." Jesse and I believed that one student, Marc, was an angel in disguise. He was tall, handsome, and very athletic, but always took up for the underdogs. One little shy boy, Charles, who was made fun of by several students, came up to me every ten minutes to tell me what time it was. He was so proud of his brand new watch. Marc befriended him in and outside of class, not caring one bit what the other kids thought.

I took two students to visit the studio of Taylor Jones, a well-known, talented young caricaturist working for *The Charleston Gazette*. He was one of several presenters who spoke to my classes about their careers as professional artists. We were honored to visit his East End studio. One of those students, Mark Wolfe, is now a successful graphic artist in Charleston and still keeps in touch with Taylor Jones.

My first husband and I moved to Columbia, South Carolina, in 1973. When I was inquiring about a teaching position in their public schools, I was told: "We've filled our ratio of white teachers." That was my first experience of being discriminated against because of my race. I worked at a local art store, which only paid minimum wage. It was such a shock and disappointment when I received my first paycheck. The earnings were a fraction of what my teaching salary was. We were only in Columbia for a year. When we returned home, luckily, I was able to get my teaching job back at Spring Hill. Having to work at minimum wage gave me a newfound appreciation for my teaching position.

The 1974 school year got off to a tumultuous start. The infamous Kanawha County Textbook Controversy had been brewing over the summer. The furor escalated when schools opened in the fall. Many parents and local preachers, mostly Christian fundamentalists, were against some of the textbooks which had been adopted by the school board. They claimed the books undermined Christianity and patriotism. When school began, thousands of parents kept their children home. Picket lines, often unruly, were set up at county schools and businesses. On September 13, Superintendent Kenneth Underwood closed schools for four days, saying: "There's apparently no way that we can have law and order. Mobs are ruling and we're extremely afraid someone will get hurt."

Radical book protestors continued to cause mayhem throughout the county. They shut down businesses and some public transportation. Schools were vandalized with dynamite and Molotov cocktails. A reporter from CBS and his crew were attacked. School buses were blasted with gunshots. Parents who kept their children in school had their cars firebombed. Fights broke out at picket lines and at a Kanawha county school board meeting. Coal miners and truck drivers held a wildcat strike. Protestors shut down mines in four neighboring counties. Following several months of heated debates, normalcy finally returned after a compromise was reached over the textbooks. Many people still believe that the controversy was racially motivated.

I continued teaching at Spring Hill for several more years. With my renewed appreciation for my job, those years were some of my best. One year, I was so prepared for my classes on the first day. Just as I was going over my class rules during first period, a cricket hiding in one of the cabinets started chirping, drowning out my voice. The kids thought that was hilarious. I was completely humiliated. I often see former Spring Hill students in public places. Many of them look nearly my age. After all, I was only seven years older than some of them.

Working on stained glass commissions started consuming my energy, so I needed to devote all of my time to that. After the first semester in 1980, I quit teaching and opened a full-time studio. To turn in my resignation, I went to the personnel director's office. As I waited to see her, I was a little apprehensive about what her reaction might be. When I gave her my reason for resigning, she leaned towards me and said: "I wish I had found some kind of niche like that." She couldn't have been more supportive.

My father and I operated the studio for six years. After closing it in 1986, I took a teaching position in a center for gifted students at Elkview Elementary. Teaching gifted children was a challenging assignment. My coworkers and I taught kindergarten through sixth grades, with each grade coming from six different feeder schools, once a week. Most of the students were excited about learning and were very motivated. All of them loved to ride the public transportation buses for a day trip to the Charleston library. They researched topics of their choice for independent study reports. We took them on many organized nature study trips, often taking the entire day.

At our center, an arrangement of stations, which students rotated around, worked exceptionally well for most age groups. The children were especially fond of problem-solving skills, computer programming, creative writing, and performing skits. I brought in a trunk of various costumes and accessories. The imaginative children impressed us with their original plays. We had quite the menagerie at the center: zebra finches, colorful betas, hermit crabs, and a spoiled gray and white Dutch rabbit, "Bun-Bun." Whenever we were quiet and near his cage, he liked to get everyone's attention. He pulled off a big piece of newspaper from the bottom of his cage. As he ran around the cage, holding the paper in his mouth, it covered his face like a mask. The kids laughed hysterically every time he did that.

Our students were invited to perform ongoing puppet shows for the Special Olympics. The director wanted the participants to have something to do while they waited for their individual events to take place. We ended up performing a show, and it was a big hit with the Special Olympians, their teachers, and parents. With grant money, I was able to purchase several well-crafted, large puppets. For many more years, my students from three different schools continued the performances.

After being at the center for three years, an art opening came up at Spring Hill. Accepting that position eliminated the need to continue taking gifted classes, allowing me to spend more time with my young sons. At the beginning of the year, it seemed like I had made the worst mistake of my life. I had been out of mainstream public education for nine years. During that time, drastic changes had taken place in our public school system. Students' behavior wasn't even similar to what I was used to from the late seventies. I was saddened and in complete disbelief at what an overwhelming transformation had taken place over those nine years. Most of my students didn't accept me at first. I had to start all over and reestablish myself at the same school where I had once been such an effective teacher. The two years which followed were much better. Although there were a few exceptions, overall, students' work ethic and behavior never reached the level that my former students had nine years earlier.

In March of 1990, West Virginia's largest teachers' union went on strike. Teachers across 80 percent of the state's counties participated in the strike. At Spring Hill, several teachers stood out in the parking lot with picket signs, while others walked by them, reporting to work. I joined the statewide march at the capitol, armed with my protest sign. Low teachers' pay was the main motivation behind the strike. It divided faculties and created hostilities against those who crossed the picket lines. I didn't witness that problem at Spring Hill, but it was very evident at other schools. More than twenty years later, some teachers still hold grudges against those "cowardly scabs."

The county school board voted to close Spring Hill in 1992. I was on the front lines fighting that cockamamie proposal. It didn't make sense to close our school and bus the students to a much older school. Eighteen years after the closing of Spring Hill, former faculty members still get together for annual Christmas dinners. That's pretty rare. Some faculties I taught with never got together for any social events.

Since my school closed, I was sent to teach at Stonewall Jackson Junior High, an inner-city school. The building was my former high school. It was comforting to return to my old stomping grounds. The way Stonewall students embraced me was beyond my wildest dreams. They were extremely receptive to someone who took a genuine interest in them. The West Side community was so supportive of the arts. I had several talented students at Stonewall who were really into drawing. Three boys, Corey, Andrew, and Roosevelt came to my room practically every morning, to show me what they had drawn the night before.

There were many students whom I felt so close to at Stonewall. I enjoyed being one of the sponsors in the Natural Helpers program. At our retreat, one enlightening activity we did was an auction, where students were given fake money and could bid on intangible items. It was heartbreaking when students bid all of their money on items such as, "Live with both parents" or "Change my appearance." On a retreat the following year, the students were so adamant about holding the auction again, that I drove back to my home to get the auction lists and money.

One day at Stonewall, my students were talking too much and not working. As a disciplinary measure, I had them read from our textbooks. I instructed each student to read aloud as we went around the room. To my astonishment, more than half of those kids couldn't read. I was so upset to have embarrassed them. One of the saddest situations at Stonewall was when a student confided in me and told me that her parents were prostituting her out every night. I contacted numerous agencies about her situation. No one would help that poor child. It was as if they didn't want to get involved or even believe her. One individual told me I had to prove that this was happening. That ordeal left me so disillusioned and disgruntled with bureaucracy.

On a chilly afternoon, a student in my class kept opening one of the windows overlooking a parking lot. Finally, I said to him, "Close the blasted window." The class got real quiet, and Randall, a rather shy student, asked in the most serious voice, "Is that a cussword?" I had to discipline another student for continuously pilfering around the room. She was autistic and was brilliant, but didn't have much common sense. If I turned my back on her, she tried to chew the steel wool. To discipline her one day, I called her parents and kept her after school for an hour. When the hour was up, she asked me if she could stay after school with me every day. So much for the effectiveness of that punishment.

One of my Stonewall students referred to me as, "The art teacher with an attitude." Sometimes you had to have an attitude to survive being there. One difficult thing about teaching at Stonewall was keeping up with the African American girls' names. In one class, I had a Shanika, Sharika, and Shamika. During my last two years there, I supervised the in-house suspension room two periods each day. That was a godsend to me, giving me plenty of time to grade papers or to work one-on-one with needy students.

After teaching at Stonewall for five years, I took a teaching position closer to home, at Elkview Middle School. It felt somewhat like a homecoming, since I had taught with several teachers on their staff before. As in other schools, once students got to know me, teaching became much easier. I especially liked the enthusiasm of the sixth graders. Students rotated around to eight different related arts classes. Whether or not they wanted to, everyone was required to take art. At the beginning of one year, a student named Lynn asked me: "Are we going to study Claudie Moneet this year?" At that point, I knew I needed to do better at teaching my students about famous artists. With the help of my son Ian, and the expertise of our county's technology gurus, Connie and Becky, I was able to design a computer lesson on famous artists. My students enjoyed using that program for many years. While teaching at the middle school, over two summers, I fulfilled my lifelong goal of earning a master's degree.

Every morning at the middle school I had hall duty for half an hour. I got so tired of breaking up fights. These days, that's a no-win situation for educators. You get accused of manhandling students if you grab them to break it up, and you get accused of not protecting students if you don't. The worse problems in class came from kids who were just waiting to become old enough to drop out of school. They would constantly misbehave, just to get suspended.

Being the Forensics coach at the middle school for five years was a fun experience. I got to work with many talented students on our team and enjoyed watching the incredible performances of students from all over the county. They competed in the poetry, prose, dynamic duo, humorous interpretation, impromptu, and sales categories. It always saddened me to see how many parents never came to watch their children perform.

In 1994, I accepted an art position at Herbert Hoover High School in our community. That was where I would finish my teaching career. For the first four years, most of my students knew me from the middle school. This was a tremendous advantage. They knew what to expect from me and what I expected from them. Like most things in life, everything is a trade-off. On the high school level, for the most part, students in the advanced art classes were at least interested in the subject. However, I was not a fan of block scheduling. No one has a ninety-minute attention span.

At Hoover, three of my favorite things I did with students were the Red Cross blood drives, Natural Helpers, and painting murals on a local bank's windows for Christmas. I was so touched to see how brave students were, in donating blood. Our Natural Helpers had retreats at Camp Virgil Tate once a year. After one retreat, several students developed a rash all over their faces. We never found out exactly what caused it, but burning poisonous wood in the bonfire was a possibility. During those retreats students got into such revealing discussions. A few years ago, they concluded that the biggest problem at our school was that no one was practicing abstinence...no one. Spending a day with students at the bank was such a nice break from the classroom.

The first few years at Hoover, I shared a small art room with my entertaining co-worker, John. After seeing what other high schools had for their art facilities, we were determined that our students should have the same provisions. With the support of our principal, school board, superintendent, and the Kanawha County Schools architect, we succeeded in getting a state-of-the-art facility built. The board carpenters custom built for us an amazing, fifteen-foot-long, sturdy wooden work table.

Once we had some space, my students designed and constructed stained glass windows for our school's library and several classrooms. We got two grants for the project and purchased distinctive Blenko glass. In the new facility, I held after-school stained glass classes for faculty members. A couple of teachers made very impressive windows for their homes. Visiting with coworkers in a stress-free atmosphere was so much fun. Several of us teachers also enjoyed each other's company as we walked around the track after school practically every day.

My favorite story from Hoover is about a loveable, laid-back, good ole boy. He was tall and lanky, handsome, very popular, and a standout athlete. In my class, he was a real overachiever, excelling above everyone else. One day, he told me, in a matter-of-fact and serious tone: "I know I'm not the brightest tool in the shed." All I could do was smile. With his spot-on statement, he had done a superb job of making his point.

During my last semester, my advanced class was perhaps the most talented group of students I ever had. There were so many students with incredible talent. They were such a pleasant change from the lackadaisical kids who were content with their mediocre work. These students were not only talented, but were also teachable. All of the great art students I have had always sought out my advice and opinion. Others thought they knew everything and were too good to improve. It pleases me that many of my former students have pursued art as a profession. Several more are currently enrolled in higher-education art programs.

Before I retired, I had several very gratifying experiences unfold at school. Lindsey, a talented former student I had in my classes for many years, visited me one day. She was taking a drawing class at West Virginia State University. "Ms. Williams, there are kids in my class who don't know how to do things that you taught us in the middle school," she said in a rather complaining tone. Another talented former student, J. D., was enrolled in a drawing class at Marshall. A friend of his delivered this message to me: "J. D.'s professor in his drawing class told him: 'I can tell your high school had a strong art program.' J. D. smiled and replied: 'I had the same art teacher for seven years.'" After hearing that, I could retire with complete satisfaction. I had accomplished my long-term goal of preparing my students with the skills they needed to be successful in future endeavors.

These days, I see many former students in the news, usually being arrested for various crimes, some more serious than others. Most of the time, I am not one bit surprised. On several occasions, students had predicted that they would end up in prison. Other times, students are in the news for their achievements. I enjoy seeing former students out in public. More than likely we exchange hugs. That's one of the things I miss about teaching…getting so many hugs every day.

Over my long teaching career, I have come up with several observations:

1. A caring, supportive principal is worth his or her weight in gold. I had many accommodating principals who were proud of the art program and strived to maintain its integrity. Others couldn't have cared less, because after all… "It's just art."

2. Even more important is an effective vice principle. The good ones are invaluable in handling discipline problems.

3. The emotional baggage some kids show up with every day is unbelievable. I had many students whose parents were incarcerated or were so messed up on drugs, that they couldn't take care of themselves, much less their kids. Many students never had an adult at home who modeled morality.

4. Students who come from bad home lives, yet have the resiliency to rise above their situations, are the fortunate ones.

5. By far, the overwhelming majority of educators I worked with were teachers because they wanted to make a difference in children's lives.

6. The art of conversation is a dying art among many young people. Towards the end of my career, several students were completely non-communicative. For so many kids, their only means of talking with others is through texting.

7. For a growing number of young people, honesty is no longer a virtue they value. Some kids could look you in the eye and lie about something, without any feelings of wrongdoing or remorse.

8. Future teachers should get a master's degree as early as possible. It's one sure way to increase your salary. If you get a master's degree in an area which will give you other options besides being a classroom teacher, it may provide a much-needed change some day.

9. When, as a teacher, you start praying for snow days more than your students do... it's time to retire.

10. Out of thousands of teaching memories I have over thirty-four years, the good far outweigh the bad.

Back to the Land

In the early seventies, I was completely enthralled with the back-to-the-land movement. My first husband, Doug, and I regularly visited several friends who had bought farmland in Lincoln County, West Virginia. The song, "Blue Sky," by the Allman Brothers, was popular back then, and that tune seemed so fitting as we drove down a dusty, country road to visit one day. We had looked at numerous pieces of land, but it was extremely difficult to find nice, affordable rural property near Charleston. After Doug and I moved back from Columbia, South Carolina, we got our first taste of gardening, in Boone County, on property his parents owned. A pleasant, elderly old-time gardener lived right beside our rather large garden plot and frequently came outside to oversee how we were doing. He liked to give us his advice.

"Those beans won't do any good if you plant them now. There's going to be a full moon tonight." That was the kind of old wives' tales he used to warn us with. We ignored everything he said, not being convinced that the waxing and waning of the moon had much to do with successful gardening. He frequently remarked: "I can't believe your garden is doing so well." Our first year, we planted 150 tomato plants and canned most of what we harvested. The garden was right beside the Coal River, so we made numerous trips up and down the steep bank, toting heavy buckets of water. Our moms helped us freeze broccoli, which we had in abundance one year. The worst part of that process was picking out the little black caterpillars, which could be so well hidden in the florets.

In the 1960s and 1970s, thousands of baby boomers from all over the country settled in West Virginia during the back-to-the-land movement. Some of these people stayed for a brief number of years, others for a longer time, and, more than forty years later, many have become permanent residents. A number of these new immigrants were artists and craftspeople who bought very isolated property. Being self-employed and living off the land, they didn't need to rely on a job away from home.

That movement was well-documented in news stories and magazines. An article in a popular women's magazine in the mid-seventies documented the story of a potter from New England and his family. They had moved to West Virginia and built their secluded home and pottery studio in rural Webster County. These days, they are prominent members of their community. He uses wood-fired kilns to fire his signature pots and has become one of our state's most distinguished and revered potters. His wife is an established attorney in the region.

When I started doing the craft shows circuit as a glass artist, I met many back-to-the-landers from the community of Chloe in beautiful Calhoun County. One family, with three kids, used to pitch a teepee in the field at the popular Mountain State Art and Craft Fair at Cedar Lakes. They camped out in it for the duration of the five-day fair. Many of the fairgoers were fascinated with the "hippies" living in the teepee. Some of the families I met have stood the test of time and still live in Chloe. Others moved back to the urban landscapes from whence they came, and the rest are scattered across the country.

It seemed like many of the people we personally knew who tried living off the land had to lower their standard of living to such extremes, that it wasn't sustainable. Others simply had to move back to where there was lucrative employment. I think some were so isolated that after a while, they missed the interaction with other people. Several of our close friends sold attractive rustic homes, which they had taken much pride in building.

After Doug and I divorced, I still had a deep-rooted yearning to live in the country. I must have inherited my ancestors' desire to live in rural West Virginia and farm the land. Continuing my pursuit for the perfect place, I finally discovered a beautiful valley farm, with eighteen acres, half an hour from Charleston. Since I had looked so long and hard for property, I purchased it, even though I was single. Peter and I would marry several years later and move to the farm, with our two young sons. Part of the eighteen acres was a nice big, flat bottom. The farm was shaped like a huge amphitheater. It had many apple trees and a gorgeous, tall, ancient cedar tree with flowering wisteria wrapped around the trunk. The old Jenny Lind house was literally built on the ground, and wasn't much, to say the least. There were several great spots for a house site. We thought the old house would make an adequate workshop after a new home was built.

Before we moved to the farm, I took our oldest son, Michael, out there with me on day trips. He played in his little walker on wheels while I worked on the house. The original home was a one-room structure made of fifteen-inch-tall, hand-hewn square logs. I tore off the old pieces of Sheetrock, which the former owners had nailed up to cover the logs. One generation's notion of modernizing the log area was completely erased in a matter of weeks. During this process, I uncovered multiple layers of old, brittle newspapers, dating back to more than a hundred years. They had been used as insulation, covering the enormous square logs.

Right before we moved in, the farmhouse was broken into, not making for such a pleasant welcome. We didn't have much inside the house at the time, but all of our belongings of any value were stolen. A gasoline-powered weed-wacker, lawnmower, and pump for the well were the things we needed and regretted losing the most. In the spring of 1985, we finally moved out there. I'm sure our families were questioning our sanity. Wanting to move out on a farm with two babies in diapers and no indoor plumbing was incomprehensible to them.

Since the inside of the house still needed quite a bit of work, all four of us slept outside on the front porch every night. We listened to the spring peepers, who were part of such a soothing lullaby, to fall asleep to each evening. Frogs and toads, owls and other night birds, and the peepers all contributed to a beautiful nighttime serenade. We resembled boot camp cadets, with our three beds lined up side by side. The porch had been open, but we enclosed it with wire screening so we wouldn't get eaten up by mosquitoes. It was actually a pleasant and memorable experience.

To start each day, we woke up to a delightful symphony from an incredible mix of numerous species of wild birds. Every morning, a team of mallard ducks quacked noisily as they waddled down the steep path from the road to the creek just a few feet away. In front of us, on the big, flat bottom blanketed with fog, we watched the curious fox making his rounds every morning. He trotted through the tall grasses and cattails along the edge of the field, with his nose held high, sniffing for any scents. Our get-out-of-bed call each morning was from our babysitter, Sondra, a teenage neighbor who lived on the next farm up the hollow from us. When we saw her walking down the path, we knew it was time to get up. Having her babysit worked out perfectly for everyone. She was happy to earn the extra money, and we were thrilled to have her, since she was so good with our boys. We continued to sleep out on the porch until the next fall, when it became too cold to stay outside.

I worked on stained glass windows in the empty log room of the house. My father and a friend of ours, Maurice, often helped me. Both men were such valuable assistants. We constructed one of our largest church commissions in that room. To be able to work on my glass, yet have my young sons nearby, was such a luxury. I could play with them whenever I took breaks and was right there if they needed me.

The first major improvement Peter and I tried to make to the farm was to have a septic tank installed. We hired our neighbor to dig a hole for it beside our house. To our grave disappointment, as soon as he dug it, the hole immediately filled up with water. That was the first of many setbacks which would follow, preventing us from making improvements to the place. The big waterhole became our permanent frog pond, surrounded with cattails and attracting monster-size snapping turtles. When he was just a few years old, our youngest son, Ian, deliberately somersaulted into the water. I was just a few feet away, up on a ladder leaned against the house. As fast as I could, I jumped in after him, not thinking once about those intimidating snapping turtles.

Shortly after we moved to the farm, we started chinking in between the big square logs. Some of the crew of timberframers Peter worked with at that time came out one day to help. We were real pleased with how the chinking turned out. The log interior was warm and homey. That area eventually became a joint bedroom and living room. We gathered old bricks from a torn-down building and made a hearth to hold the black Vermont Castings wood stove. It was our savior while we were stranded out there during heavy snows and power outages, and with frozen gas pipes.

An old well house sat near our home, right off of the back porch. We constantly had to fetch buckets of water for bathing and doing dishes. Heating big pans of water every day for bathing was such a grueling, time-consuming ordeal. Often, we filled a large, round, metal washtub beside the wood-burning stove to bathe both boys.

One of my favorite things about our farm was getting to garden together as a family. Even when they were very young, Michael and Ian helped me plant seeds in the little dirt troughs, and as I hoed, they helped pull weeds. For several years, we planted multiple rows of gigantic sunflowers. As I looked out our window at the kitchen sink, that was such a visual treat, to see row after row of majestic sunflowers swaying back and forth. For several years, Peter planted a patch of greens near the frog pond. It was such a luxury to be able to pick fresh greens for salads each evening. He had a variety of lettuces, herbs, and other kinds of greens, like chard and beet greens.

I especially loved being able to walk over to the main garden and pick fresh, sweet ears of Seneca Chief corn and Big Boy tomatoes for dinner. When we had friends out for supper one night, they couldn't believe what a different, delicious taste freshly- picked ears of corn had. As for fresh tomatoes, I agree with Guy Clark's lyrics: "Only two things that money can't buy...and that's true love and homegrown tomatoes." I'm sure those of you who have grown your own tomatoes can relate to that.

One day at the farm, I was approached by a man named Junior and his son, Timmy. They were cattle farmers over the hill from us in the nearby community of Sissonville. After chatting with them, they proposed a trade we couldn't resist. In exchange for using our pasture for their herd of cattle, they would help with the upkeep of the farm. Meeting them was one of the best things that happened to us. The maintenance of the farm was more than we had expected, so we were grateful for their help. The two of them and their friend, Robert, replaced fence posts and barbed wire, put up sturdy metal gates, and mowed the fields for hay.

We liked having the cows around, but it was a sad time when the men rounded up the calves and took them to the auction house. Listening to the desperate cries of the forlorn mother cows, missing their babies, was heart-wrenching. These tormenting sounds lasted for several days. Junior offered to give us a side of beef when they had some of the herd slaughtered. We simply weren't interested in consuming any of those cows for dinner. It was too much like eating one of your pets.

After we lived on the farm for a little more than a year, we hired a local handyman to help us hook up running water. That made a huge difference in daily chores. I was both happy and angry when we got the water hooked up: Happy to finally have it, yet angry to see how easily and quickly it could have been hooked up all along. After we had running water for several years, if we had extremely dry summers, then in the fall our dug well dried up. We had to bring in gallons of water from wherever we could, until the well filled back up.

During snowstorms, our sons ran around the house, collecting water in buckets. When the warm afternoon sun slightly melted the top layer of the deep snow, there were several places where the runoff dripped from the roof. Knowing how valuable water was to us, they voluntarily collected it whenever the snow began to melt. One winter, they got overly-adventurous and tried to use the slanted roof of the chicken coop as a ski ramp. They thought their sled would soar into midair, like an Olympic downhill skier. Instead, the sled careened off of the roof and made a nosedive right into the snow, breaking one of Michael's front teeth.

Peter started back to college after we had lived at the farm a few years. That period was a difficult time for everyone. The boys were still very young, so Peter went to bed early, then got up to study once they fell asleep. Regrettably, building a new house was put on hold. He told the kids: "As soon as I graduate from school, we will build our new house." At that time, we only had one vehicle. Peter dropped me off at a bus stop in Charleston and I rode a public transportation bus to my teaching job. He took the boys to my parents' house, and then drove up to West Virginia Tech, about forty minutes away. Some nights, when he had an evening class, I waited at school until ten o'clock for him to pick me up. After three long years, he graduated. Both boys and I went up for his graduation. It was a joyous occasion for all of us. The next morning, Ian showed up at our bedside with a hammer in his hand, saying: "Come on, Pop, let's start building the house." That's how literally he had taken Peter's promise.

In the winter months, except on weekends, we were never at home during the daylight hours. It was dark when we left so early every morning. When I taught at Elkview, Pete dropped me off at school several hours before it started. Out of boredom, I painted floral designs in the ladies' restroom. At nighttime, it got dark so early that we never made it home while it was still daylight. It seemed nonsensical to live on a farm if we could never enjoy being there.

For the longest time, we lived at the farm without a television. That suited all of us just fine. The boys played every day in their "fort" up on a plateau where the hillside leveled off. In our yard they had a large sandbox, a blue plastic swimming pool with a slide, a nice big playhouse, and a swing set. When they swung on their glider swing, they loved for me to grab them as they rocked back and forth. I acted like I was going to pinch their bellies and yelled, "I want your ticket." They thought that was hilarious and begged me to do it over and over.

For years, we pulled the boys around the farm in a little red, wooden Radio Flyer wagon. Ian had a Big Wheel tricycle, and we listened to the sound of it rolling up and down the gravel driveway nonstop. They both had little metal lawnmowers, which made such a loud, annoying sound, but they had so much fun using them. When they were a little older, we bought them a battery-operated, kid-size red Jeep. They drove themselves around in it, up and down the driveway and in circles around the big grassy bottom.

Michael and Ian enjoying a cruise in their red Jeep at the farm, 1991

When they were still pretty young, Peter had a friend Steve help him build a nice bedroom for the boys. They tore down walls and finished it out with Sheetrock. In the process of tearing out old walls, they discovered several mice skeletons. I painted a mural of cartoon characters on the wall and displayed all of their toy trains on a shelf above the windows. Their curtains and bedspreads had bright, colorful train designs. I attached glow-in-the-dark stars to their ceiling, which produced a neat effect at nighttime. They were delighted with their new bedroom.

Before the boys were in grade school, a sign outside a local church a few miles from the farm caught their attention. It was advertising their Vacation Bible School with a jungle theme. Michael and Ian wanted to go to the VBS, so I took them. Since they had such a good time, we started going there regularly. The church had an active youth group with dedicated leaders, a wonderful pastor, and good Sunday school teachers. The boys enjoyed participating in many of their activities and attending the church camp, Camp Whitney.

Our own Christmas pageant in the boys' bedroom, 1987.

Every summer, for the finale to VBS, the church had a big covered-dish dinner. That was always a feast for the taste buds. Michael and Ian sang and participated in Christmas pageants, and went camping, swimming, and picnicking with the youth group. I enjoyed helping the pastor's fiancée paint the stage backdrops for Christmas plays and VBS stages. We still tease Ian about the year when he had a speaking part as a shepherd in the Christmas play, and said: "The angel rapeared." That was before he was even in grade school. Michael orchestrated a Christmas pageant in their bedroom which they performed just for me. He assigned Ian the part of Mary, coerced Peter into being "Jofus" (that's how Ian pronounced it), and he, of course, was a wise man.

Dealing with our treacherous, steep driveway was often a harrowing experience. Before we owned a four-wheel-drive vehicle, it proved to be nearly impossible to climb many snowy mornings. By the time we finally made it up the driveway, my nerves were completely shot. From the passenger side, I could look over the steep embankment, which was just one slip away from our tumbling over it. One day, when I was teaching at a school in Charleston, the most spectacular snowfall began. My classroom had an entire wall of windows, so we could look out and watch the gigantic snowflakes as they came down. The snow began to accumulate quickly. School was dismissed right away, and by the time I had made the dangerous trek out to the farm, the driveway was already covered with a deep blanket of snow. As I headed over the steep drop at the top of the driveway, my little blue Subaru got hung up on top of the snow. It couldn't budge. Our driveway never got direct sunlight, so snow would linger on it, well after it had melted everywhere else.

The boys rode the school bus every morning, and, like other families, sometimes we missed the bus. We raced down the road on those mornings, trying to catch up to that elusive, big yellow bus. When we knew the bus had a fairly long stop with several kids waiting to get on board, Michael and Ian jumped out of the car and raced to the bus door. Occasionally, during extremely bad snows, I rode the school bus to work, while I was teaching at the center for gifted students in Elkview. Rob was the school bus driver on our road and was the most laid-back, polite, and kind gentleman you could ever hope to meet. He was a nice-looking older man and was a biker. You never saw him wear anything other than a black leather jacket and the complete biker's outfit. To those who didn't know him, he could look pretty intimidating.

One day when I was riding with him, he ranted on and on about how upset he was when he saw that vandals had smashed in our mailbox. I had painted a picture of our farm on the side of the box. It was the view looking down on the farm, from the top of our driveway. "That was the prettiest box on the road. They didn't have to ruin it," Rob said in disgust. Smashing mailboxes along the road with a baseball bat was, unfortunately, a fairly popular sport among bored teenagers living in the boondocks. I was just amused that Rob had appreciated the painting, and was so put out about it being destroyed.

At the Gifted center, I found a circular, Styrofoam incubator in storage, so I asked our sweet custodian, Charlie, to bring us some chicken eggs we could hatch. All of the students faithfully watched over the eggs with much anticipation. After exactly twenty-one days, seven tiny gold, black, and white chicks started pecking their way out of the shells. We watched as, one by one, they success-fully broke open the shells and wriggled their way to freedom. I kept them at school for a few days, and then soon took them home.

These baby chicks were so cute and fluffy and followed us wherever we went. The boys had such fun with them. Then, the chicks started getting bigger. Charlie had failed to mention one minor detail about the eggs…the males were the kind they bred for fighting gamecocks. Once they were nearly fully grown, we noticed that the males were becoming very aggressive. They acted as though they wanted to charge us sideways. When they grew to be adult size, they did try to spur us.

Whenever we came home during the daylight hours, the big, black, aggressive rooster, Darth, tried to terrorize us. He jumped on the hood of the car when we parked, waiting for us to get out. We weren't going to be intimidated by roosters, so we built cages for them. It was a little hurtful to see how those cute baby chicks, who were so friendly, turned against us, as adults. The roosters were the best watchdogs we could possibly have. During the night, they crowed at any critter passing through. Listening to them crow at the break of dawn every morning is something I still miss.

The hens weren't one bit aggressive and ran around the yard, scratching in the grass, wherever we went. At nighttime, they jumped up to perch on top of the play yard fence, beside the house. One of our favorite hens was Punker, a golden Polish variety, with a fantastic plume on the top of her head. She got her name from resembling a Punk rocker. I used to take her to Stonewall, the inner-city junior high where I taught for five years. She developed quite a cult following with the students. Stonewall had its own morning televised newscast. Punker and I appeared as guests on the morning news once a year. Many of the students were fascinated with her and spent their entire lunch break in my room, just so they could play with her. None of the students had ever been around a chicken, much less one which looked so funny. They thought it was hilarious that she followed me like a puppy, up and down the hallways and around my classroom.

Punker outlived all of the other hens and roosters. We kept her as a pet even after we moved from the farm. She ran around our chain-link-fenced yard with all of the other pets, often chasing after our dogs and cats. When all of us were out in the yard together, one of her favorite things to do was to jump on top of the boys' heads. I would have never believed anyone, if they had told me that one of those baby chicks would live for thirteen years. She was such a great pet.

On the farm, we could tell when snakes were climbing around the branches of our apple trees. The birds protested and squawked so loudly at them, with such a distressing sound. One of the most awe-inspiring sights I have ever witnessed in nature was two medium-size, silvery black snakes slithering back and forth, side by side, in perfect synchronization. They were only an inch or two apart, and as they swiftly glided across the yard with identical movements, they were an incredible sight to behold.

We enjoyed watching the little house wrens build their nest on the back porch in a hanging clothespin bag made from a child's shirt. They stuffed their nest with all kinds of soft tidbits of feathers, fur, and hairs. We had a front-row seat in watching the progression of their nest. It was an exciting morning when the four baby wrens started leaving their nest. One at a time, they perched on the opening of the nest, fluttered their wings, then were off for their debut flight.

When we first moved to the farm, we took great pleasure in watching all of the hummingbirds as they visited our sugar water feeder. The second year, it wasn't such a pleasurable experience. One territorial, vicious male stayed on the clothesline and guarded the feeder with such ferociousness. He attacked any other bird that came nearby. We soon took down the feeder, not willing to watch such unpleasant drama unfold every day.

One of the most curious critters we encountered at the farm was a little kitchen mouse. Our old house wasn't very tightly constructed, and every night, as we were in the kitchen area, he climbed out from the space between the window frame and the wall. Sitting up on the top of the circular wall clock, he just looked down upon us for hours at a time, as we ate or sat around the big wooden table. It seemed as if he just wanted to hang out with us every night, or was curious to see what we were doing.

While we lived at the farm, we had numerous animals show up. We took all of them in, but two were extra special. The cutest little calico kitten won the hearts of our two boys when they got off of the school bus one afternoon. She had been dropped off along the road at the top of the hill and was smart enough to latch onto Michael and Ian. As they walked down the steep bank to our house, she followed them. We called her "Callie," and she literally grew up with my sons. She was such a pampered, well-loved cat, living for more than fifteen years.

Another afternoon, we spotted a young golden retriever mix puppy looking down on us from the bank next to the woods. She was probably attracted to the sounds and actions of the kids playing. We called her to us, and she became one of our favorite pets for years. She had a litter of pups, which we found homes for, but kept one for our own. Unfortunately, we had to keep her on a leash because she would run up to the road, where one day she got hit by a car. I always thought that was one of the biggest ironies about moving to the farm...I couldn't wait to move out to where our dogs would be able to run free. I never dreamed we would have to keep them tied up. We tried keeping her in a fenced yard, but she could easily climb the fence and escape.

My mother gave us a television one year as a Christmas gift, because she thought the boys were "missing out on so much" by not having one. There was no cable out there at that time. We had to climb up a ladder which leaned against the house to rotate the antenna on top of the roof. After doing this for so long, we knew exactly what position to turn it to for each channel. The television was mostly used by Ian and Peter to play the Mario Brothers Nintendo game. One year they really got hooked on that.

Listening to the rain hitting the metal roof of our farmhouse during the night was such a comforting sound. One night, however, the weather delivered all four of us an experience we will never forget. It was early on a springtime evening, when the kids and I were out in the yard. Peter came up to me and said we needed to seek shelter as fast as we could. The ominous sky was turning so dark, and strong winds were blowing in from the East. We had the boys put on their little West Virginia University football helmets. The four of us hurried to the front log room and crawled under our double bed. For what seemed like an eternity, we clung to each other under the bed. We shuddered as the strong winds roared through and we felt our little farmhouse shaking and rattling all around us. When the winds subsided, an eerie hush fell over the farm.

I peeked out of the bathroom window to assess the damage. I thought our black pony was lying dead on the ground in the yard. That mass of darkness turned out to be the dirt around the root system of one of the many trees which had been uprooted. The most disappointing destruction happened to the old cedar tree near the house. In a matter of seconds, a tree which had been around for more than a hundred years had been snapped in half like a toothpick. Clearly, it had been a twister which ripped through the area, touching down with a hit-and-miss pattern. Our neighbors' farm was unscathed. They ran over as soon as they could to help with the aftermath of destruction. Down the road five miles, an 84 Lumber warehouse storage building was completely flattened. My pet rabbit was still sitting on a table outside in his wire cage, untouched. Yet, five feet away, the well house, made of steel rebars and cinderblocks, had been twisted and destroyed.

I still pursued the possibility of getting a new house built on the farm. We picked out a model and bought the blueprints for a modular home, the kind of stick-built houses made in sections. As we decided more definitely about it, we even visited the company's factory in Virginia. The quality of the craftsmanship was impressive. One evening, the boys and I met with the contractor, who was in charge of getting the house sections delivered and assembled. We picked out our wooden kitchen cabinets, linoleum, and Formica countertops. Michael and Ian picked out the carpet for their own bedrooms. They could not have been more ecstatic. To our disbelief, a few weeks later, the contractor told us that he didn't think it was feasible to deliver the large sections down our steep driveway. The boys and I were devastated.

Shortly after that, my maternal instincts took over and told me it was time to move someplace where our sons could live in a nice home. It seemed obvious we were not going to get a house built at the farm. In 1993, the boys and I moved into a brick apartment in Elkview. They enjoyed living in a neighborhood with other playmates, and were so proud of having their own nice, big bedrooms.

We occasionally went out to the farm to visit Peter and our pets, who weren't allowed in the apartment.

Peter eventually moved with us into a house we purchased in the same neighborhood. Unfortunately, the driveway culvert at the farm was washed out during a horrible flood that hit the area about twenty years ago. Since then, we haven't been able to drive down to our farmhouse. For years, I have wanted to sell the farm. Both boys have insisted that we keep it, so they could build out there some day. No one really knows what the fate of our farm will be. I am so eager to see someone move out there and turn it into a tranquil country home again. When I first bought the place, I had an inspector for the local health department test the well water. He went on and on about what a gorgeous piece of property I had. It will be so wonderful to finally see it restored to how beautiful it once was.

Motherhood and Parenting

Ian and Michael with me at Momaw's and Popaw's house, 1994.

Ever since I can remember, having children was one of my ambitions. Being a mother has been the most endearing and challenging experience of my life. To say that Peter and I weren't perfect parents would be a profound understatement. We must have done something right, though, seeing what remarkable young men our sons have become. Many people have congratulated us on our "wonderful sons."

When Peter and I first met, we were in our thirties. We both wanted to have children, so that seemed like the right thing to do. I decided to have my first baby at a local birthing center. We had faithfully attended Lamaze classes, which taught us how to do the fast panting and exhaling exercises. Those were supposed to help me endure labor. Every day during my pregnancy, I had morning sickness. Once the vomiting was over, I could get on with the business at hand. At that time, my dad and I were running our stained glass studio. He fixed himself a pot of coffee as soon as we stepped in the door. Simply smelling his coffee gave me such a nauseous feeling, it expedited my sickness every morning.

Our first son, Michael, was appropriately born on Labor Day, in 1983. When I started going into labor at home, I was having a difficult time getting into a comfortable position. Peter jury-rigged a contraption on the bed to help support my back. It was an upside-down wooden chair with a piece of plywood attached to it. After eighteen hours of being in labor at home, with no real progress in dilating, the midwife on call suggested that we come to the center. My parents and sister, who were so excited about this baby, met us there. With the onset of each contraction, I had such excruciating back pain. My support group took turns rubbing my back as hard as they could. That was the only thing which helped me cope with the pain.

Several hours of this agonizing ordeal went by. I was still not dilating, even though the piercing contractions kept coming. At that point, I was completely drained. Our midwife, whom we were very fond of, continued leafing through her enormous childbirth manual for techniques on speeding up the dilation process. After trying several suggestions from the manual, with no luck, I felt like it was time to go a different route. When she suggested nipple massaging, I was far too exhausted to wait around and see if that might work. I had been in labor for so many hours that I needed immediate results.

We summoned an ambulance, and in a matter of minutes I was being admitted to a hospital. I was given some kind of shot to help me start dilating. Our midwife came along, and that was a real comfort for me. She waited with us for what seemed like an eternity in a pre-delivery holding room. When there was an opening and a doctor available, I was wheeled into a delivery room. By that time, I had been in labor over twenty-four hours. After wanting a child for so many years, it was quite ironic that I was too exhausted to enjoy his birth. The delivery doctor, whom I had never met, joked about needing ribbons for the baby's long, dark hair. After the delivery, when the nurse said, "Here's your baby boy," I was so completely drained, that I couldn't even look at him.

Of course, after a few hours of rest, I got to hold my bundle of joy. I was as proud and happy as any mother could be. The next day, Pete and I took Michael and moved in with my parents, who had offered their assistance. For me, the days immediately after childbirth were nearly as difficult as the birth itself. One of the doctors at the hospital had warned me about four physical complications and mental problems which commonly occur after childbirth. I had all of them. Eventually, after a few days, my postpartum blues improved, and we were able to go to our own house.

Michael had a wicked case of colic, which began a few days after he was born. Every single evening, Peter and I dreaded the nighttime approaching. Michael's uncontrollable crying started when it got dark and lasted all night. The only way we could survive was for each of us to take shifts. Thankfully, we discovered that if we placed him in a crank-up baby swing, it would put him to sleep. After much desperate searching, we finally found one which swung for a longer period of time. That swing was our godsend.

The Town Center mall, in downtown Charleston, opened shortly after Michael was born. At that time, it had a few vacant storefronts. The mall management invited local craftspeople to fill in those spaces, rent free. Eight of my artist friends and I opened the Creative Collection. We took turns manning the shop. Ed, one of the craftsmen, displayed handsome, hand-built furniture from his woodworking shop. Whenever I manned our store, Michael napped in the wooden baby crib from Ed's shop. One year, when I was an exhibitor at the Mountain State Art and Craft Fair, Peter and I kept Michael in his playpen with us in our booth. Hundreds of fairgoers jokingly asked, "How much is the baby?" Being able to have my children with me, wherever I worked, was something I never took for granted.

Michael's first words were, "Nan Mom," which was what he called me for some time. That was the likely combination from hearing people calling me both Nancy and Mom. Whenever we held him up to a mirror and asked him, "Who is that?" he replied, "Mike Mike." That became his nickname for many years. On a camping trip in New Hampshire, Michael spoke his very first sentence. "I love you, chocolate milk," came out as clearly as could be. He had directed that towards me. We thought it was a pretty clever way of bribing me into giving him his favorite drink.

Fifteen months after Michael was born, our youngest son, Ian, came along. By that time, I was thirty-five, and my age put me in the "danger zone" for having children. This round, my pregnancy was extremely well-monitored. I chose to go with the more traditional childbirth route and qualified to be a patient at the West Virginia University medical teaching center. I was seen by a terrific group of young doctors doing their residency. During one visit, right before my due date, Dr. Bush couldn't get a response from the baby when he held a loud radio up to my stomach. He sent me immediately to the lab for an amniocentesis. Seeing that nineteen-inch needle coming towards me was frightening, to say the least. To my surprise, the procedure was virtually painless. That afternoon, I received a message saying the doctor wanted to induce labor the next morning.

My two experiences with childbirth were as different as night and day. Our friend Pam babysat Michael while my family and I headed to the hospital. She couldn't believe that he could read at such a young age. Actually, at only fifteen months, he couldn't read at all. He had simply memorized all the pages of his books.

At the hospital, the comforting sounds of Christmas carols filled the hallways. It was a few days before Christmas, and everyone was in the holiday spirit. I was to have my labor induced at six in the morning. The fluid they gave me worked wonders. This delivery happened so quickly, it was done and over with in a flash. My parents had run downstairs to the snack bar to pick up something for lunch. By the time they came back upstairs, the delivery was over. In the delivery room, my squawking baby firmly grasped the scissors in the doctor's hand before he could cut the umbilical cord. To my amazement, as soon as he was cleaned off and placed on my stomach, he immediately crawled right up to my breast and started nursing. Seeing this newborn, who knew precisely what to do, seemed nothing short of a miracle. At first we named our newborn son "Matthew," but in a few weeks, we realized he looked and acted more like an "Ian."

Since Michael and Ian were so close in age, it almost felt like we were raising twins. Even as an infant, Ian was fascinated with his older brother, continuously watching his every move. Perhaps that is why he went through normal stages of development at such an accelerated pace. He never, ever crawled. That stage was completely bypassed, and he went straight to walking. Peter and I had to tie a net over the top of his crib every night to keep him from climbing out. Being the little Houdini that he was, Ian still managed to escape several times.

Ian was just six months old when we moved to our farm. From his highchair one day, he spoke his first words. As if it were one word, he blurted out, "I want down," with the emphasis on "down." That became his favorite saying, even after he learned many more. He disliked the confinement of being strapped in a highchair or shopping cart. Many times from his highchair, he held out his arms towards me and said, "Hold you, Mommy, hold you." That was his way of saying he wanted me to hold him. He was always climbing and getting into everything.

When the boys were little, they loved for me to sit them on my lap, facing me, and bounce them while repeating the familiar lyrics: "This is the way the lady rides, this is the way the gentleman rides, but this is the way the cowboy rides." The bouncing pace for the lady and gentleman was a slow, rhythmic beat. The cowboy part was fast and uncontrollable, making them laugh hysterically. One day in the kitchen, while both boys were in their highchairs, Ian proclaimed, "Kids like you, Mom." We had such fun together. I often made their sandwiches into funny faces, or arranged their food in some wacky, different way. Every night, before they went to sleep, I read them a bedtime story. Recently, I came across a couple of their favorite books. Remembering those cherished times brought back such fond memories.

We had many out-of-town relatives visit us at the farm. Peter's sister, Linda, and her family visited one summer, when the boys were still pretty young. They pitched a tent and slept in the yard. Our neighbors' dogs attacked their tent in the middle of the night. That was a pretty nightmarish experience for them, not knowing what kind of animal it was. When they were ready to leave and we were saying goodbye, Linda got such a kick out of Michael yelling out to them, "I love you to pieces."

Pete's other sister, Judy, and her family came down from Massachusetts for a visit, just days after the twister touched down on the farm. It uprooted nearly every tree in our yard. We had worked so hard at making the grounds really look nice for company. All of that effort was ruined in a matter of seconds. Peter's brother, P. M., came down from Vermont to visit for several days. An avid runner, he ran the five-mile length of our road and back every morning. He thought it was hilarious to hear how the boys had picked up such a country accent since the last time he had seen them. P. M. is a pediatrician, and after observing Ian for a few days, he pointed to him and predicted: "Fifty stitches by the age of five."

Michael and Ian enjoyed growing up in the country. We didn't live in a great house, but we had a beautiful farm and enjoyed being out there together. On one lazy afternoon, the four of us were visiting in the shade under one of our apple trees. Out of the blue, Michael, who was only two, announced: "Today's sermon is on 'Why God Created Ice Cream.' " Then he proceeded with his sermon.

I looked forward to burning trash in the burn barrel practically every night. That was my guaranteed quiet time. All of us liked gardening, sleigh riding, and the peace and tranquility from our bucolic lifestyle. The kids spent most of their time playing outside. It pleases me that as adults, both boys have chosen to live out in the country.

When Michael was a baby, Peter took him to "Water Babies" swimming classes. A few years later, we enrolled both boys in classes at a local pool. Michael was so put out one night with his instructor, who had made him jump into the deep water of the diving section. At that time, he and I used to say to each other, "I love you this much," as we stretched out our arms as wide as possible. After the swimming class, going home in the car, Michael asked: "Know how much I love my swimming teacher?" I turned around for his answer, and he said, somewhat angrily: "This much," with his hands practically touching.

During the summer months, the boys and I went swimming at Coonskin Park almost every day. We waited out many thunder and lightning storms in the bathhouse lobby. When the kids were little, I took them into the women's dressing room with me. They loved taking hot showers after we swam, especially when we didn't have running water at home. We also liked to go roller skating. One night, after a skating party for his kindergarten class, Ian said: "I was the best skater there, among the kids who had to hang on to the rail."

My sons and I spent a lot of time traveling in the car, often singing songs together. Both of them still remember the lyrics to a goofy little brainwashing tune I had made up. We sang it all of the time: "I like to share, I like to share my things with you. If you want to read my book, just ask me. If you want to play with my toy, just ask me, because I care about you." That was more than twenty years ago, and unfortunately, the tune has been etched into our memories forever. I always doubted the effectiveness of my lesson on sharing.

As a family, we made a concerted effort to spend Sunday afternoons together. This took precedence over everything else. We often made the loop on the scenic nature trail at Coonskin Park or hiked the dense woods at Kanawha State Forest. Sometimes we let the boys ride their bikes on the shady road between the river and golf course at Coonskin. On hot summer days, we often took them swimming at Sutton Lake. I'm glad we set that as a priority. Those Sunday outings were some of our best times together.

A few weeks before he turned three, Michael kept saying he wanted "Spensia" for his birthday. I wasn't sure what that was, until we were going by a local toy department, and he said, "There's Spensia, Mom." I looked over and saw the four-foot stuffed clown, which he had told me he wanted for his birthday. It had been a while since he had first mentioned it. I had told him back then that it was too "expensive." He thought I was calling it "Spensia." Since we couldn't afford the clown, Mom and I made a close facsimile to it, which he loved.

For several years, Michael was into his first of many "phases." Everything he was interested in had something to do with clowns and circuses. He often placed all of his stuffed animals in a spread-

Michael with "Spensia" at his third birthday party, 1986.

out circle around him. With his whip in hand, he pretended to be his idol, the famous animal trainer, Gunther Gebel-Williams. For his fourth birthday, I thought it would be a great surprise if I dressed up like a clown. The party was in a picnic shelter at Coonskin. I made myself up like a clown and went early to hide in the woods behind the shelter. When my parents arrived with the kids, I came out of the woods, calling to Michael and wishing him happy birthday. My cool surprise backfired. He was terrified at the sight of seeing a strange clown coming out of the woods. I thought he would be delighted to have a clown at his party, and never dreamed I would frighten him. He didn't even recognize my voice. What was I thinking?

When the boys were three and two, we drove up to visit Peter's family. Everyone had gathered for Christmas at his mother's house in Manchester, New Hampshire. Our dog had just given birth to a litter of seven puppies, so we brought her, the puppies, and my pet Dutch rabbit on the trip with us. The cousins loved playing with the bunny and newborn puppies. All of the children had such a good time playing together. The trip home turned out to be quite the comedy of errors, although there was nothing funny about it at the time. As we were heading home, coming through Pennsylvania, a winter blast of snow and ice moved in, out of nowhere. Numerous wrecked vehicles were scattered all along the interstate. Like all of the other motorists were trying to do, we thought it would be wise to get off of the highway and stay the night, letting the storm pass. We stopped at many motels, but no one had any vacancies. Finally, we found a room.

The next day, the snow storm continued. At Wilkes-Barre, our car broke down. We had to be towed to a local mechanic, who replaced the electronic ignition switch. Michael started coughing uncontrollably, so we took him to an emergency clinic. The doctor there sent us to Wilkes-Barre General Hospital, where they immediately admitted him. He was diagnosed with asthma. We had quite an unexpected delay in Pennsylvania, as the doctor kept him in the hospital for five days. I stayed with him the entire time, sleeping in a recliner next to his bed. Probably out of sympathy, a local veterinarian took in our menagerie at a minimal cost. When we finally arrived home, and started down our driveway, that little primitive farmhouse, down in the valley never looked so appealing and comforting.

Sometimes we took the boys into town to watch the Fourth of July fireworks at Watt Powell Park. For several years in a row, by the time we got to Charleston, they were so sound asleep, that they slept through the show, loud booms and all. On New Year's Eve one year, we drove them into town to the Steak and Ale restaurant for a fancy meal. I will never forget how their eyes lit up when the waiter walked up to our table and presented to them the enticing tray of elaborately-decorated dessert delicacies.

While the boys were two and three, I was required to take gifted education classes. The classes were one night a week. On those nights, Peter, or "Pop," had to fend for himself, taking care of the boys. For some reason, they loved tattling on him and couldn't wait for me to come home so they could do so. One night, I parked at the end of the driveway, and the two little tattletales ran up to my car and protested, "Pop just fed us scraps." Peter had fixed leftovers for dinner, and they thought he was shirking his parental duty. Another time, Ian ran up to me as soon as I got home and said: "Mom, Pop said 'Right up your alley' to me." In his think-ing, that was some kind of vulgar expression. Peter had simply tried to tell him that he would probably be interested in something, because it was the kind of thing he liked.

On Christmas Eve one year, we took the boys to Coonskin Park to visit with Santa. Out in the parking lot, they saw tracks in the snow and were certain those were reindeer tracks. During the ride home, both boys looked up to the night sky and said they were pretty sure they could see Santa's sleigh. For most Christ-mas Eves, my parents came out to the farm and spent the night. They helped assemble toys, bikes, kid-size tractors, and anything else that needed to be done. One year, there was a little parking garage and a bicycle which needed to be assembled. About half-way through the tedious assembling, Peter lost his patience and, sounding like Scrooge, screamed, "I hate Christmas." We were all thankful that the kids were sound sleepers.

When he was two, Ian got a soft, fluffy, white stuffed cat one year from Santa. The only gift he paid any attention to was that cat. He carried it around for months, draping it over his arm. Eventu-ally, it was literally worn out. One of the hardest times in dealing with Santa gifts was the year Ian asked for a real pot-bellied pig. We actually went to look at one that was advertised in the local ad bulletin. It was as big as a full-blown hog and didn't look anything like pictures of those cute little piglets. Santa left Ian a note, explaining that there simply wasn't a place to keep a pig. I'm sure he was disappointed, but soon got over it.

We had a small tape player, and one Christmas morning I recorded the boys' conversations as they went in to see what Santa had left them. On the tape, my sister had asked Michael what Santa brought him. In a low, down-and-out voice, he answered: "Oh, just a bike, a drum set, and a Lite-Brite." For some reason, at the last minute, he had asked for a glass crystal. He was sulking because he didn't get one. I asked him if he had checked out his stocking. He walked over to the stocking and, in the loudest, most excited voice imaginable, he screamed, "Oh look, I got a crystal!" We had more fun playing that tape over and over again for many years, laughing hysterically every time.

One Christmas Eve, I was burning the midnight oil, finishing a black satin magician's cape for Michael and a purple wizard costume for Ian. At that time, Michael was into his "magician phase." We had traveled to Huntington to check out the inventory of tricks at Magic Makers. Practically all of his presents had to do with magic. He became pretty good at his magician's routine, performing it for the other teachers' kids where I taught. In the sixth grade, he performed a magic act in his school's talent show.

Another year, he began going through his "Indian phase." Santa brought him a big rawhide drum and Indian plaques. Mom made him an Indian outfit. My sister and I had driven up to a gift shop across from New River Gorge Bridge. It had all kinds of rustic wooden plaques, many of them with decals of Indians. After Michael saw the ones Santa left him, he said: "Whichever elves painted these, they sure did a good job."

For Halloween the next year, I made him some elaborate tail feathers to complete his Indian outfit. He and I spent scorching August afternoons at the annual Pow Wows at Oakes Field in South Charleston. Those were the highlight of the year for Michael. He diligently observed and took in all of the male dancers' moves and the drummers' chants and beats. He could accurately mimic the male Fancy Dancers, with their stomps and circular swooping movements. For quite some time, we had the pleasure of listening to his Indian chants coming from the back seat whenever we were traveling in the car.

Ian was always curious about everything. When we went to Camden Park, a local amusement park, he got down on the pavement, looking under the merry-go-round, to see how it worked. As a three-year-old, he called out for me, holding up a blue, individually wrapped, unopened sanitary pad, saying: "We don't know about these, Mom." Peter and I always got a kick out of such a little guy using rather big words. He often made up his own words too, such as, "No, I amn't."

He could be pretty headstrong. When we went to his preschool's Christmas program, at Humphreys Methodist church, Ian stretched out on the bottom shelf of a bookcase, refusing to perform with the class. One year he insisted on wearing a little pair of leather boots every day until they were too worn to wear. On trips, he often refused to go into restaurants if he didn't like their food. At McDonald's one afternoon, he was crying about something, and I remember telling the girl taking our order: "We want a Happy Meal and a Not-So-Happy Meal." One night, while the boys were spending the night with "Momaw and Popaw," my mom called at three o'clock in the morning. Ian had a severe earache and was asking for me. I made the trip from the farm into Charleston and took him to Thomas Hospital's emergency room. The doctors stopped the ache by simply blowing hot air from a hair dryer into his ear.

Ian "fishing" at his fifth birthday party, 1989.

At Coonskin pond one day, Ian invented what he called a "bar-may" fishing pole. It was just a piece of fishing line with a hook on the end of it. Another kid, who was fishing nearby, came over and was so impressed with Ian's invention. He called out to several other kids who came over and marveled at the bar-may pole, too. Ian was thrilled with his instant celebrity status. He often gave himself haircuts, and then came to me, begging me to miraculously "fix" them. For his birthday parties in December, we usually went to Chuck E. Cheese's or Putt-Putt Games and Golf. His favorite toys were the fishing game, where you catch the colorful fish with a little fishing pole, a kid-size tractor, and a noisy chainsaw. Even today, he is quite the "tool guy."

One fall day, we took the boys out in our fishing boat at beautiful Summit Lake, in Greenbrier County. Ian was only five, and always seemed to have the fishing gods on his side. He caught three impressive rainbow trout and was so cocky that as he reeled them in, each time he yelled: "No net, no net." There were many onlookers for this remarkable episode, since the lake was surrounded by people fishing from their lawn chairs.

Michael, Ian, and I were riding around Charleston one afternoon and had stopped at a traffic light. Beside our car was a homeless man standing on the median. Ian looked over at him and said, in disgust: "Look at that... 'Homeless vet.' " The man was holding a sign which read: "Homeless vet, will work for food." Ian had always been a kindhearted child, so I was somewhat puzzled by his reaction. I asked him what he meant. He so seriously replied: "You know, with all of that knowledge, he could work on *someone's* animals."

When I picked up the boys from the Third Base after-school program one afternoon, Michael was so mad about what Ian had done at school that day. He said: "Mom, Ian bought posters and pencils for everyone in his class at the book fair today." This came as a surprise to me. Looking at him in the rearview mirror, I asked Ian, who was in kindergarten: "How did you do that?" He just smiled and said: "You know, Mom." Right then, I remembered giving both boys a check before school to pay their lunch bills. Then I realized Ian had given the book fair volunteers his check. Like the big-time spender in a bar who announces: "The next round is on me," he so generously bought everyone in his classroom something…with his lunch bill money.

When the boys were in their early years in grade school, while we lived at the farm, we took a family trip to Washington D.C. Peter had a business meeting to attend, so we tagged along with him. We stayed in a swanky, upscale hotel in the Washington suburbs. As soon as we pulled into the unloading area, the boys raced inside to check out the place. In a few minutes, they came running back, excitedly explaining that it was real fancy inside, with men dressed up in black tuxedos. Ian loudly cautioned us: "Even if you don't know what to do in there, act like you do." I think that's a pretty good approach to life itself.

The boys thought it was so nice of the hotel to provide us with a little refrigerator which was full of snacks and drinks. While Pete attended his meeting, the kids and I explored the usual tourist stops and museums in downtown Washington. Near the Ford Theater, we were caught in a downpour and purchased an umbrella from a street vendor. I gave the man $20 for the $12 umbrella. Obviously not understanding simple math, he asked me: "Now, what's the sitchiation?" He had no idea how much change to give me. That incident made quite an impact on my sons.

At the farm, from a litter one of our cats had, Michael and Ian each picked out a beautiful gray, long-haired male cat. Michael named his "Buddy," and Ian named his "Mr. Look-Around," because he liked to watch the food go around in the microwave. We called him "Looky" for short. Both of their cats, not quite a year old, became very irritated by the little stray calico kitten the boys brought home one day. She thought their bushy, long tails were great play toys. The madder they got, the more their tails swished back and forth, and the more she chased them.

After the gray cats had put up with her abuse for a few weeks, they both disappeared. That wasn't real uncommon, living out in the country, since there are wild animals who prey on smaller domestic ones. Michael accepted the fact that his cat was probably gone for good. Ian was completely heartbroken and determined to find Looky. He insisted that Peter go with him and scour the steep hillside behind the house. Sadly, their day-long, grueling search was unsuccessful.

A few days later, Ian pointed to a road near their school and asked if we could go up there to search for Looky. Since we were about half an hour from the farm, I asked him why he thought his cat might be up there. "Because of the sign," he replied. I looked over to a sign which read, "Lots for Sale." He had misread it as,

Ian and Michael out on the farm, with Buddy and Looky, 1990

"Lost for Sale." Ian had conjured up an image of a place where lost items and animals were for sale. To this young, heartbroken child, perhaps it was his last hope in trying to find his beloved Looky.

Eventually Little League sports started dominating our lives. Ian played on a midget league football team, and both boys played baseball and basketball in a community league. For kids, the quality of these experiences depends largely on the coaches and the civility of the parents. Thankfully, most of our boys' coaches were extremely dedicated, with a team attitude instead of a win-at-all-costs approach. For me, the worst part about this experience was getting upset over the adults in the stands, screaming unkind remarks to their children or the officials. Ian tried out for All Stars one year and had more hits than anyone else at the tryouts. He didn't make the team, but several adults who were present told him he played better than the ones who had made it. The days when he played midget football games seemed like a never-ending marathon. The boys were required to attend all three age group's games. That made for such a long day.

Our boys went to Frame Elementary, about nine miles from the farm. It was a small, community school. We were very pleased with the education and attention they were receiving. After Michael and Ian were there a few years, the county school board started making plans to consolidate Frame and three other Elk River area grade schools into one gigantic elementary center. We were promised, among other things, that students would learn Japanese at this new facility. Peter and I became very active in fighting this consolidation. We joined a host of other community members of all ages who were taking a stand against closing the four schools. All of the research we had read said smaller schools were the best environment for young children. Practically every waking moment was spent on this battle, when we weren't at work. We wrote numerous letters to the editor, attended many meetings, and pleaded our case before the school board.

One school board member, John Luoni, came around to admitting: "Their argument makes more sense than ours." Our group, Save Our Schools, or SOS, took the school board to court, but the judge ruled in favor of our opponent. He said they had already invested too much time and money into the project. We campaigned vigorously and were successful in getting two school board members voted in. When they took office, there was a huge controversy as to whether or not they should recuse themselves from voting on consolidation because they had a "conflict of interest." Young kids, fifteen miles away, were bused down to a school right outside of Charleston. Neither of our sons learned Japanese. And, to this day, no one can convince me that mega elementary schools are better than smaller, community ones for young children.

I believe the best thing that came out of this experience was the lesson all of our children gleaned during the battle. They learned the value of assuming the role of being proactive. All of our children spent many tiring nights at SOS meetings and school board hearings. They got a first-hand glimpse of what it was like to stand up for one's convictions. Several community members and I worked diligently in persuading the school board to let us use one of the closed schools for a community center. With the help of then superintendent, Dr. Jorea Marple and her liaison, Doug Walters, we were able to open the Elk River Community and Education Center. It remains to be a much-used faculty for Elkview residents of all ages.

When the boys were in the fourth and fifth grades, they and I moved into a red brick apartment in Elkview's Walker Addition. No progress had been made in getting a house built at the farm. I wanted to live in a home where the boys would invite friends over to visit and spend the night. They loved running around the neighborhood and having other kids to play with. After living there a year, we bought an older stucco house in the same neighborhood. One year, Michael and Ian walked over to a nearby gift shop and purchased a Dreamsicles figurine to give me for a Christmas present. A sympathetic shopper had overheard them saying that they didn't have enough money to buy it, and pitched in the amount they were lacking. That little angel, holding a heart in each palm, is one of my treasured mementos from their youth.

The boys played basketball or jumped on our big trampoline nonstop with two friends, Brian and Chris. When I hear the sound of basketballs being dribbled by my neighbors' kids, it brings back such fond memories. I miss those days when I heard that same sound on the concrete in front of our house from morning until bedtime. Ian became pretty good at basketball, from playing so much. One night in Clendenin, during a middle school game, he had a great night with three three-point baskets.

While both boys were in middle school, I took them to a Marshall home football game to watch Randy Moss and Chad Pennington play. They were an incredibly-talented, rare duo. It was a terrible game for Marshall until the fourth quarter, when they came from behind for a victory. I also took them to the state capitol grounds to hear President Clinton speak. One little elderly woman behind us coaxed me into forcing my way through the crowd, so they could meet him. They did get to shake hands with the president and thought that was a pretty big deal.

When the opening came up, I took a teaching position at the middle school where both of my boys attended. Michael was happy to have me as his art teacher, but for Ian, it was a different story. He was scheduled to be in my art class for four and a half weeks. The day he was to start my class, he walked into my bedroom and said: "I just can't do this, Mom." I assured him that we would survive our short time together. We did survive, but he was never really comfortable with the situation. He still complains that I gave him the hardest test he ever had.

The boys and I looked at so many homes to buy, trying to find a nice place within our budget. On three occasions, we placed bids on houses, but someone beat us to it. Those disappointments were devastating to all three of us. We were so thrilled when we finally succeeded in finding a nice home. When Ian was in the eighth grade and Michael was in the ninth, they and I moved into our dream home. It had a huge hot tub, family room, nice, big yard, and seemed to be a perfect match. To us, it had the feel of a beach house. The boys had many friends over and hosted several parties. Michael's bedroom had a balcony outside of his sliding glass doors. One night, he and I pitched our sleeping bags out there and slept under the stars. We wanted to watch the meteor showers that were supposed to occur. Nature put on quite an impressive show. Neither of us will ever forget that spectacular sight.

Our front yard was quite large, and the boys took turns mowing it. Michael had plenty of room to practice his golf swing and became one of the best golfers on his high school team. He represented his school in the state tournament during his tenth grade year. I was so relieved when he got his driver's license and was able to drive himself to practices, which were quite a long distance away.

My sons went through the typical sibling-rivalry. One afternoon, they got into a spat on the driveway. We had just come home from the grocery store. I broke up the fight with the only thing I had in my hand, a bag of groceries with a carton of eggs in it. They still remind me that I hit them with eggs. One of our favorite annual rituals was going shopping for back-to-school clothes. I loved every minute of those trips, and treasure the memories. Similarly, I enjoyed the bittersweet shopping excursions we took when each kid moved into his first apartment at college. Those were expensive trips, since they needed so many different things.

The most nerve-racking time for me as a mother was when both boys were learning to drive. I did my fair share of slamming my foot down, as if there were a brake on the passenger's side. Grabbing the handle on the door was another reaction I had. A few times, there was a communication breakdown, and I didn't know that one of them was spending the night with a friend. With much angst and apprehension, Peter and I drove up and down the roads the next morning, looking for any signs of a wreck.

When both boys headed off to West Virginia University, I had a severe case of the Empty Nest Syndrome. All of a sudden, the kids who had been such a huge part of my daily life for nearly twenty years were gone. No more taking them to the swimming pool, to movies, to the skating rink, to Little League games, to the beach, to go camping, and on and on. Michael studied at Stellenbosch University, in South Africa, during his junior year, as part of WVU's study abroad program. He liked everything about his stay in South Africa. That year was a memorable, life-changing experience for him.

These days, Michael and Ian both live out of town. They and their girlfriends come to visit occasionally. It's so great, just hanging out with them. Sometimes we rent a cabin for a few days at beautiful Canaan Valley, in Tucker County. Frequently, we have side-splitting Scrabble games. I usually try to pass off made-up words, which they challenge. We always have a good time visiting with each other, and especially enjoy going out to eat. I like to visit them in Morgantown, where there are so many unique eateries.

As a former teacher, I'm very aware of the numerous, serious problems many parents have had in raising incorrigible children. I realize how fortunate we have been, having such incredible sons. It has been my privilege being their mom. They have been the delight of my life and are such a blessing to me.

A Weighty Situation

Like so many of us baby boomers, I am overweight. Of course, my mental image of myself is still young and thin, like I was for many years. I'm often taken aback when I try on clothes in front of a three-way mirror. That's always somewhat of a shocking reality check. Sometimes I walk by a mirror in a department store and don't recognize my bigger self.

When I was in my twenties, I weighed 120 pounds for the longest time. The Wrangler jeans I wore for many years were size 12. I could eat anything I wanted, and never had to worry about gaining weight. Then the old metabolism slowed down. In my forties, I maintained a weight of 169 for many years. I would be pleased to weigh that again.

Just as I am sure many of you have done, I have squandered so much money trying to lose weight. My hard-earned money was thrown out the window on gadgets from convincing infomercials, fees for ridiculously-expensive, yet promising, weight loss programs, and pricey exercise equipment. I use my treadmill every day...as a clothes valet. Upstairs, my son's enormous home gym unit is another clothes rack. Over the years, I have purchased a ridiculous amount of exercise and weight loss DVDs and videos. My goals were ambitious and sincere... when I first bought them. Any commitment and determination to use those proved to be extremely short-lived. I got discouraged when I didn't see immediate results.

The greatest disappointment for me in these weight loss endeavors was when I spent hundreds of dollars on a much-advertised program. It had worked wonders for two acquaintances. They had nothing but praise for the program and had lost a considerable number of pounds. As soon as I handed over the check to the consultant, at that very moment, I realized what a huge mistake my decision was. I quickly lost interest in participating in the program. Each week, a consultant was supposed to praise you and ring a bell if you had lost weight. One week, I so proudly had lost five pounds, but when I weighed in, there was no bell ringing, no fanfare, no hoopla whatsoever. Not even an "atta girl." What a disappointment! I had paid all of that money, recorded everything I had eaten, lost five pounds, and then received absolutely zero amount of praise for my accomplishments.

Many of us wish we could look like the beautiful, bikini-clad Valerie Bertinelli, touting her weight loss success in a commercial. One of those programs where you eat the food that you purchase from that company sure worked wonders for her. One of my friends is currently experiencing some weight loss success on a similar program. She spends more than six hundred dollars a month buying the food. Personally, I think my bikini-wearing days are over, no matter whose food I eat.

When I took my mom to her hair appointment recently, I noticed that one of the hairdressers, who is my age, had lost quite a bit of weight. She and her two sisters were on a particular diet where they dripped some special elixir under their tongues each morning. All of them had tremendous success on that diet. In a heartbeat, I was ready to buy that expensive, mysterious potion. I wanted so badly to enjoy the same successes which they were celebrating. Then she explained how they were only allowed to eat five hundred calories each day. Gee, I could drip water under my tongue and go on a starvation diet on my own, without paying big bucks to do so. That's the problem, though. We think that somewhere there is a quick-fix to losing weight, when in reality, there is no panacea.

If I can feel my little tummy roll resting on my lap, I know something needs to change. It's time to get out my peculiar-looking, inflatable Bean and start exercising on it again. Another warning sign is not being able to look over that belly roll and see my toes when standing straight up. That's my reminder to start working on the gut-control exercises and watching my food intake. I am so sick and tired of doing the recommended exercises to tone my triceps, without seeing any results. They look exactly like how my mom's arms did most of her adult life before she started shrinking. A friend of mine just bought some new gadget which is supposed to shake that flab away. I'm eagerly waiting to hear of her miraculous results.

The onset of spring is always a difficult time for those of us who have a weight problem. During the winter, thick down jackets, sweaters, and sweatshirt hoodies do such a fantastic job of hiding those extra little rolls and problem areas. Every year, I get caught off guard. In the blink of an eye, spring arrives, and it's time to shed those accommodating cover-ups and expose the not-so-flattering shape. It's embarrassing for me to see the excessive amount of clothes I have kept in storage for way too many years. I refuse to get rid of them, thinking that they will fit me again someday, "when I lose the weight." There are so many clothes in storage which I don't or can't wear. I could easily start my own secondhand clothing store.

All of us plus-size women need to protest about the lack of selection we have in the "Big-But-Beautiful" sections of our larger department stores. We need to march en masse on the National Mall to tell the clothing industry that we are fed up with this size discrimination and aren't going to take it any longer. Plus-size women deserve the same amount of selections and attractive clothing choices as our thinner counterparts. It seems like these smaller plus-size sections of department stores are completely disproportionate to the number of plus-size women.

Everything is relative when it comes to the weight issue. I was observing people at a popular Southern beach a few years ago and was so saddened to see how many people, young and old, were morbidly obese. When I was teaching, we had several male and female students who were easily twice my size. If they are so large now, what will they look like in twenty years? I don't have much tolerance for people who question how we in the United States have developed such a severe teen obesity problem. The latest statistic I heard was that over 40 percent of American youth are obese. Our generation didn't have that problem when we were young, and clearly there are several contributing factors which help to explain this difference.

One of my pet peeves, as an educator, was to witness how school systems contributed to this epidemic. At several schools where I taught, pizza was an everyday lunch choice for students. The cafeterias usually had another line available, which offered other choices, but even in that line, once a week, pepperoni rolls, pizza, and pizza bread were standard offerings. As if that weren't bad enough, some schools sold pizza slices as a fundraiser during morning and afternoon breaks. When I asked my students at one school what they usually ate at home for supper, a surprising number of them answered, "Pizza." So, for many of them, they had pizza for two meals a day, several days a week. One only has to look at how many calories there are in pizzas to understand how this phenomenon has undoubtedly contributed to childhood obesity. Don't get me wrong. I love a good slice of pizza as much as the next person. Thin-crust veggie pizzas are my favorite. Having said that, I think pizza intake has to be done in moderation.

Of course, the introduction of fast food restaurants into our society has had a profound impact on our youth obesity epidemic. With most parents working full-time, it's just so handy for them to zip in the drive-through and grab something for dinner that their children will eat. Typically, this is fries, burgers, and soft drinks or milkshakes. When I was in junior high school, my doctor put me on a diet to help me gain weight. I had to drink a milkshake every day. Sure enough, I gained weight. During our youth, many of us walked home for lunch, and practically all of us ate a nutritious home-cooked supper every night.

The elephant in the room, which is the main contributor to our nation's youth obesity epidemic, is the sedentary lifestyles our young people have led, in some cases for their entire lives. This younger generation is so inactive, compared to how we were. Sure, there are some exceptions, and they usually don't have a weight problem. So many young people spend all of their spare time in front of computers, playing video games, watching television, or texting friends on their cell phones. For the most part, they aren't running around the neighborhood playing like we did when we were their age. As kids, we walked almost everywhere we went. We were required to participate in gym class, and opting out was never a consideration.

One of my favorite visualizations I use when motivating myself to lose weight is one I saw on the Oprah show: Imagine carrying around a five-pound bag of sugar for every five pounds of excessive weight you have. If I could lose thirty pounds and get rid of six of those sugar bags, I'm sure my energy level would sky-rocket. Think about our teens who are a hundred pounds overweight. They are carrying around the equivalent of twenty of those five-pound bags of sugar. No wonder they're so lethargic and walk like they can barely move. That makes me tired just thinking about it. For them, and many other Americans of all ages, it's their exhausting, everyday reality.

On Aging

My mom, Betty Williams, age 87, January 2011.

"Getting old is no fun," my dad used to tell me, during his last few years, before he died at the age of seventy-nine. I always reminded him: "There are many people who would have loved to have had that problem." So many remarkable people in my lifetime never made it to middle age, much less old age. It didn't matter if they were famous, wealthy celebrities or ordinary folks. This remains to be one of the real mysteries of life to me: Who is afforded the gift of time, and who is not? There seems to be no rhyme or reason to it. Many individuals who were as worthy as anyone to live long prosperous lives were deprived of that opportunity in a heartbeat, often at a very young age. Meanwhile, others who appear to be the personification of evil live on, well into old age.

A friend of mine from high school and I started e-mailing one another recently. He and I hadn't communicated with each other since we graduated in 1967. We were discussing our high school classmates who have passed on. To our astonishment, there were so many. A number of them have been gone now for a very long time. When we were children, my sister and I and all of our friends used to lament about people from our church in their sixties who had died: "At least they got to live a long life." That's what we thought back then, when the life expectancy was much lower than it is today. These days, many of us baby boomers are dealing with our own aging, plus coping with elderly parents. In addition to those conditions, some of us still have children at home and others are raising grandchildren.

Recently, I told my sons that I would want them to try to find another Dr. Kevorkian if I ever got to the point where I had no quality of life. It's like my friend explained. He was a few years younger than I and recently passed away. After ten long years, he finally lost his brave battle with cancer. The cancer had left him paralyzed. From his bed at the Hospice House, he told me that his doctor offered to give him treatments which might prolong his life for two months. He opted to not take them, saying, "This isn't living."

Our mom recently turned eighty-seven. It is very difficult to watch her quality of life deteriorate so rapidly. She refused to have much-needed knee surgery years ago and is now paying the price for that decision. Until recently, she was able to get around on a walker. Now, she's in severe pain when she tries to walk. Her legs and feet refuse to move for her, confining her to a wheelchair. She's totally dependent on someone else. It must be unbelievably frustrating to lose your mobility and independence, especially after being so active. Recently, we met with a funeral director and Mom picked out her casket. I can't imagine how that must have felt. At least my sons won't be concerned with that. They can put my ashes into any ole jar or container.

Often I am so disappointed with myself in how quickly I lose my patience in dealing with her. As a school teacher, I had to practice a lot of patience, so this is somewhat surprising to me, to see how quickly she upsets me. No matter what I do for her, it seems like she is never satisfied. She questions everything I do, like why I took a particular route, driving her to the beauty parlor. For her and my sister and me, our roles have completely reversed. Our mother who once bathed and dressed us now needs our help with those everyday tasks.

Mom is insisting on staying in her own home, even though she falls several times a day. Her face is usually black and blue, bruised from falling. It's a miracle that she hasn't broken any bones. People often scowl at me, when I take her out in public. They act as if I had physically abused her. Caregivers come in for several hours each day, and my sister and I alternate every other day, taking long shifts. She really needs around-the-clock assistance. Several of her friends recently moved into a swanky assisted living home, in her neighborhood. I doubt that she would qualify to be accepted by any assisted living facility now. One administrator explained that they require their residents to be mobile. She certainly doesn't fit into that category these days.

About a year ago, my sister and I took her to tour another assisted living home. We wanted to see if she might like to live there. She begrudgingly agreed to go, but was clearly put out with the entire notion. The facility seemed like a nice place, with an exceptionally-accommodating staff. Still, it somewhat resembled a scene from *One Flew Over the Cuckoo's Nest*. None of the residents had the mental capacity, or desire, to carry on a normal conversation. Clearly, Mom, who is still sharp as a tack, would have been out of place there.

Since there is already a shortage of nursing homes and assisted living manors, one can only imagine how severe this problem will be, when many of us baby boomers will need those facilities. Now is the time for enlightened and insightful developers to be on the cusp of accommodating the aging of our generation. They need to construct more self-contained walking communities with one-story houses. Contractors should get a head start on building additional nursing homes and assisted living residences. These facilities will be dire necessities in the not-too-distant future.

I often worry about how our country and our children's generation will survive, bearing the costs of Social Security, Medicaid, and Medicare for all of us. I can't fathom what a financial burden our generation will be, due to our sheer numbers. To say it will have a profound impact on the economy would be a gross understatement.

My first encounter with aging came several years ago, when I was diagnosed with macular degeneration. This was such a shock to me, since I had perfect vision up to that point. I recall how matter-of-factly the optometrist explained that one in every five people who have the debilitating disease will lose their eyesight. He never mentioned there were vitamins which could keep the disease from progressing. Nowadays, I have difficulty seeing to drive in the dark, especially in the rain, when the headlights reflect on the wet pavement. Thankfully, my disease hasn't progressed in five years. The vitamin regimen, which my current optometrist has me on, probably contributed greatly to that success.

The week before I retired, I went to the Department of Motor Vehicles to get my driver's license renewed. No surprise to me, I failed the vision test. I thought this was the kiss of death...to think that I had worked my entire adult life, then not be able to drive once I retired. That disability certainly would have been life-changing. It was such a blessing when I passed the eye exam in the optometrist's office. He gave me a different prescription for glasses and a note to get my license renewed. What a relief that was. I had been sweating bullets, thinking I may have my driving privileges revoked. At that point, I understood how my parents must have felt, when my sister and I told them they couldn't drive anymore.

For the last ten years, I have had to wear reading glasses. The hardest thing about that is keeping up with where I last placed them. When I was teaching, my students frequently brought my glasses up to me, asking, "Are you looking for these?" It's hard on my eyes to spend long periods of time in front of a computer. I am often embarrassed to see how many e-mails I have sent out which were riddled with typos, even though I had proofread them numer-ous times. Just as in reading highway signs, I simply don't see some of the letters. These days, I often need two pairs of glasses to read or carry out routine tasks. Phone books require the two pairs, plus a huge magnifying glass. Publishers and manufacturers should make their products more boomer-friendly. In my younger days, I used my sewing machine frequently. Nowadays, threading the needle is nearly impossible.

Like many of us, I have arthritis in my knees, and just discov-ered it a few years ago. I was going to a water aerobics class twice a week, and hadn't the first inkling that there was a problem with my knees. After half an hour of rigorous exercising in the water, my knees started hurting and telling me they were tired of being jumped on. Upon my first visit to a joint specialist, he told me I had arthritis in both knees, as well as a Baker's cyst behind my right knee.

With aging, I have developed several obsessive-compulsive disorders, or OCDs. I am such a germaphobe these days, constantly needing to wash my hands. Touching the doorknob to exit a public restroom is something I avoid at all costs. Putting on lipstick is another one of my OCDs. I don't actually care whether or not my lips are pink. They just need to be moistened. I feel lost if I don't have my lipstick with me.

I also have a few pet peeves, which have intensified with age. The misuse of the pronunciation "pitcher" when referring to a picture or photograph drives me nuts. And have we become so lazy, as a society, that we are just going to drop the contraction "n't" from the phrase, "I couldn't care less?" Over the last few years, that phrase has gradually evolved into, "I could care less." Doesn't that bother anyone else? To say "I could care less" completely eradicates the original intent of the phrase. It becomes a contradiction. And, please, friends, stop sending me those "inspirational" e-mails, which end with some kind of jinx. I'm not interested in hearing: "If you don't send this to twenty people in the next five minutes, something terrible will happen to you."

What I miss the most about my youth is having a limber body. Even though I exercise by walking at least five days a week and trying to swim frequently, this sixty-year-old body keeps getting stiffer and less agile. Sometimes, just walking up and down the stairs can be a challenge. I miss being able to lean over and cut my toenails without it being so difficult.

About a year ago, I watched a television special on Alzheimer's. The show featured a man who was in the early stages of the disease. He was standing in front of his bathroom mirror and sink, repeating the same tasks over and over. To my dismay, I am right there, in the same situation as he was. I often forget if I have washed my face with my expensive cleanser, and, more frightening, I forget to take my medications completely, or can't remember if I have already taken them.

Admittedly, I fit into the category of "cell phone refusenik." My TracFone accompanies me on trips in case of emergencies. I am just not interested in getting a cell phone. My problem isn't with cell phones, per se. I simply resent having to listen to other people's loud, private conversations everywhere I go. It feels as though my personal space and privacy have been invaded. Not long ago, Mom and I were dining at a local restaurant. A large man in the booth behind us talked on his cell phone during our entire meal. He was extremely loud, and his choice of words was very offensive. No one in the restaurant was brave enough to confront him and tell him to be quiet and watch his language. He was a pretty imposing character and looked like he wouldn't take too kindly to that suggestion.

I always like to imagine how ridiculous it would have looked for all of us, as kids, to be carrying around and talking on the old black "Banjo" telephones, like the ones we grew up with. That would have been so absurd. Everyone would have asked: "Why do they need to be talking on the phone everywhere they go, and all of the time? How could they possibly have so much to talk about?" I used to have some pretty lengthy phone conversations with my boyfriends, but certainly didn't talk on the phone nonstop.

One good thing about aging is receiving perks, like senior discounts at grocery stores and movies, and getting a reduction in the YMCA monthly membership fee. I have found the freedom of being retired to be a real luxury, especially since I had never had the privilege of not working before. Life is less hectic and not as stressful. Predictably, my blood pressure improved dramatically with my retiring from teaching. Another benefit of aging is getting more pleasure out of the simple things in life. All winter long, I enjoyed my daily treks through the deep snow to my two birdfeeders. Listening to and watching the numerous birds who seem to be showing their gratitude by singing all day, gives me great pleasure.

Michael Feldman's humor and wit on his public radio show *Whad'Ya Know?* is something I look forward to every Saturday morning. His laugh is contagious. For several decades, I have cleaned my kitchen every week, as I listen to the two-hour-long show. I also enjoy listening to his announcer, Jim Packard, and the arrangements from his talented music trio of pianist John Thulin, bassist Jeff Hamann, and "the Funky Drummer," Clyde Stubblefield. The show's quiz segment and interviews of callers can be so off the wall. Feldman recently interviewed a man who uses a trolling motor down in his hot tub to stir up the water. When Michael asked him if that wasn't dangerous, the man replied: "Hmm...I never thought of that before." During every show, he interviews authors or other interesting personalities.

On Saturday nights, I'm thoroughly entertained by the hilarious, complicated, convoluted tales from America's favorite storyteller, Garrison Keillor. His public radio show, *A Prairie Home Companion*, is such a delightful blend of his monologues and stories, and guest musicians, often joined by Keillor. My favorites are his Guy Noir episodes and the tales from Lake Woebegone, "where all the women are strong, all the men are good looking, and all the children are above average."

On the same PBS station, Keillor's show is followed by *The Mountain Stage* show, "From the Mountain State of West Virginia." This awesome production is the brainchild of Andy Ridenour and musician Larry Groce. Celebrating its twenty-five-year anniversary a couple of years ago, the show features an eclectic blend of incredible music. It is a wonderful venue for music legends, as well as up-and-coming musicians. The members of the house band, the Mountain Stage Band, are such outstanding musicians. Charleston is fortunate to have them and their pianist, Bob Thompson, and his band, The Bob Thompson Unit.

I don't watch much primetime television, but my one visual treat every week is CBS's *Sunday Morning* show, with its bow-tie-clad host, Charles Osgood. This program has an entertaining, uplifting blend of features on art and artists, music and musicians, news, and human interest stories. Nancy Giles and Ben Stein offer their varying, insightful opinions and commentaries. Bill Geist's humorous stories often showcase some of the most bizarre events and places all across the country. I still like watching Oprah to get inspired by many of her segments and guests.

Walking, swimming, and taking hikes are my favorite pastimes. For me, being out in the woods, communing with nature, is such a spiritual, uplifting experience. Staying at home makes me perfectly content, too. Sometimes I'll put on oldies music, other times, I'll listen to a completely different genre. The music selection changes with my mood. As I relax in my recliner and sip on a cup of hot tea, my two cats stretch out on my lap. I savor every moment. One day, I may pursue my lifelong dream of moving to a beach community. Taking long morning and evening walks beside the ocean is something I think I could get used to.

A few years ago, I purchased some tap shoes with jingle taps, the real noisy kind. That was one thing I've always wanted to do. I lay my big square of plywood down on the living room carpet, put on Chet Atkins' and Tommy Emmanuel's CD, *The Day Finger Pickers Took Over the World*, and have the best time tapping to their music. Of course, I don't really know what I'm doing, since I never had tap lessons. It's still great fun and good exercise. That's one item on my bucket list to check off.

Lately, I have been involved with people all across our state in fighting a situation which we believe is unjust. It has been inspirational to deal with like-minded individuals who have dedicated so much of their time, energy, and money to this worthwhile endeavor. As a group, we were able to get legislation passed, which will benefit landowners across our state for years to come. Social conditions which need to be changed or challenged will often consume much of my time and energy.

Just recently, I've started communicating over social media sites with former childhood neighbors and high school friends. Rekindling old friendships has been a real pleasure for me. We have especially enjoyed sharing photographs from our younger days. It's interesting how it seems like the older we get, the more our desire increases to reconnect with our roots.

My favorite story on aging comes from a recent tour of a local assisted living facility. One of the directors of the place was showing my sister and me around. He took us into several apartments, explaining the different sizes and rates. We walked into one room, and he told us that the lady who had lived in that particular apartment for several years had recently moved out. "She left to marry her high school sweetheart. She was eighty-five," he mused. The moral of this story is: "To those of you who think that you have missed the boat on finding true love in your life...it's never too late."

Connect with the author on Facebook,
on the page, *If You Remember Metal Skates.*

Postscript

On January 4, 2013, my sweet mother, Betty, passed away peacefully in her sleep. My sister, Jean, and I were by her side. She had been in a nursing home for a year and several months. During that time, Jean and I took turns visiting with her, so one of us was there every single day. For some reason, about a year ago, she lost her ability or desire to talk. If she did try to speak, it was usually so faint that no one could hear her. That must have been tremendously frustrating for someone who liked to talk as much as she did. Occasionally, we were able to hear what she was saying, but those days were few and far between.

When Jean and I went to visit her, we never knew what to expect. Some days she was so alert, and other times, she kept her eyes closed and head bowed, almost as if she were "zoning us out." On rare occasions in the dining room she fed herself, but most of the time someone had to feed "Miss Betty." She often pocketed food in her mouth, only to have it ooze out, sometimes hours later. During activities, she could last for several rounds during the Spelling Bees, yet she could never release the plastic horseshoes to throw them around the stake.

Shortly after she was there, I bought her a pretty little blonde-haired doll, which she fondly called Cindy. She loved that doll and seemed to have more fun with it. I think all of the staff and residents alike got a kick out of watching Mom play with Cindy. Everyone loved Betty. Many of the residents remarked about how beautiful she was. The nursing assistants liked getting her "all dolled up" every day, wearing a cute outfit and a headband with a flower in her hair. I often wondered if she was considered "the perfect resident" because she couldn't yell at the staff or complain about anything, like other residents did.

Most of the time, Mom appeared to be content at the nursing home. She obviously loved many of the workers there. Until she could no longer help pull herself up out of the car, we were still able to take her to church and for short trips around town. One day I thought she seemed especially alert, while we were visiting in the front lobby. Then, to my surprise, she looked over at me and asked: "Is you mother in here too?" She frequently spoke of her own mother and told me a few times that she had spent the night with her. One day she somewhat angrily insisted that I take her to town so she could visit her daughter Nancy. I could never convince her that I was that person.

Mom turned eighty-nine in October, a few months before she died. We had a party for her and she seemed to enjoy herself. The next day, while I was visiting with her in her room, she tapped me on the leg and asked: "You gonna miss me?" I was completely caught off guard. "*Miss* you?" I asked. "Where you going? You'll probably outlive all the rest of us." Our family actually did believe that. Other than having dementia and bone-on-bone in her knees, she didn't have any physical ailments. Her body must have been telling her something that we couldn't see. If she only knew *how much* she was going to be missed... by Jean and me, her grandsons, and everyone else who loved her.

When Mom started declining so rapidly, many of my friends who had lost their mothers, advised me to cherish every moment I had with her. I did indeed cherish my time with her, yet one can never anticipate the emptiness which remains when our mothers are no longer with us. My, how we take everything for granted. At Christmastime, Mom had been nonresponsive for several days. Upon hearing the voices of her two grandsons, she slowly opened her eyes. We were so ecstatic and filled the room with such loud, robust cheers. It must have sounded like our favorite team had just made a touchdown. What I wouldn't give to see those little eyes open one more time.

These days I feel a little bit like Emily, in the play, *Our Town*, yearning to return to my youth, just to relive one more day. Let me go back to our happy home once again, with my family and friends and little dog Skipper, to our mundane, uneventful lives. This time I promise to soak up and savor every single detail, since the first time around I was completely oblivious to all that was precious around me.

When Mom died, we opted to have a celebration of her life, instead of a traditional funeral. Teary-eyed people came out of the woodwork, bravely standing up and telling of the good deeds Mom had done for them and what an influence she had on their lives. Others told of how she had befriended them at church, when they were newcomers and didn't know anyone. The service was a beautiful tribute to a special lady and the Christian stewardship she showed to so many. She was a wonderful mother and grandmother who gave my sister and me, and my sons many fond memories to cherish forever.

None of us would have ever dreamed that my cousin Joyce, who is mentioned in this book numerous times, would have died from a brain tumor six months before Mom passed. She was my sister's age and was more like a sister to us growing up. Joyce lived her life as a devout Christian, serving God every day through her life. Mom and I liked to watch her outstanding performances when she portrayed Mary Todd Lincoln at Civil War reenactments. Joyce was a remarkable cook, talented seamstress, and was dedicated to her family and friends. She was so proud of this book and promoted it every chance she had. Joyce was an inspiration to many people.

In closing, I would like to share this message with my female readers, especially the younger ones: "If you ever find yourself in an abusive relationship, do everything you can to get out of it. At the very first sign of controlling or aggressive behavior, separate yourself from that person." I know this is easier said than done, but there are many groups who help women in this situation. So, seek help, if need be. My parents and I had to take out a restraining order on a man I dated in college. He had seemed like such a nice guy, until I broke up with him. Then, he became irate and threatened to harm me. Quite frankly, for some time, he made my life a living hell. I knew I had no choice but to leave him. In retrospect, I am so thankful I did. The number of deaths every year from domestic violence is staggering. Please, don't become another statistic.

Nancy Williams

February, 2013